Essentials

of PSYCHOLOGICAL ASS

D1118277

Everything you need to know to adm..........., ...et, and score the major psychological tests.

I'd like to order the following
ESSENTIALS OF PSYCHOLOGICALL ASSESSMENT:

❑ **WAIS®-III Assessment / 28295-2 / $34.95**
❑ **CAS Assessment / 29015-7 / $34.95**
❑ **Millon Inventories Assessment / 29798-4 / $34.95**
❑ **Forensic Psychological Assessment / 33186-4 / $34.95**
❑ **Bayley Scales of Infant Development-II Assessment / 32651-8 / $34.95**
❑ **Myers-Briggs Type Indicator® Assessment / 33239-9 / $34.95**
❑ **WISC-III® and WPPSI-R® Assessment / 34501-6 / $34.95**
❑ **Career Interest Assessment / 35365-5 / $34.95**
❑ **Rorschach® Assessment / 33146-5 / $34.95**
❑ **Cognitive Assessment with KAIT and Other Kaufman Measures**
   38317-1 / $34.95
❑ **MMPI-2™ Assessment / 34533-4 / $34.95**
❑ **Nonverbal Assessment / 38318-X / $34.95**
❑ **Cross-Battery Assessment / 38264-7 / $34.95**
❑ **NEPSY® Assessment / 32690-9 / $34.95**
❑ **Individual Achievement Assessment / 32432-9/$34.95**
❑ **TAT and Other Storytelling Techniques Assessment / 39469-6 / $34.95**

Please send this order form with your payment (credit card or check) to:
JOHN WILEY & SONS, INC., Attn: J. Knott, 10th Floor
605 Third Avenue, New York, N.Y. 10158-0012

Name _____

Affiliation _____

Address _____

City/State/Zip _____

Phone _____ E-mail _____

❑ **Would you like to be added to our e-mailing list?**

Credit Card: ❑ MasterCard   ❑ Visa   ❑ American Express
(All orders subject to credit approval)

Card Number _____

Exp. Date _____ Signature _____

TO ORDER BY PHONE, CALL 1-800-225-5945
Refer to promo code #1-4081

To order online: www.wiley.com/essentials

Essentials of Neuropsychological Assessment

Essentials of Psychological Assessment Series
Series Editors, Alan S. Kaufman and Nadeen L. Kaufman

Essentials of WAIS®-III Assessment
by Alan S. Kaufman and Elizabeth O. Lichtenberger

Essentials of Millon Inventories Assessment
by Stephen N. Strack

Essentials of CAS Assessment
by Jack A. Naglieri

Essentials of Forensic Psychological Assessment
by Marc J. Ackerman

Essentials of Bayley Scales of Infant Development–II Assessment
by Maureen M. Black and Kathleen Matula

Essentials of Myers-Briggs Type Indicator® Assessment
by Naomi Quenk

Essentials of WISC-III® and WPPSI-R® Assessment
by Alan S. Kaufman and Elizabeth O. Lichtenberger

Essentials of Rorschach® Assessment
by Tara Rose, Nancy Kaser-Boyd, and Michael P. Maloney

Essentials of Career Interest Assessment
by Jeffrey P. Prince and Lisa J. Heiser

Essentials of Cross-Battery Assessment
by Dawn P. Flanagan and Samuel O. Ortiz

Essentials of Cognitive Assessment with KAIT and Other Kaufman Measures
by Elizabeth O. Lichtenberger, Debra Broadbooks, and Alan S. Kaufman

Essentials of Nonverbal Assessment
by Steve McCallum, Bruce Bracken, and John Wasserman

Essentials of MMPI-2™ Assessment
by David S. Nichols

Essentials of NEPSY® Assessment
by Sally L. Kemp, Ursula Kirk, and Marit Korkman

Essentials of Individual Achievement Assessment
by Douglas K. Smith

Essentials of TAT and Other Storytelling Techniques Assessment
by Hedwig Teglasi

Essentials of WJ III™ Tests of Achievement Assessment
by Nancy Mather, Barbara J. Wendling, and Richard W. Woodcock

Essentials of WJ III™ Cognitive Abilities Assessment
by Fredrick A. Schrank, Dawn P. Flanagan, Richard W. Woodcock, and Jennifer T. Mascolo

Essentials of WMS®-III Assessment
by Elizabeth O. Lichtenberger, Alan S. Kaufman, and Zona C. Lai

Essentials of MMPI-A™ Assessment
by Robert P. Archer and Radhika Krishnamurthy

Essentials of Neuropsychological Assessment
by Nancy Hebben and William Milberg

Essentials of Behavioral Assessment
by Michael C. Ramsay, Cecil R. Reynolds, and Randy W. Kamphaus

Essentials

of Neuropsychological Assessment

Nancy Hebben and
William Milberg

 John Wiley & Sons, Inc.

Library of Congress Cataloging-in-Publication Data:
Hebben, Nancy.
    Essentials of neuropsychological assessment / Nancy Hebben and William Milberg.
        p. cm. — (Essentials of psychological assessment series)
    Includes bibliographical references and index.
        ISBN 0-471-40522-1 (pbk. : alk. paper)
        1. Neuropsychological tests.   2. Neuropsychological tests—Evaluation.   3. Clinical
neuropsychology.   I. Milberg, William.   II. Title.   III. Series.

    RC386.6.N48 H43 2002
    616.8′0475—dc21

                                                                        2001046814

This book is dedicated to our most important collaborative works:
Our two beautiful sons,
Jan and Aron

CONTENTS

	Series Preface	xi
One	Introduction to Neuropsychological Assessment	1
Two	The Discipline of Neuropsychological Assessment	25
Three	Essentials of the Interview and Clinical History	41
Four	Essentials of Test Selection, Administration, and Scoring	67
Five	Essentials of Interpretation	131
Six	Special Issues in Neuropsychological Assessment	159
Seven	Essentials of Report Writing	181
Appendix A	A General Guide for Neuropsychological Assessment	207
Appendix B	Essentials of the Neurobehavioral Syndromes	211
	References	217
	Annotated Bibliography	227
	Index	233
	About the Authors	247

SERIES PREFACE

In the *Essentials of Psychological Assessment* series, we have attempted to provide the reader with books that will deliver key practical information in the most efficient and accessible style. The series features instruments in a variety of domains, such as cognition, personality, education, and neuropsychology. For the experienced clinician, books in the series offer a concise, yet thorough way to master utilization of the continuously evolving supply of new and revised instruments, as well as a convenient method for keeping up to date on the tried-and-true measures. The novice will find here a prioritized assembly of all the information and techniques that must be at one's fingertips to begin the complicated process of individual psychological diagnosis.

Wherever feasible, visual shortcuts to highlight key points are utilized alongside systematic, step-by-step guidelines. Chapters are focused and succinct. Topics are targeted for an easy understanding of the essentials of administration, scoring, interpretation, and clinical application. Theory and research are continually woven into the fabric of each book, but always to enhance clinical inference, never to sidetrack or overwhelm. We have long been advocates of "intelligent" testing—the notion that a profile of test scores is meaningless unless it is brought to life by the clinical observations and astute detective work of knowledgeable examiners. Test profiles must be used to make a difference in the child's or adult's life, or why bother to test? We want this series to help our readers become the best intelligent testers they can be.

In *Essentials of Neuropsychological Assessment,* the authors have presented an overview of the assumptions, logic, knowledge base, and skills underlying the practice of neuropsychological assessment. This book describes how clinical history, behavioral observations, and formal test results are used to make inferences about the contribution of brain damage to psychological functioning, as well as how to report this information in a manner that will be useful to referring professionals and clients. Practical and conceptual issues related to neuropsychological assessment in geriatric, pediatric, forensic, and other specialized settings are discussed. In each chapter the reader is given additional sources of information that can be used to deepen knowledge of these areas. The reader is also provided with a discussion of the professional development and training of neuropsychology and extensive information about resources for test materials, journals, and textbooks in the area.

Alan S. Kaufman, PhD, and Nadeen L. Kaufman, EdD, Series Editors
Yale University School of Medicine

Essentials of Neuropsychological Assessment

One

INTRODUCTION TO NEUROPSYCHOLOGICAL ASSESSMENT

OVERVIEW

It is difficult to pinpoint the factors that have made neuropsychology one of the fastest growing and perhaps largest single specialties within the discipline of clinical psychology today. Although many of the techniques and concepts that form the basis of modern practice of neuropsychological assessment were established between the world wars, it is probably not coincidental that clinical neuropsychology saw its emergence as a coherent discipline in parallel with the cognitive revolution in psychology (i.e., the change in focus from behaviorism to cognitivism) and the explosion of the technology of neuroimaging, both of which began in the mid-1970s. To comprehend the remarkable rate of growth in this field, one needs only to read the foreword of the first general textbook on clinical neuropsychology (Reitan & Davison, 1974). Even in 1974, Reitan and Davison heralded the "large growth in substantive knowledge" in neuropsychology and neurosciences preceding the landmark event of the first American Psychological Association (APA) Symposium on Clinical Neuropsychology in 1970. Their text introduced the power of empirically based approaches to neuropsychological assessment to what was probably the first large postwar wave of clinicians who identified themselves as specialists in neuropsychology. It now seems to be a gentle irony that at the time of that writing, fewer than six journals focused on clinical or experimental neuropsychology and the related medical discipline of behavioral neurology. As the new millennium begins, slightly more than 25 years later, more than 100 journals deal with the brain or brain-behavior relationships.

History of Clinical Neuropsychology

In the early 1970s the professional identity of a neuropsychological specialty was just emerging. In 1967 The International Neuropsychological Society

(INS) began its evolution from a few disparate, informal, and geographically scattered groups of psychologists interested in the relationship between brain and behavior into the first scholarly/professional society explicitly dedicated to neuropsychology. By 1973, around the time of the publication of Reitan and Davison's textbook, approximately 350 members of INS represented the United States, Canada, Great Britain, Norway, and a number of other nations. Today, INS, the principal scientific society of neuropsychology, has more than 3,000 members (Rourke & Murji, 2000).

In 1975 a group of clinically oriented neuropsychologists organized the National Academy of Neuropsychology (NAN), largely to help clinicians keep up with the growing number of techniques and findings directly related to clinical practice. Today NAN has more than 3,000 members.

By 1980 neuropsychology had become sufficiently established as a specialized area of interest to organize its own division (Division 40) of the American Psychological Association, and in 1996 APA officially recognized neuropsychology as a specialty area. Division 40 (Clinical Neuropsychology) consists of a wide variety of psychologists involved in both clinical practice and research and serves to represent neuropsychology within the larger association of psychologists in the United States. Division 40 had approximately 433 members in its charter year and has grown to more than 4,000 members as of this writing (Puente & Marcotte, 2000). Although some clinicians are members of more than one group, memberships in INS, NAN, and Division 40 do not completely overlap. As a definitive sign of the establishment of neuropsychology as a recognized clinical specialty, the American Board of Clinical Neuropsychology (Meier, 1998) was formed in 1981 and began to offer diplomate status in clinical neuropsychology in 1983, after coming under the auspices of the American Board of Professional Psychology (ABPP). As of April 2001, 418 clinical neuropsychologists in North America and overseas held this board certification, signaling advanced competence (L. A. Bieliauskas, personal communication, April 27, 2001). Clinical neuropsychology is the second largest board-certified specialty within ABPP after clinical psychology. In 1982 the American Board of Professional Neuropsychology (ABPN) was also established to award board certification for competence in clinical neuropsychology. By April 2001 ABPN had awarded diplomate status to 234 neuropsychologists who had completed the requirements for board certification (J. J. Blase, personal communication, April 26, 2001). Rapid Reference 1.1 pro-

≈*Rapid Reference 1.1*

Major Historical Events

- 1967 International Neuropsychological Society formed
- 1970 First APA Symposium on Clinical Neuropsychology
- 1975 National Academy of Neuropsychology formed
- 1980 Division 40 (Clinical Neuropsychology) of APA created
- 1981 American Board of Clinical Neuropsychology formed
- 1982 American Board of Professional Neuropsychology formed
- 1983 ABCN offers diplomate status under ABPP
- 1996 APA recognizes clinical neuropsychology as a specialty area
- 1997 Houston Conference on Specialty Education and Training in Clinical Neuropsychology convened

vides a brief chronology of the development of clinical neuropsychology as a separate discipline.

Perhaps the emergence of clinical neuropsychology was inevitable, given the increasing centrality of biology and medicine in science itself and what has become an almost universal interest in the problems of neurobiology in such diverse scientific disciplines as physics (e.g., Penrose, 1997) and philosophy (e.g., Churchland, 1989). It is safe to say that a discipline that only 25 years ago was considered as esoteric and arcane as alchemy by many psychologists and physicians is now an established and respected part of the assessment, treatment planning, and rehabilitation of children and adults with histories of psychiatric, neurological, or developmental problems, or a combination of these.

Definition of Clinical Neuropsychology

Neuropsychology is usually broadly defined as the study of brain-behavior relationships. Of course, this definition does not capture the multiplicity of questions and approaches that have been used to explore how the central nervous system represents, organizes, and generates the infinite range of human capabilities and actions. Modern neuropsychology includes the study of the classic problems of psychology—attention, learning, perception, cognition, personality, and psychopathology—using techniques that include the methods of experimental psychology as well as the methodologies of test construction and psychometrics. Its scientific palate includes such state-of-the-art technologies as functional neuroimaging and computational modeling.

This book presents some of the core concepts of the particular discipline of clinical neuropsychological assessment. According to a consortium of representatives of a number of professional neuropsychological organizations that convened in 1997 in Houston, Texas, clinical neuropsychology can be defined as "the application of assessment and intervention principles based on the scientific study of human behavior across the lifespan as it relates to normal and abnormal functioning of the central nervous system" (Hannay, et al., 1998, p. 161). In practice, this translates into using standardized psychological tests, which are usually designed to assess various aspects of human cognition, ability, or skill, to provide information to a variety of clinical questions about the central nervous system. Less often, tests of personality or affective behavior have been adapted as neuropsychological instruments.

Historically, the tests used by neuropsychologists were usually not developed for the purpose of assessing brain damage, and in many cases they reflect clinical assessment traditions more than basic research in cognition or neuroscience. For example, the Wechsler Adult Intelligence Scale (Wechsler, 1955) and its successors were developed as tests of intelligence, primarily to aid in the identification of mental retardation and to facilitate academic, military, or vocational assessment (Kaufman & Lichtenberger, 1999; Matarazzo, 1972). The Seashore Rhythm Test, a traditional component of the Halstead-Reitan Battery, was part of a test of musical aptitude (Saetveit, Lewis, & Seashore, 1940).

DON'T FORGET

Neuropsychology is the study of brain-behavior relationships. Clinical neuropsychology is "the application of assessment and intervention principles based on the scientific study of human behavior across the lifespan as it relates to normal and abnormal functioning of the central nervous system." (Hannay et al., 1998, p. 161)

What all tests used by neuropsychologists have in common (or should have in common) is known reliability and validity as predictors of the presence of brain damage. Minimum requirements for neuropsychological tests are sensitivity to the presence of brain damage and the ability to distinguish correctly the presence of brain damage from normal brain functioning. Over the years, these basic criteria for neuropsychological tests have grown to include the ability to predict the site and severity of brain damage and, in some cases, the more controversial ability to predict the specific cause or etiology of brain damage. During the inception of the first formally validated neuropsychological tests, the sensitivity of neuropsychological instruments was gauged by their agreement with the clinical judgments of neurologists (Reitan & Davison, 1974). As neuroimaging and other technologies have advanced, so has the expectation that neuropsychological tests will be sensitive to changes observable with increasingly sensitive and detailed views of brain structure and physiology. Today, it is not uncommon to see neuropsychological instruments used to detect the presence of brain damage in both research and clinical settings. As we discuss in Chapter 5, this is a controversial development from which many practitioners distance themselves. Its existence, however, is a reflection of the respect these instruments have gained.

Some clinicians advocate using a fixed battery of tests to anchor and compare observations across different patient populations, whereas other clinicians advocate using tests that are dictated by the specific referral question or unique presentation of the patient. Clinical neuropsychological assessment may employ clinical interview and behavioral observation techniques that have not necessarily been subject to the usual methodological standards of test construction but are usually considered indispensable in providing rich descriptions of a patient's behavior. Many clinicians employ unique variations on standardized tests or procedures developed on the fly in an attempt to capture qualitative features specific to the patient in question. The advantages and disadvantages of these approaches are discussed later in this chapter.

Uses of Neuropsychological Assessment

One can identify at least seven different but related purposes or uses of neuropsychological assessment. These categories are derived from what are probably the most common clinical referral questions presented to neuropsychologists as well as from the information presented in many neuropsychological reports. These categories of use can arise in a number of different contexts, including medicine, law, education, and research. These categories are presented here in the order reflecting the logic in which clinical inferences are typically made.

1. *Describing and identifying changes in psychological functioning (cognition, behavior, emotion) in terms of presence/absence and severity.* Although the raison d'être of clinical neuropsychology is to predict the presence of brain damage, the ability to describe function precedes this seemingly core purpose of neuropsychological tests. Neuropsychologists are usually expected to provide a description of a patient or client by identifying cognitive strengths and weaknesses and then by making the basic inference of whether the patient's current status represents a change from some previous, usually not precisely defined, baseline or premorbid level of functioning. When children are evaluated and there is little basis to estimate premorbid abilities, clinicians may attempt to infer change from expected developmental milestones. The issues of strengths and weaknesses and the presence or absence of change are addressed before any other inferences regarding brain function or recommendations for interventions may be considered. The neuropsychologist must try to infer what part of the current observations reflects the patient's "normal" allocation of intellectual functions versus what parts of the current observations show changes attributable to brain dysfunction. Accurate description and reference to correct normative standards for the individual are the most basic and critical purposes of neuropsychological assessment.

2. *Determining the biological (i.e., neuroanatomical, physiological) correlates of test results: detection, gradation, and localization of brain damage.* After they have described the patient's behavior, neuropsychologists typically try to determine whether the pattern of test results, clinical behavior, and particular historical context of the observations can be attributed to abnormal brain function. Such abnormalities may be the presence of a structural brain lesion, a developmental disorder, or, in some cases, neurochemical lesion. Part of this determination is trying to ascertain what region of the brain is involved.

3. *Determining whether changes are associated with neurological disease, psychiatric conditions, developmental disorders, or nonneurological conditions.* The next kind of inference that clinical neuropsychologists often try to make or are asked to make concerns the likely etiology or etiologies that produced the changes described. In the case of neurological

disorder and known history, this can sometimes be done accurately. This is particularly true in cases in which the behavioral changes involve unusual and dramatic phenomena that have historically been related to the presence of lesions in specific parts of the brain and are usually caused by a highly limited set of etiologies. For example, nonfluent aphasia symptoms (e.g., hesitant, agrammatic speech) are most likely related to a limited set of diseases that, if present by history, can be considered causative of the observed changes in language. Many changes in neuropsychological functions, however, may be caused by psychiatric, motivational, developmental, or cultural factors and may not be attributable to a specific neurological etiology even when present by history. Often, neuropsychological test findings are nonspecific to etiology and may be related to a host of factors, such as depression, anxiety, sleep deprivation, or even chronic pain. In these instances, the neuropsychologist must work as an investigator to review the test findings thoroughly in the context of the patient's history.

4. *Assessing changes over time and developing a prognosis.* One of the most useful applications of neuropsychological assessment is to track improvements and decrements in performance over time. This helps in determining the etiology and progression of a disease, developing social or financial plans for a patient, and tracking whether treatment or efforts toward rehabilitation are effective.

5. *Offering guidelines for rehabilitation, vocational/educational planning, or a combination of these.* The ability to provide inferences regarding etiology and descriptive power has made neuropsychological assessment a popular tool in rehabilitation and educational planning. Therapists and teachers can often use a patient's profile of strengths and weaknesses to develop and optimize rehabilitation and educational programs. Knowledge of which problems or weaknesses are attributable to brain damage and which are likely the result of nonneurological sources can help a therapist allocate time and resources toward the treatment priorities that are most likely to be effective.

6. *Providing guidelines and education for family and caregivers.* In a similar vein, neuropsychological data can help families and caregivers to under-

stand the strengths and weaknesses of their loved ones and to cope with patients who may suffer from challenging limitations on independent functioning. Beleaguered family members are less likely to be angry with a patient when they understand that symptoms that appear to be related to motivation or personality are actually causally related to a disease state. An understanding of the prognosis of the illness can also be invaluable to families who must plan their use of finances and future care.

7. *Planning for discharge and treatment implementation.* Neuropsychological deficits can sometimes be insidious and difficult to describe, even for sophisticated clinicians. An understanding of a patient's capabilities can help the clinician assess the degree to which a patient is going to comply with treatment recommendations and medication use, as well as the extent to which the patient or the patient's family may need continued supervision after discharge.

Rapid Reference 1.2 provides a quick summary of the uses of neuropsychological assessment.

In the ensuing chapters of this book, we review the essential information about neuropsychological assessment techniques that clinicians need in order to help in the description, diagnosis, and treatment process of patients.

≡ Rapid Reference 1.2

Uses of Neuropsychological Assessment

- Describing and identifying changes in psychological functioning
- Determining the biological correlates of test results
- Determining whether changes are associated with neurological disease, psychiatric conditions, developmental disorders, or nonneurological conditions
- Assessing changes over time and developing a prognosis
- Offering guidelines for rehabilitation, vocational and/or educational planning
- Providing guidelines and education to family and caregivers
- Planning for discharge and treatment implementation

THEORETICAL AND RESEARCH FOUNDATIONS OF MODERN NEUROPSYCHOLOGICAL ASSESSMENT

Much of clinical psychology has drawn from the psychology of learning and cognition, developmental psychology, social psychology, and psychodynamic traditions for its scientific paradigms and language. Clinical neuropsychology adds to this mixture the paradigms of biology and medicine in order to grapple with the problems of human psychopathology.

The problems that are the focus of modern clinical neuropsychology have been described for centuries and have captured the imaginations of physicians and philosophers. A detailed history of neuropsychology (Benton & Adams, 2000) is not within the focus of this book, but an examination of several modern conceptual and investigative trends is important to help practitioners understand the source of many of the assumptions and practices currently in use.

Holism versus Localization

Observations of behavioral changes that occur following injuries to the head can be found in the earliest written records of history, including translations of 5,000-year-old Egyptian medical documents (as described in Finger & Stein, 1982). The idea that thoughts, memories, and sensations somehow originate in the brain, however, did not gain wide acceptance until the beginning of the 17th century, although some still believed Aristotle's declarations regarding the heart's role in understanding human behavior and motivation (Finger & Stein, 1982). By the 19th century, there was little contention with the idea that the brain was the center of consciousness, memory, language, feelings, and passions, but there has never been complete agreement on how these basic categories of psychological function are actually accomplished. Although the levels of technology and sophistication have evolved dramatically over the centuries, the conceptualization of how the brain organizes its task as the organ of the mind boils down to two prevailing views that still guide the organization of research, theory, and clinical practice of neuropsychology.

Perhaps the most intuitively appealing and most clearly stated notion is that of a localized correspondence between structure and function. This idea suggests that different psychological functions are subserved by distinct and separate structures in the brain. The idea of localization found its clearest statement in the writings of the French physician and physiologist Franz Joseph Gall in the latter half of the 18th century. Gall (1835) argued that separate organs within the brain controlled such faculties as wisdom, poetic ability, religiousness, language, and memory. This position's appeal lies in its ability to account for the countless observations of variations in symptoms accompanying variations in brain lesions. Since Paul Broca (a dedicated follower of Gall) masterfully documented the association of damage to the left frontal cerebral hemisphere of humans with the loss of the capacity to speak, much of neuropsychological research has attempted to document correspondences between other psychological functions and focal brain lesions.

Much of today's research is guided by the doctrine of localizationism, in which the description and localization of function are a primary goal of neuropsychological assessment. This idea has found its most modern form in the relatively new subdivision of neuropsychology, sometimes called cognitive neuroscience, which uses neuroimaging techniques such as magnetic resonance imaging (MRI) and positron-emission topography (PET) to detect minute changes in blood flow to relatively circumscribed areas of the cerebral cortex. Much of the literature using this technology documents increasingly specific localization of blood-flow changes associated with increasingly specific experimental measures of cognition. The goal of much of this research is to create detailed charts of cognitive localization in the brain. The strongest form of localization theory appears in the work of Jerry Fodor (1983), who introduced the concept of *modularity*. Modularity refers to the idea that localization is a necessary consequence of the distinct processing requirements of the sensory systems and such higher order cognitive functions as language. Fodor argued that the physical requirements of processing information in different sensory modalities mandate distinctly adapted and localized neural mechanisms. He proposed that language, which requires the use of specific, automatically accessed rules, also requires specific and localized neural mechanisms.

Localizationism is not the only conceptualization of how the brain is organized. As Pierre-Marie Flourens (1824), Hughlings Jackson (1894), Kurt Goldstein (1939), and Alexander Luria (1966) argued, however, the localization or correlation of symptoms or behavior with lesions (or even documented changes in blood flow) does not necessarily prove that the function of that behavior is localized in the observed brain structure. Although these writers acknowledged that lesions might have effects that differ as a function of location, they believed that brain function itself always involved multiple structures working together. This position is often associated with Kurt Goldstein's term for this principal: *holism*. The following example illustrates the central principle of holism: Although a loose screw might be responsible for a malfunction that prevents an automobile engine from starting, it would be erroneous to localize the function of locomotion in the screw itself. A symptom may arise because an important component of a larger network of functions is disrupted or because only the most complicated and susceptible or weak "function" of many functions subserved by the same area is disrupted. Imagine concluding that piano playing (a relatively complex motor skill) was localized in the fingers, but that scratching (a relatively simple motor skill) was not because a sprain disrupted one but not the other. This was essentially Hughlings Jackson's argument regarding Broca's and others' localization of expressive language (a relatively complex cognitive skill) to a specific part of the frontal lobes, when evidence showed that patients with lesions in Broca's area could articulate words in an emotional or even musical context.

In 1929 Lashley published research showing that highly focal ablations of brain tissue had only mild and temporary effects on the recovery of maze learning in rats (Lashley, 1929). As a result, he concluded that the brain followed the principle of mass action and that different brain structures had the potential to take over the same function. His conclusion was a major influence on Ward Halstead's creation of the first psychometrically sound neuropsychological test battery and forms the basis of many of the instruments and standards for test construction used today. For example, the Halstead-Reitan Battery, a widely known and used approach to neuropsychological assessment, is based largely on nonlocalizationist assumptions (Reitan & Wolfson, 1996).

One of the most sophisticated approaches applied to the study of brain-behavior relationships is the development of computer models, constructed out of building blocks that function and interact very much like neurons, that imitate cognitive function and dysfunction. There has been remarkable success in making computer models that mimic various aspects of cognition and changes in cognition following brain lesions.

Many of these models do not use the assumptions of modularity or localization of function; instead, they are constructed using assumptions of mass action and equipotentiality (see Anderson, 1995). In the literature of functional neuroimaging, a view is also emerging that most functions should be conceptualized as distributed among neural networks (Damasio, 1995). Some researchers also make arguments against strict localizationism based on the fact that many functions substantially return after brain injury. Such recovery may indicate that other parts of the brain are doing the job of the damaged tissue (Finger & Stein, 1982).

The localizationist view is currently the most popular way of conceptualizing the results of neuropsychological tests. It is common to make the inference that a change in test performance (or pattern in performance across tests) is an indication that some function (presumably measured by the impaired test performance) is localized in a specific region of the brain. Even the Halstead-Reitan Battery has been adapted to this tradition. However, the clinician should be cautioned (or at least aware) that such direct inferences may be simplistic and inaccurate. Test performance is not necessarily an indication that a function is localized in a specific part of the brain. Moreover, predictions that may be accurate in one context (e.g., during the acute phase of a lesion) may not be accurate in another (e.g., several years after a lesion occurs, in children, or even in older adults). As Luria, Damasio, Finger, and Stein have argued, neuropsychological test performance and symptoms may reflect the disruption of an organized, distributed network of structures that participate in the function in question. The symptoms of brain damage may reflect the disruption of a system rather than a single localized function.

Empiricism versus Cognitivism in Test Construction

Much of the variation in today's approaches to neuropsychological assessment is layered on the foundation of two issues: how behavior should be conceptualized (empiricism or functionalism) and how brain organization should be conceptualized (cognitivism).

Most of the neuropsychological assessment techniques used currently are derived from the psychological/philosophical tradition of empiricism/functionalism. This means that tests are constructed using the ideas that prediction of performance is primary and that test content and psychological meaning are secondary. In contrast, tests from the cognitive tradition are constructed primarily to measure specific psychological, usually intellectual or perceptual functions; clinical prediction is a secondary or derived goal. A detailed discussion of these issues would be too digressive for this text, but neuropsychologists should have some general understanding of the basic interpretative and methodological assumptions that organize contemporary approaches to neuropsychological assessment.

Where do all the tests and measures that are used by neuropsychologists come from? A fair discussion of this seemingly simple question could easily consume this volume and would likely lead to a full-fledged barroom brawl if presented to more than two neuropsychologists at a time. It is raised here just to make the point that clinical neuropsychology derives its techniques in much the same way as do other clinical disciplines. In many cases, tests are used because they work or were thought to work based on previous observations. The term *empiricism,* the idea that knowledge is derived from direct experience, refers to this approach to creating tests. The empirical (or *functional*) approach is perhaps the most easily defended and most identified with nonlocalizationist approach to neuropsychology. Ward Halstead and his most famous student, Ralph Reitan, adopt (sometimes implicitly) the view that much of the brain follows the principle of mass action; thus, the primary consideration in selecting neuropsychological instruments is their observed sensitivity in detecting brain damage. Once a set of optimal measures are derived, they are used to test a variety of populations; in many cases, the primary goal is the detection of changes associated with brain pathology.

This process represented the primary trend in American neuropsychology well into the 1970s. Today, because localizationism has become the mainstream view of brain function, many of the tests that come from the Halstead-Reitan tradition are used to predict or detect the presence of focal lesions. In most of these cases, empiricism nevertheless rules: The tests themselves (and how they are derived or created) are not as important as their ability to predict the presence of brain damage or their empirically demonstrated validity.

Independently constructed theories of cognitive function or dysfunction, which include sensitivity to brain damage as an important but secondary consideration, provide another source of neuropsychological tests. Many modern tests were created in this way. For example, the Boston Diagnostic Aphasia Exam (BDAE; Goodglass & Kaplan, 1983) and the California Verbal Learning Test (CVLT; Delis, Kramer, Kaplan, & Ober, 1987) were created primarily using prevailing theories of language and memory, respectively, and in both cases were created to measure specific aspects of function known to be affected by brain damage. In these cases, the tests' construct validity or theoretical interpretation was as important as was their sensitivity to the presence of brain damage. Literature documenting the sensitivity of the tests' tasks to the presence of brain lesions came primarily after their creation. In both cases, the assumption was made (either explicitly or implicitly) that the psychological functions measured were cognitive domains that could be affected independently by brain damage. Further, it was assumed that the functions associated with these tests could be localized.

An understanding of these historical distinctions is helpful in understanding the strengths and weaknesses of neuropsychological tests. Some tests are excellent detectors of brain damage but may be difficult to use as tools for describing abilities or as sources of real-life recommendations. Other tests do not demonstrate sensitivity to brain damage as clearly but may provide clear, descriptive measures of a psychological domain; these measures can then be used to make recommendations for rehabilitation or treatment planning. Ideally, tests should be sensitive to the presence of brain damage and theoretically coherent while also being functionally descriptive and ecologically valid (Sbordone, 1996; Sbordone & Guilmete, 1999); however, because of their historical origins, in practice many tests are compromised or limited to one of these two goals.

THE MAJOR NEUROPSYCHOLOGICAL ASSESSMENT APPROACHES: THEIR HISTORY, DEVELOPMENT, STRENGTHS, AND WEAKNESSES

In this section we briefly review the background of the major testing approaches used in contemporary neuropsychology practice. Rapid Reference 1.3 provides publication information for the Halstead-Reitan Neuropsychological Battery (HRB), the Luria-Nebraska Neuropsychological Battery (LNNB), and the Boston Process Approach (BPA).

Halstead-Reitan Neuropsychological Battery

The discipline of using psychological tests to assess systematically the effects of brain damage originated in the midwestern United States in the late 1930s and early 1940s. In the years between the two world wars, clinical neurologists

≣Rapid Reference 1.3

Publication Information for the Three Major Approaches to Neuropsychological Assessment

HRB

Reitan, R. M., & Wolfson, D. (1993). *The Halstead-Reitan Neuropsychological Test Battery: Theory and Clinical Interpretation.* Tucson, AZ: Neuropsychology Press.

LNNB

Golden, C. J., Purisch, A. D., & Hammeke, T. A. (1985). *Manual for the Luria-Nebraska Neuropsychological Battery: Forms I and II.* Los Angeles: Western Psychological Services.

BPA

Kaplan, E. (1988). A process approach to neuropsychological assessment. In T. Boll & B. K. Bryant (Eds.), *Clinical Neuropsychology and Brain Function: Research, Measurement and Practice* (pp. 125–167). Washington, DC: American Psychological Association.

in Great Britain (e.g., Hughlings Jackson and the appropriately named Henry Head and W. R. Brain) and Europe (e.g., Von Monakow, Kurt Goldstein, and Balint) had already created an extensive history of the effects of brain damage on language, attention, vision, and personality. Ward Halstead, however, worked in relative isolation from these observations and developments. Although his ideas were influenced by Karl Lashley's concepts of mass action and equipotentiality, Halstead started with a relatively blank slate, putting together after much trial and error a battery of psychological tests that, taken together, could be used by clinical neurologists and neurosurgeons to distinguish patients considered to have brain damage from patients with no known history of disease. After trying and rejecting hundreds of tests that did not perform the basic job of discriminating normal adults from brain-damaged adults, he put together a battery of tests originally developed for a variety of purposes. For example, his battery included the Seguin-Goddard Form Board, a test that originated in the mid-19th century as a measure of so-called feeble-mindedness (Seguin, 1907), the Seashore Rhythm Test from the Seashore Test of Musical Aptitude (Saetveit, Lewis, & Seashore, 1940), and modifications of other tests (e.g., Boston University Speech Sound Perception Test) as well as tests that he originated, such as the Finger Oscillation or Finger Tapping Test

(Halstead, 1947), and the most original, the Category Test (Halstead, 1947). From these tests he constructed an index of impairment that could be used to predict the presence of brain damage. In the early 1950s his former graduate student, Ralph Reitan, continuing in this perfect example of the empiricist tradition, modified and systematized Halstead's original battery to include observations of left- versus right-sided motor performance, a sensory-perceptual examination, and an aphasia screening examination (Reitan, 1955). He also developed a set of test norms for the battery after administering the battery to patients with focal and diffuse brain damage and to a group of normal controls. In addition, he developed indexes of brain damage, permitting localization and inferred causality. The resulting fixed battery of tests, widely known as the Halstead-Reitan Neuropsychological Battery (HRB), stimulated a remarkable body of research as Halstead's original methods were applied to different patient populations, such as children and patients with epilepsy psychiatric illness.

The HRB is clearly empiricist with a clearly nonlocalizationist origin. The fixed battery approach pioneered by Halstead and Reitan has the advantage of providing a standard set of measures by which different patients can be compared. After the measures are established, it is easy to extend the scope of the battery to new populations and to collect extensive norms. Although the advantage of stability and comparability is clearly the strength of a fixed battery approach, this particular battery has found itself decreasing in popularity in recent years for a number of reasons. The practical problem with the purely empiricist approach is that it does not necessarily lead to the most efficient or interpretable measures. The HRB is extremely long and tedious for some patients, leading to reports of noncompliance and discomfort, particularly in older and more impaired patients. In today's environment of limited or capped payment of medical expenses, batteries of this size are difficult to justify economically. In addition, it is sometimes difficult to describe what the constituent tests are measuring other than the obvious intuitive characteristics of the tasks. In many cases, the relevance of task performance is difficult to tie to real-life situations.

Although not strictly antilocalizationist, the research tradition of the HRB has allowed for the prediction of focal lesions only as they emerge from the variables available in the battery. This has led to the development of a variety of prediction formulae and decision rules that have been offered in order to predict the presence of focal lesions. These formulas, which are difficult to interpret, sometimes appear to be random comparisons of tasks (e.g., Parsons, Vega, & Burn, 1969) or do not generalize beyond the populations in which they were validated. In recent years, as more cognitively based approaches have emerged, some psychologists have attempted to relate the tests and findings of the HRB to the cognitive domains of language, memory and other functions (Reitan & Wolfson, 1996), although such tasks as the Aphasia Screening Test and even the venerable Category Test seem anachronistic in view of the evolution of the concepts of language and executive functions these tests were designed to assess. Still, the wealth of referent validating data, the fact that the battery may be administered by a technician, and the convenience of receiving training in this approach have made the HRB a model for other approaches.

Luria-Nebraska Neuropsychological Battery (LNNB)

Alexander R. Luria, a Russian neuropsychologist, was a contemporary of Ward Halstead. Although Luria worked at roughly the same time as Halstead, he took a very different approach from his American colleague to the development of techniques for assessing the effects of brain damage. Luria published in the Soviet Union, where scientists felt great pressure to relate research to the Pavlovian concepts of conditioning and inhibition. He and his mentor, Vygotsky, were staunch cognitivists who concerned themselves with the formulation of rich descriptions of the development and structure of human mental functions. Luria's model of brain organization was a direct reflection of the concept that human mental faculties were composed of elementary intellectual building blocks; these components could be used to solve the problems of action and thought in a variety of different manners. Cognition was a dynamic process that varied as function of development, the demands of a particular problem situation, and, in the case of Luria's neuropsychology clinics, of the presence of brain damage.

Luria described his approach in some detail in his landmark book, *Higher Cortical Functions,* published in English in 1966. He described hundreds of tasks that could be used in a seemingly infinite array of patterns in order to characterize the details of the effects of brain damage in each particular case. This approach was acknowledged as brilliant and insightful but was seen as forbiddingly complex and impractical for the average clinician, who would not have the mentorship available to develop the skills needed to apply these methods reliably. In addition, the standard set by the Halstead-Reitan approach made many clinicians suspect that Luria's inherently variable methodology could not be subjected to conventional means of assessing reliability and validity.

Although Luria's conception of brain organization and his approach to the development of cognitive theory were remarkable in that they foreshadowed much of what characterizes modern cognitive neuropsychology and experimental psychology research, his approach to assessment would have remained an exotic curiosity if not for a Norwegian student, Anne-Lise Christensen, who after apprenticing herself to Luria, introduced to the United States a detailed description of Luria's test techniques, entitled "Luria's Neuropsychological Investigation," that included a set of materials (stimulus cards, photographs, etc.) to which Luria alludes in *Higher Cortical Functions*. Charles Golden, a Nebraska-based neuropsychologist who was an expert in the Halstead-Reitan approach, used these materials along with Thomas Hammeke and Arnold Purisch to develop a new battery of tests. Golden hoped both to take advantage of Luria's knack for developing tasks that seemed to reveal the details of basic brain functions and retain the rigorous empirical tradition of the Halstead-Reitan Battery.

The publication of the Luria-Nebraska Neuropsychological Battery (LNNB) (Golden, Hammeke, & Purisch, 1978) represented a controversial landmark in the development of neuropsychological test methods. Golden's method, which combines items that can discriminate between subjects with brain damage and normal subjects into scales named after various cognitive or functional domains such as reading and writing, was severely criticized for not representing the concepts advocated by Luria. Luria, for example, described a variety of variations of how a seemingly simple function like writing can break down depending on the specific underlying brain lesion or system that was disrupted. Luria mentioned basic orthography (the development of letters and words as holistically represented symbols), the association of sound with letter and word, and so forth as potential components of writing that may be affected independently as a reflection of the type and localization of a lesion. According to Golden's critics, combining the tasks that Luria used to develop a description of variations in a function into a single scale subverts Luria's goal of finding the correct descriptive recipe for every variation in performance. The LNNB has also been criticized for its lack of sensitivity to certain problems such as language. Although the Luria-Nebraska Neuropsychological Battery never gained the popularity of the Halstead-Reitan Battery, it developed a loyal following who appreciated its relative brevity and the increasing base of empirical findings to support its validity as a neuropsychological instrument. Although many psychologists would argue that the Luria-Nebraska Battery represents a failed attempt to make Luria's methods more accessible and reliable, most would admit that it provides some hope that more efficient, empirically based approaches to assessment can be developed.

Boston Process Approach (BPA)

While the Halstead-Reitan Neuropsychological Battery was establishing itself as the benchmark method for assessing brain damage, a critical mass of investigators had begun to work on the problems of brain/behavior relationships in the Boston area. Researchers and clinicians interested in language, memory, perception, and other classic psychological issues coalesced under the charismatic leadership of Norman Geschwind, one of the great behavioral neurologists of the 20th century, and Harold Goodglass, a clinical psychologist who brought the study of aphasia into the realm of psychology. In Boston, American psychology's then-new focus on cognition had begun to revolutionize studies of the brain. Geschwind and Goodglass came from different disciplines, but both researchers approached the task of studying the brain as a process of analysis and reduction to basic elements. Influenced by German neurology, theoretical linguistics, and cognitive psychology, this work used an experimental approach different from that of the Halstead-Reitan tradition. Davis Howes, Jean Gleason, Edgar Zurif, and Sheila Blumstein joined Dr. Goodglass's efforts to adapt the methods of psychophysics, linguistics, and developmental psychology to revolutionize the study of aphasia. At the same time, Nelson Butters' and Laird Cermak's studies of memory and amnesia helped bring the subject of brain damage to the attention of mainstream experimental psychology.

It was in this atmosphere that Edith Kaplan, a graduate student of developmental psychologist Heinz Werner, came to work. Dr. Kaplan, working as an assistant to Dr. Goodglass, brought to the Boston Veteran's Affair Medical Center an acute eye for observing patients' behavior and Heinz Werner's lesson that different cognitive processes could be used by different individuals to solve the same problem. Werner taught that cognitive development was characterized by changes in the means by which children solved problems. Encouraged by the sympathies of other clinicians and researchers with whom she worked, Dr. Kaplan applied Werner's ideas to patients who had undergone a newly-developed neurosurgical treatment for epilepsy involving the cutting of the corpus callosum, the major neural bridge between the two cerebral hemispheres. She noticed that the patients solved a puzzle construction task called Block Design from the Wechsler Adult Intelligence Scale (WAIS) differently when the task was placed to the right of the patient from when the task was placed to the left of the patient. Over the next twenty years, Kaplan compiled hundreds of such observations, which she imparted to students and other psychologists through supervision and seminars. In 1991 she published a complete modification of the Wechsler Adult Intelligence Scale–Revised (WAIS-R) in the Wechsler Adult Intelligence Scale–Revised Neuropsychological Instrument (WAIS-R NI), reflecting her adaptations and observational recommendations (Kaplan et al., 1991). The Boston Process Approach, as these methods were dubbed in 1986, (Milberg, Hebben, & Kaplan, 1996) has at its core the idea that task performance is more important than the task itself. In practice, although most patients would receive a core battery of tests including the WAIS, the Wechsler Memory Scale, the Rey-Osterrieth Complex Figure, and other tests, Dr. Kaplan would use what would be considered a *flexible battery approach*. This approach adds measures from a long list of tests borrowed from various domains to reflect referral questions and to follow up on the observations made with the initial battery given.

Initially, the Boston Process Approach was criticized for not having supporting norms or sufficiently detailed standard methods to assess the psychometric properties of reliability and validity. A growing body of research in the last twenty years, however, supports Kaplan's observations (e.g., Bihrle, Bellugi, Delis, & Marks, 1989; Freedman et al., 1994; Joy, et al., 2001; Wecker et al., 2000). In addition, some researchers have recently attempted to quantify the BPA (Poreh, 2000). Nevertheless, the Boston Process Approach never sparked the explosion of research that the Halstead-Reitan Battery did and still suffers from relatively limited normative information. The WAIS-R NI (Kaplan et al., 1991) is one of the few examples of tests published with some standard information about reliability and standard errors of measurement. Even this landmark test, however, does not provide reliability and validity information for the hundreds of observations that Kaplan and her students used for making clinical inferences. In spite of these significant limitations, the approach has gained increasing popularity in recent years because it provides clinicians with much greater descriptive power than either the Halstead-Reitan or Luria-Nebraska batteries. To many it is seen as a modern version of the methods taught by Luria, using conventional, familiar neuropsychological instruments and techniques that are more readily learned and adapted. Rapid Reference 1.4 provides a summary of the principal advantages and disadvantages of the major approaches to neuropsychological assessment.

Other Approaches and Contributions

In addition to the Halstead-Reitan Neuropsychological Battery, Luria-Nebraska Neuropsychological Battery, and the Boston Process Approach, a number of laboratories have made significant contributions to test practices, providing tests and clinically available data that have proven useful in a number of settings. In many cases, these laboratories have produced a wealth of supportive data and have made substantial contributions to both experimental and clinical research.

Because of the limits of space in this text, we have painted some of these remaining contributors to clinical neuropsychology with relatively broad strokes, grouping together individuals who otherwise deserve individual mention:

- *Contributions from Canada.* A number of major contributors to clinical assessment resources have been located in Canada. These contributors include the laboratory of Brenda Milner, who conducted hundreds of studies of the neurosurgery patients at the Montreal Neurological Institute. She and her colleagues and students, including Doreen Kimura and Sandra Witelson, were responsible for producing highly sophisticated tests of executive and motor functions and memory (e.g., Design Fluency Test, Dichotic Listening, and Dichaptic Perception Test).
- *Contributions from Europe.* A number of countries, including France (e.g., Hecaen), Italy (DeRenzi, et al.), Norway (Klove), and Germany (Poeck), have supported acclaimed laboratories in neuropsychology,

≡ *Rapid Reference 1.4*

Advantages/Disadvantages of Major Approaches to Neuropsychological Assessment

Halstead-Reitan Battery

Advantages

- Empirically designed battery with nonlocalizationist origins
- Wealth of validating data
- Reliability and comparability across different patient groups
- Ability to be administered by a technician

Disadvantages

- Length and inefficiency
- Complex measures; difficulty of knowing which functions are being measured
- Difficulty of economic justification, often because of length

Luria-Nebraska Battery

Advantages

- Empirically designed battery based on Luria's measures
- Single scales for various functional or cognitive domains
- Relative brevity of administration time
- Increasing base of empirical findings

Disadvantages

- Not an accurate reflection of Luria's method
- Not as popular as Halstead-Reitan battery
- Single scales inconsistent with Luria's view of individual variation

Boston Process Approach

Advantages

- Frequent use of adaptations of validated measures
- Flexibility in matching tests to referral question
- Great descriptive power

Disadvantages

- Produces a relatively limited set of normative data for qualitative findings
- Depends upon observational skills for its use
- Requires specific training

contributing important tests of language, memory, and visual functions (e.g., Token Test and the Grooved Pegboard Test), as well as scoring schemes for apraxia (e.g., Poeck, 1986).

- *Contributions from Britain.* Great Britain has supported several internationally famous neuropsychology laboratories. The laboratory of Elizabeth Warrington, for example, has been responsible for several generations of major contributors to clinical and experimental neuropsychology. The group of psychologists working at the Rivermead Rehabilitation Hospital published a number of well-normed tests of functions that are designed to represent real life situations (e.g., Warrington Recognition Memory Test and The Rivermead Behavioural Memory Test), including a battery of tests to assess memory and attention. These tests, which reflect contemporary ideas derived from cognitive neuropsychology, are highly adaptable to the purposes described earlier in the section entitled, "Uses of Neuropsychological Assessment." They deserve to be considered by any practicing neuropsychologist and may become (in terms of popularity) the Halstead-Reitan Battery of the future.

- *Contributions of Arthur Benton.* The Arthur Benton Laboratory in Iowa City, Iowa, deserves special mention (Benton, Sivan, deS Hamsher, Varney, & Spreen, 1994). Dr. Benton pioneered the development of highly specific descriptive tests of cognitive functions (e.g., Line Orientation and the Benton Visual Retention Test). It is not clear why these tests did not gain more popularity, other than the sheer force of data supporting the Halstead-Reitan Battery, which appeared contemporaneously with many of Benton's tests. He designed and normed memory and visual functions tests that are still very useful in special clinical testing situations.

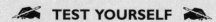

TEST YOURSELF

1. **The majority of tests used by neuropsychologists were not usually developed for the purpose of assessing brain damage.** True or False?

2. **Tests such as the Boston Diagnostic Aphasia Exam and the California Verbal Learning Test were constructed with sensitivity to brain damage as the primary consideration.** True or False?

3. **Which neuropsychological test battery is the best example of test development based on an empirical approach?**

   (a) Luria-Nebraska Neuropsychological Battery

   (b) Halstead-Reitan Battery

   (c) Boston Process Approach Battery

   (d) Luria Neuropsychological Investigation

4. **What is a clinical neuropsychologist?**

   (a) A psychologist board certified in clinical neuropsychology by the American Board of Professional Psychology or the American Board of Professional Neuropsychology

   (b) A psychologist with a doctorate in clinical neuropsychology

   (c) A psychologist licensed as a neuropsychologist in his/her state

   (d) All of the above

5. **Holism theory suggests that different psychological functions are subserved by distinct and separate structures in the brain.** True or False?

6. **Localization theory holds that brain lesions may have effects that differ as a function of location, but that the brain involves multiple structures working together.** True or False?

7. **Ideally, neuropsychological tests should be sensitive to the presence of brain damage and have ecological validity.** True or False?

Answers: 1. True; 2. False; 3. b; 4. d; 5. False; 6. False; 7. True

Two

THE DISCIPLINE OF NEUROPSYCHOLOGICAL ASSESSMENT

EDUCATION AND KNOWLEDGE BASE

Before we discuss some of the specific skills required for the collection and interpretation of neuropsychological test data, we should consider the knowledge, training, and experience that the professional skills necessary for the practice of neuropsychology. Until recently, the skills necessary for competence as a neuropsychologist were acquired on the job—few graduate programs or predoctoral internships provided formal skills in this area. Many members of the generation of neuropsychologists trained shortly after World War II were largely self-taught or were guided by mentors who directed them toward texts and medical school courses helpful to the development of what were effectively apprenticeship roles. A traditional path was to obtain a doctoral degree in clinical psychology and then to receive specialty training in neuropsychology. Because of the lack of specific guidelines on training in neuropsychology, those choosing to call themselves clinical neuropsychologists had widely disparate backgrounds and experience. Many were simply psychologists who administered neuropsychological tests, others were psychologists who had taken a weekend workshop in neuropsychological assessment, others were clinical psychologists with specialized training in neuropsychology, and a minority were psychologists, board-certified in clinical neuropsychology following credential review and examination.

In 1987 a joint task force sanctioned by the International Neuropsychological Society (INS) and Division 40 of the APA published the first formal guidelines on the education, accreditation, and credentialing of neuropsychologists (Adams & Rourke, 1992), setting some basic standards for training in clinical neuropsychology. The committee concluded that doctoral training in neuropsychology should prepare students for "health service delivery, basic clinical research, teaching and consultation" relevant to neuropsychology. Such graduate study should include a core of generic clinical and general psychology courses accompanied by "specialized training in the neurosciences as well as basic human and animal neuropsychology" along with "specific training in clinical neuropsychology."

These standards were most recently updated in September 1997 in Houston, Texas, by a delegation of 40 neuropsychologists representing Division 40 and the National Academy of Neuropsychology (NAN), as well as directors of training programs in neuropsychology at the doctoral, internship and postdoctoral levels (Hannay, et al., 1998). The consensus report of The Houston Conference, as this meeting is now known, mandates that education and training in clinical neuropsychology follow the scientist-practitioner model (Belar & Perry, 1992). The scientist-practitioner model, which was adopted in 1949 at the Boulder, Colorado, conference on doctoral education and training in clinical psychology, specified that clinical psychologists should be trained first as scientists and second as practicing professionals. As applied to neuropsychology, this model dictates that education and training in clinical neuropsychology integrate all aspects of general neuropsychology. Professional education and training would begin with doctoral education and continue through internship and postdoctoral residency education and training. The Houston Conference defined a clinical neuropsychologist as a "professional psychologist trained in the science of brain-behavior relationships. The clinical neuropsychologist specializes in the application of assessment and intervention principles based on the scientific study of human behavior across the lifespan as it relates to normal and abnormal functioning of the central nervous system."

The Houston Conference envisioned that education and training in the specialty field of clinical neuropsychology would be necessary for individuals who engage in clinical neuropsychology, those who supervise clinical neuropsychologists, as well as those who call themselves clinical neuropsychologists. According to this delegation, education and training in the specialty of clinical neuropsychology is also essential for psychologists involved in the education and training of others in the specialty of clinical neuropsychology.

In keeping with the earlier 1987 standards, the Houston Conference recommended a particular knowledge base necessary for clinical neuropsychologists: a generic psychology core, a generic clinical core, a specific neuropsychology core, and a specific core for the study of brain-behavior relationships. This knowledge base is acquired through doctoral courses and other didactic methods. The generic psychology core comprises courses drawn from a general psychology curriculum, including courses in statistics, research design, and methodology; learning, cognition and perception; the biological basis of behavior; social psychology and personality; lifespan development; history; and cultural and individual differences. For practicing neuropsychologists, a working knowledge of these areas is not a mere academic exercise. Clinical decision making in both clinical psychology and neuropsychology requires an understanding of basic statistical and psychometric concepts, the norming and standardization of tests, and the use of normative data in making clinical judgments.

It could be argued that neuropsychological assessment is a direct application of cognitive psychology, because a knowledge of modern concepts of such functions as attention, memory, and language are needed to interpret and explain correctly the content of most neuropsychological instruments. For example, an understanding that memory may be dissociated into processes important for the encoding, storage, and retrieval of information and that these functions may be related to different brain systems, guides the interpretation of such clinical measures as the Wechsler Memory Scale–Third Edition (WMS-III). A course in the biological basis of behavior is requisite for understanding the biological or physiological functions that may be disrupted by brain damage; such a course provides considerable information on the neuroanatomical connections between various cortical and subcortical structures. Knowing that the frontal lobes are intimately connected with these cortical and subcortical structures, for example, is critical to understanding the far-reaching effects of lesions in this area. An understanding of personality, social behavior and lifespan development also provides essential information that clinical neuropsychologists use to understand test performance and to make recommendations that take into account the overall context of behavior presented by a patient. What may appear to be deficits on a neuropsychological test for a young adult, for example, may be a reflection of normal development for a child on the one hand or normal aging for an elderly adult on the other hand. Coursework in cultural and individual differences is a prerequisite for understanding test findings as they apply to a particular patient because tests may contain cultural biases.

The Houston Conference also recommended a core of courses typically offered as part of a clinical psychology program, including psychopathology, personality theory, psychometrics theory, interview and assessment techniques, intervention, and ethics. This recommendation reflects the view that clinical neuropsychology should be regarded either as a subspecialty within clinical psychology or as a separate specialization having requirements similar to those of clinical psychology. The clinical neuropsychologist needs to understand all the manifestations and variations of personality and psychopathology, as well as how these issues can affect test performance and human adjustment. The clinical neuropsychologist must have skill in interviewing techniques and assessment procedures, a sound foundation in test theory, and a good basic understanding of professional ethics.

Neuropsychological test performance can be affected by nonneurological factors, and neurological disease may mimic nonneurological conditions. For example, high levels of anxiety and depression can impair test performance in the absence of neurological disease, and patients with brainstem and basal ganglia lesions may have symptoms that mimic depression. Because neuropsychological test performance is not affected only by neurological conditions, the clinical neuropsychologist must always make neuropsychological judgments in the context of clinical judgments about psychopathology.

In addition to more general clinical coursework, a clinical neuropsychologist requires knowledge in several particular specialized areas. The Houston Conference recommended that the specialty curriculum include topics that provide foundations for the study of brain-behavior relationships. These topics include functional neuroanatomy, neurological and related disorders, nonneurological conditions affecting central nervous system (CNS) functions, functional neuroimaging, neurochemistry, and neuropsychology of behavior. A working knowledge of neuroanatomy, neuropathology and neurosciences provides a brain-behavior framework for the judgments that a clinical neuropsychologist makes. Specialty training in clinical neuropsychology might also include coursework on the neuropsychology of perceptual, cognitive and executive functions, as well as research design and methods specific to the study of brain-behavior relationships.

Additionally, the Houston Conference recommended that clinical neuropsychology programs include courses specific to the discipline of neuropsychology, including specialized neuropsychological assessment and intervention techniques, research design and analysis in neuropsychology, professional issues and ethics in neuropsychology, and practical implications of neuropsychological conditions. Unique to neuropsychology, these courses expand upon basic education and training in clinical psychology and provide a knowledge base for the specialty of clinical neuropsychology.

The Houston Conference also mandated that clinical neuropsychologists acquire skills in basic areas germane to neuropsychology through the aforementioned core coursework in graduate school and through other didactic training. In the area of assessment, the Houston Conference stated that clinical neuropsychologists should possess skills in information gathering, history taking, test selection, test administration, interpretation and diagnosis, treatment planning, report writing, feedback, and recognition of multicultural issues. In the area of treatment and intervention, the necessary skills included identification of intervention targets; specification of intervention needs; formulation, implementation and monitoring of intervention plans; outcome assessment; and recognition of multicultural issues. In the area of consultation, the Houston Conference named important skill areas such as effective basic communication, determination and clarification of referral issues, knowledge of referral sources regarding neuropsychological services, communication of evaluation results, and education of patients and families regarding services and disorders. In the area of research, important skills to acquire were named as selection of research topics; review of the scientific literature; design, execution, and monitoring of research; outcome evaluation; and communication of results. In the areas of teaching and supervision, the Houston Conference recommended that skills be acquired through methods of effective teaching, plan and design of courses and curricula; use of effective educational technologies, and use of effective supervision methods.

In 1987, the Joint Committee suggested that training in clinical neuropsychology include an internship devoting at least 50% of one-year, full-time training experience to neuropsychology and at least 20% of the training to general clinical training. Perhaps feeling that this recommendation was too narrow, the Houston Conference proposed that the percentage of time devoted to clinical neuropsychology "should be determined by the training needs of the individual intern." It also recommended that the internship be completed in an APA- or Canadian Psychological Association– (CPA–) approved professional psychology training program. This means that graduate training in neuropsychology should also occur in an APA- or CPA-approved program in clinical or counseling psychology. Students can gain experience through attendance at neurobehavioral rounds, neurology rounds, and neuropsychological case conferences, as well as through hands-on testing and supervision.

Recognizing that the skills needed for independent practice in neuropsychology could not typically be acquired with only a one-year internship, the Houston Conference suggested that specialty training be completed with a two-year postdoctoral residency in neuropsychology. They recommended that accreditation of such programs be based on the presence of a board-certified clinical neuropsychologist, that the program be held at one or more training sites, that on-site supervision be provided, that access be available to clinical services and training programs in medical specialties and allied professions, and that interactions with other residents be required. The Houston Conference indicated that a "significant percentage of time" should be spent in clinical service, research and education. Preferably, the neuropsychologist should train in a medical setting and gain exposure to a wide variety of patients with neurological and psychiatric disorders.

These training experiences are necessary to attain the advanced skills required for advanced understanding of brain-behavior relationships, as well as for independent neuropsychological evaluation and treatment. By virtue of their education, training, and experience, graduates of residency training must be both capable of scholarly activity and eligible for licensure or certification in the independent practice of psychology. In addition, upon the training's completion, the neuropsychologist should be eligible for board certification in clinical neuropsychology by the American Board of Professional Psychology.

Recognizing that education and training do not end with the completion of a postdoctoral residency, the Houston Conference indicated that the clinical neuropsychologist would be expected to engage in continuing education "to enhance or maintain the already established competence of clinical neuropsychologists by updating previously acquired knowledge and skills or by acquiring new knowledge or skills" (Hannay et al., 1998, pp. 164–165). They cautioned that continuing education by itself is not sufficient to retrain as a clinical neuropsychologist or to acquire the skills necessary to educate and then "identify oneself as a clinical neuropsychologist" (Hannay et al., 1998, p. 165). Rapid Reference 2.1 provides a summary of the Houston Conference guidelines for specialty education and training in the field of clinical neuropsychology.

≡ *Rapid Reference 2.1*

The Houston Conference: Guidelines for Specialty Education and Training

Knowledge Base

- Generic psychology core
- Generic clinical core
- Foundations for the study of brain-behavior relationships
- Foundations for the practice of clinical neuropsychology

Skills

- Assessment: Information gathering, history taking, selecting and administering tests, interpreting data, making a diagnosis, treatment planning, report writing, providing feedback, and recognizing multicultural issues
- Treatment and interventions: Identifying intervention targets, specifying intervention needs, formulating, implementing, and monitoring intervention plans, assessing outcomes, and recognizing multicultural issues
- Consultation: Communicating effectively determining and clarifying referral issues, knowing referral sources, communicating results and recommendations, and educating parents and families
- Research: Selecting research topics; reviewing literature; designing and executing, and monitoring research; evaluating outcomes; and communicating results
- Teaching and supervision methods of effective teaching, planning and designing courses and curricula, using effective educational technologies and supervision methods

Doctoral education in clinical neuropsychology at regionally accredited university

Internship training in clinical neuropsychology in APA or CPA accredited program

Residency education and training in clinical neuropsychology for equivalent of two years full-time

Continuing education in clinical neuropsychology

Source: Hannay et al. (1998).

DEFINITION OF A CLINICAL NEUROPSYCHOLOGIST

With recognition of the specialty of clinical neuropsychology by the APA and the CPA, defining who is a clinical neuropsychologist has taken on increased importance. The Houston Conference has set out the preceding specific guidelines for that purpose. The National Academy of Neuropsychology has also drafted an official position on the definition of a clinical neuropsychologist (Weinstein, 2001). NAN takes the position that:

> A clinical neuropsychologist is a healthcare professional within the field of psychology with a specialty in the applied science of brain-behavior relationships. The field of clinical neuropsychology uses this knowledge in the assessment, diagnosis, treatment, and/or rehabilitation of patients across the lifespan with neurological, medical and psychiatric conditions, as well as other cognitive and learning disorders. The clinical neuropsychologist uses one or more psychological, neurological, cognitive, behavioral, and/or physiological principles, techniques and tests to evaluate patients' cognitive, behavioral, and emotional strengths and weaknesses and their relationship to normal and abnormal central nervous system functioning. The clinical neuropsychologist frequently uses this information provided by other medical/healthcare providers to identify and diagnose impairment, and plan and implement intervention strategies. Clinical neuropsychologists are independent practitioners (healthcare providers) of psychology and clinical neuropsychology (Weinstein, 2001, p. 9).

According to NAN's draft statement, the minimum educational and training criteria for a clinical neuropsychologist include state licensure as a provider or practitioner in psychology or neuropsychology, a doctoral degree in psychology from an accredited university training program, an internship in a clinically relevant area of professional psychology, and two years (with at least one year at a postdoctoral level) of full-time specialty training in neuropsychology with supervision by a clinical neuropsychologist. NAN also recommends that clinical neuropsychologists undergo board certification through examination, peer review, and formal verification of credentials to demonstrate "further evidence of advanced training, supervision, and applied fund of knowledge in clinical neuropsychology."

NAN's draft statement does not differ significantly from the definition of a clinical neuropsychologist adopted as the official position of the Division of Clinical Neuropsychology (Division 40) of the APA on August 12, 1988 (Division 40, 1989):

> A Clinical Neuropsychologist is a professional psychologist who applies principles of assessment and intervention based upon the scientific study of human behavior as it relates to normal and abnormal functioning of the central nervous system. The Clinical Neuropsychologist is a doctoral-level psychology provider of diagnostic and intervention services who has demonstrated competence in the application of such principles for human welfare following:
>
> A. Successful completion of systematic didactic and experiential training in neuropsychology and neuroscience at a regionally accredited university;
> B. Two or more years of appropriate supervised training applying neuropsychological services in a clinical setting;
> C. Licensing and certification to provide psychological services to the public by the laws of the state or province in which he or she practices;
> D. Review by one's peers as a test of these competencies.

Attainment of the ABCN/ABPP Diploma in Clinical Neuropsychology is the clearest evidence of competence as a Clinical Neuropsychologist, assuring that all of these criteria have been met.

TRAINING, EXPERTISE, AND CREDENTIALS

Most programs that offer specialty training for clinical neuropsychology students are PhD or PsyD programs in clinical psychology. These programs provide students with the opportunity to specialize in clinical neuropsychology in the context of general clinical training. A few have been specifically accredited as clinical neuropsychology programs. Some neuropsychologists come from degree programs other than neuropsychology, obtaining specific coursework outside their degree programs.

Although the latter was a more common training route for the first postwar

CAUTION

Remember: The term *neuropsychologist* is not well regulated. Most states do not prohibit licensed psychologists from performing so-called neuropsychological evaluations and calling themselves neuropsychologists regardless of their specific training.

generation of neuropsychologists, most students do not choose this route today because these students have difficulty in obtaining internship and practicum training. Training programs that obtain APA accreditation must usually take students from clinical psychology, counseling psychology, or clinical neuropsychology programs, making it difficult (if not impossible) for students without clinical degrees to gain admission. It is difficult to estimate precisely how many doctoral students graduate with specialties in clinical neuropsychology from accredited programs each year. Data from a list of clinical neuropsychology training programs maintained for Division 40 of the American Psychological Association by Lloyd I. Cripe and available in updated form on the Division 40 website (http://www.div40.org) cites 39 accredited programs offering doctoral training in clinical neuropsychology that admit between 169 to 189 new students each year (Cripe, 2000). This is likely an underestimate because this list does not include all doctoral programs that offer some or all of the recommended coursework in neuropsychology. The list of training programs also contains 55 internship offerings and 85 postdoctoral programs. *The Clinical Neuropsychologist* (TCN) lists the name of the program and its directors, along with the types of patients served, the types of disorders typically seen, and the specialty areas of the program. The list also specifies additional program details, such as the number of positions available and the length of the program, as well as whether the director of the program is board certified.

Neuropsychological assessment requires that practitioners be able to evaluate and recognize behavioral, personality and psychiatric consequences of neurological disorders and attribute correctly behavioral or cognitive symptoms to neurological versus nonneurological causes, or a combination. Training in clinical psychology programs provides many prerequisites for developing such skills. Furthermore, many doctoral programs offering specialty training in clinical neuropsychology are parts of universities that have programs in medicine or strong affiliations with independent local medical schools; such associations ensure that necessary coursework and practicum experiences are available.

Doctoral programs in clinical psychology with a specialty in neuropsychology or doctoral programs in clinical neuropsychology typically require five years for completion. Internships usually occur in the fourth or fifth year, most often in general hospital or medical center settings. These settings allow access to a broad range of patient populations and should offer experience with patients with a wide variety of neurological and psychiatric disorders.

Practitioners in neuropsychology must usually obtain state licensure in psychology. With the exception of Louisiana, most states do not offer specific licensure in neuropsychology, leaving the representation of professional expertise in neuropsychology to the ethical judgment of the psychologist. Technically, one could argue that the only professionals who can call themselves clinical neuropsychologists are those with one or more of these qualifications: a doctoral degree in clinical neuropsychology, licensure as a clinical neuropsychologist, or board certification in clinical neuropsychology. However, the only credential that currently demonstrates recognized competence in neuropsychology is the achievement of board certification or diplomate status through peer review and examination.

Today, diplomate status certifying competence to practice neuropsychology is offered by the American Board of Clinical Neuropsychology (ABCN) and by the American Board of Professional Neuropsychology (ABPN). Both governing bodies do so on the basis of a review of credentials, work samples, and some form of examination, often leading to confusion among practitioners and the public. Some significant differences exist between the procedures for obtaining diplomate status from these two boards.

ABCN offers its diplomate status under the auspices of the American Board of Professional Psychology (ABPP). ABPP has its own general standards and criteria for all diplomates that are implied in the ABCN degree. These standards include completion of basic and more advanced coursework in psychology along with supervised training and receipt of a doctorate in psychology. ABCN requires coursework relevant to the specialty of neuropsychology in the areas of basic neurosciences, neuroanatomy, neuropathology, clinical neurology, and neuropsychological assessment, in addition to more clinically based courses such as psychopathology as well as psychological assessment and intervention.

> **DON'T FORGET**
> ....
> Diplomate status certifying competence to practice neuropsychology is offered through examination only by the American Board of Professional Neuropsychology (ABPN) or by the American Board of Clinical Neuropsychology (ABCN) under the auspices of the American Board of Professional Psychology (ABPP).

ABCN also requires a doctoral degree in psychology and licensure or certification in psychology. The ABCN degree also requires postdoctoral experience in psychology. There is no formal supervision requirement for individuals who obtained their doctorate before 1981. For those who completed their doctorate between 1981 and 1989, the supervision requirement is 1600 hours at the pre- or postdoctoral levels. For those who obtained their doctorate after 1989, the supervision requirement is 2 years of clinical neuropsychological training, of which one year may be predoctoral. For both groups, supervision must be done by a clinical neuropsychologist. After successful completion of the credential review, the applicant must pass a stringent 100-item, multiple-choice written examination to demonstrate his or her breadth and depth of knowledge in clinical neuropsychology; if successful on the examination, the applicant is invited to submit two work samples for review. These samples must include the raw data as well as justification for both the procedures used and the conclusions drawn. ABCN uses specific criteria to evaluate the work samples and if two of three reviewers approve the samples, then ABCN invite the candidate to sit for an oral examination covering fact finding, work samples, ethics, and professional responsibility. The pass rate for the work samples was 75% in 1998; pass rates for the written and oral examinations are usually in the 60–70% range (Ivnik, Haaland & Bieliauskas, 2000).

Board certification in clinical neuropsychology by ABPP is a credential designating competence to practice; additionally, "The APA recognizes the significant service to the profession and to the public that is rendered by the American Board of Professional Psychology" (APA Association Rules, Section 130-2). Board certification in clinical neuropsychology by ABPP is comparable to board certification in various medical specialty areas by the American Board of Medical Specialties (ABMS), the only specialty certification organization recognized by the American Medical Association (AMA). Board certification in clinical neuropsychology by ABPP is a recognized credential denoting competence for work in many different arenas (e.g., the courtroom and HMOs). The credential confers preference in faculty positions in psychology training programs and increased pay in the armed services; it also ensures licensure reciprocity in many states (Ivnik, Haaland & Bieliauskas, 2000).

ABPN also requires that the applicant have a doctoral degree in psychology and current licensure or certification to practice psychology in a state, province or territory. In addition, ABPN requires professional experience in neuropsychology, for a minimum of 5 years, of which 1 year may be a supervised neuropsychological internship. The applicant must also have been engaged in providing neuropsychological services for a minimum of 500 hours per year during the past 5 years. In addition, ABPN requires involvement in continuing education in neuropsychology either by taking or teaching APA- (or CPA-) approved continuing education courses. As part of the application process, ABPN requires a written response to a clinical scenario and submission of two work samples for review by a panel of examiners, but does not require a formal written examination. After successful completion of the work sample review, the applicant is invited to an oral examination covering the areas of core knowledge, work samples, and ethics. The pass rate for second submission of work samples was 80% in 1999 and 2000; pass rates for the oral examination in the same time period averaged 95% (personal communication, Blasé, 2001). Board certification in clinical neuropsychology by ABPN indicates an advanced level of competency as a clinical neuropsychologist.

ABCN and ABPN differ in their requirements for board certification, but both require the production of work samples and oral examination. Most importantly, both of these boards are different from the so-called vanity boards that require only submission of an application and payment of a fee for board certification. These vanity boards do not require a demonstration of competence through peer review or examination.

ORGANIZATIONS

Clinical neuropsychologists have several major organizations available for affiliation, including the International Neuropsychological Society (INS), the National Academy of Neuropsychology (NAN), and Division 40 (Clinical Neuropsychology) of the American Psychological Association (APA). The purpose of the INS is to promote research, service, and education in neuropsychology and to encourage and enhance the worldwide exchange of information about brain-behavior relationships among scientific disciplines involved in brain-behavior research. INS meets twice each year; the annual meeting is in February and takes place in the United States or Canada, and the midyear meeting usually occurs in July and is most often in a European country. The membership directory for INS lists over 3,000 members from all over the world from Argentina to Yugoslavia, with most members from the United States.

NAN had 3,303 members at the time of publication of its 2000–2001 mem-

DON'T FORGET

The major organizations for clinical neuropsychologists are
- International Neuropsychological Society (INS)
- National Academy of Neuropsychologists (NAN)
- Division 40 of the American Psychological Association (APA)

bership directory. The objectives of NAN include preserving and advancing knowledge of the assessment and remediation of neurological impairments by psychological means; fostering the development of neuropsychology as a discipline, science and profession; and joining with other professional groups to exchange information in pursuit of the advancement and development of neuropsychology. NAN has held annual meetings each fall (October or November) since 1981.

In addition, neuropsychologist members can join Division 40 of the APA, the Division of Clinical Neuropsychology. According to APA bylaws, Division 40 was developed "to enhance the understanding of brain-behavior relationships and the application of such knowledge to human problems." Division 40 seeks to advance "clinical neuropsychological practice, scientific research, and professional education in the public interest." Each summer at the annual meeting of the APA, Division 40 presents scientific symposia in the area of clinical neuropsychology for education, training, and the promotion of the exchange of scientific research.

NEUROPSYCHOLOGICAL RESOURCES

Books

Many books on clinical neuropsychology can serve as reference books or resources for the clinical neuropsychologist. Rapid Reference 2.2 provides a sampling of essential works for the clinical neuropsychologist.

Journals

Enhancement of one's knowledge base requires keeping current with the latest scientific research. Numerous journals are available for that purpose. Rapid Reference 2.3 lists journals important for the continuing education of the clinical neuropsychologist.

Sample of Clinical Neuropsychology Sourcebooks

- Grant, I. G., & Adams, K. M. (1996). *Neuropsychological Assessment of Neuropsychiatric Disorders* (2nd ed.). New York: Oxford University Press.
- Heaton, R. K., Grant, I., & Matthews, C. G. (1991). *Comprehensive Norms for an Expanded Halstead-Reitan Battery.* Odessa, FL: Psychological Assessment Resources.
- Heilman, K. M., & Valenstein, E. (1993). *Clinical Neuropsychology* (2nd ed.). New York: Oxford University Press.
- Jarvis, P. E., & Barth, J. T. (1994). *The Halstead-Reitan Neuropsychological Battery: A Guide to Interpretation and Clinical Applications.* Odessa, FL: Psychological Assessment Resources.
- Lezak, M. D. (1995). *Neuropsychological Assessment* (3rd ed.). New York: Oxford University Press.
- Loring, D. W. (Ed.). (1999). *INS Dictionary of Neuropsychology.* New York: Oxford University Press.
- Mitrushina, M. N., Boone, K. B., & D'Elia, L. F. (1999). *Handbook of Normative Data for Neuropsychological Assessment.* New York: Oxford University Press.
- Spreen, O., Risser, A. H., & Edgell, D. (1995). *Developmental Neuropsychology.* New York: Oxford University Press.
- Spreen, O., & Strauss, E. (1998). *A Compendium of Neuropsychological Tests: Administration, Norms, and Commentary* (2nd ed.). New York: Oxford University Press.

Sample of Relevant Journals

- *Applied Neuropsychology*
- *Archives of Clinical Neuropsychology*
- *The Clinical Neuropsychologist*
- *Cortex*
- *Journal of Clinical and Experimental Neuropsychology*
- *Journal of Forensic Neuropsychology*
- *Journal of International Neuropsychological Society*
- *The Journal of Neuropsychiatry and Clinical Neurosciences*
- *Neuropsychiatry, Neuropsychology, and Behavioral Neurology*
- *Neuropsychologia*
- *Neuropsychology*
- *Neuropsychology Review*
- *Psychological Assessment*

🖎 TEST YOURSELF 🖎

1. **A clinical neuropsychologist is anyone who administers neuropsychological tests.** True or False?

2. **The knowledge base for a clinical neuropsychologist should include**
   (a) statistics and methodology.
   (b) neuropsychological assessment techniques.
   (c) psychopathology.
   (d) functional neuroanatomy.
   (e) all of the above.

3. **ABCN and ABPN differ in their requirements for board certification but both require the production of work samples and oral examination.** True or False?

4. **Licensure in clinical neuropsychology is widely available and is the single best credential available to clinical neuropsychologists.** True or False?

5. **The Houston Conference did not consider which of the following necessary in the education and training of a neuropsychologist?**
   (a) Doctoral degree in neuropsychology from a regionally accredited institution
   (b) Internship training in clinical neuropsychology
   (c) Core coursework in psychometric theory
   (d) Residency training in clinical neuropsychology

Answers: 1. False; 2. e; 3. True; 4. False; 5. a

Three

ESSENTIALS OF THE INTERVIEW AND CLINICAL HISTORY

OVERVIEW

A detailed reconstruction of a patient's medical, social, cultural, intellectual, and emotional past is an integral piece of the puzzle of neuropsychological assessment. Most of the clinical issues assessed by the neuropsychologist occur in the fabric of many years of development and experience. In some instances, an individual's life may be changed in only a few moments by a brain injury or stroke. In other cases, the changes in neuropsychological functions wrought by diseases of the central nervous system may unfold over months or years. A disease of the central nervous system may affect a mature adult differently from a developing adolescent, who may in turn be affected differently from a preverbal child. The patient's history and clinical interview provide the data essential to an understanding of the characteristics and time course of a patient's illness; they may also provide critical clues as to diagnosis and prognosis. The history and clinical interview also supply information about psychological or medical conditions that can affect cognitive and emotional functioning and therefore can affect test performance. Finally, the patient's educational, social, and developmental history informs the clinician about what the patient was like before the illness or injury, so that the clinician can compare current and past function. In many cases, history may be as (or more) important as formal test results themselves as a source of answers to the questions described in Chapter 1. In addition to the clinical history, astute observations of a patient's behavior before, during, and after a test session not only provide important clues to aid in the interpretation of neuropsychological test results, but may even supercede those results in drawing conclusions about core clinical referral issues.

> ## CAUTION
>
> Neuropsychological test results cannot be interpreted in a vacuum. Neuropsychological test results can only be interpreted within an historical context.

To understand these statements, we must examine the basic logic of neuropsychological test interpretation. Neuropsychological tests are psychological tests that have been shown to be sensitive to the presence of functional compromise in the central nervous system. However, it is only within the context of a patient's history that a diagnosis can be made. In order to allow for a correct interpretation of the test results, the neuropsychologist must follow a particular series of steps in analyzing the data.

First, historical information and behavioral observations are obtained through clinical interview, record review, and reports of significant others. Then a battery of tests is administered to a patient to obtain a sample of behavior. The tests are scored and the results tallied. Next, the scores obtained from the patient are compared to normative data consisting of test scores of adults or children who are similar in age, education, and (if possible and relevant) cultural background. Typically, such normative test data are obtained from samples of adults or children who have either some documented history of brain damage, or who are considered normal (with no documented history of brain damage). In most (but not all) cases, tests are scored for correct responses so that high scores reflect better performances than low scores. If the patient's scores on an individual measure or on multiple measures are lower than would be expected for a normal person of that age or education and are within the range of the scores of patients with brain damage, then the neuropsychologist must decide whether the presence of brain damage can be inferred for that patient. Can this fundamental neuropsychological inference be made simply because the patient has obtained an abnormal score (the concepts of *normal* and *abnormal* are discussed further in Chapter 5)? The short answer to the question is no. The ability to make such an inference under the circumstances described is difficult and in most cases cannot be made on the basis of the test scores alone. The process of making clinical neuropsychological judgments involves the integration of details of the patient's past and current life circumstances with empirical test data.

THE ROLE OF HISTORY

The ability of a neuropsychological test (or any clinical test for that matter) to predict or decide the clinical category to which a patient belongs can be divided into two quantifiable criteria: *sensitivity* and *specificity*. Sensitivity is the probability that the test detects or classifies a condition that is actually present. Specificity is the probability that the test correctly detects or classifies a normal performance. Tests that are specific minimize the number of normal performances that are classified as abnormal. Tests that are sensitive classify a patient as belonging to a particular group.

Consider making the decision that an individual test score belongs to a healthy person (HP) or a person with brain damage (BD). Sensitivity is the proportion of individuals with BD that the test will correctly identify as having BD, whereas specificity is the proportion of individuals who are HP and are correctly identified as HP. Values for sensitivity and specificity may vary between 0 and 100%. A test may be sensitive but not specific; that is, a test may correctly identify individuals with BD as BD, but may also misclassify HP individuals as being BD. A test may also be specific but not sensitive; that is, the test may have a low rate of misclassifying HP individuals as BD but may also have a low rate of correctly classifying patients with BD as having BD. Well-designed tests usually try to maximize both criteria, allowing trade-offs to reflect the consequences of making an incorrect decision.

The ability of a test to be sensitive and specific is greatly affected by the proportion of actual individuals in the clinical and nonclinical categories. When a condition is very rare, tests tend to be less specific (i.e., they tend to classify more individuals into the clinical group) than when the condition is more common. When a condition is very common, a test (assuming it is less than perfectly sensitive) tends to miss the occurrence of the condition. We return to the topic of base rates and diagnostic accuracy in some detail in Chapter 5, but as a general rule the patient's history provides information that allows a clinician to estimate the likelihood that a given individual is part of a particular diagnostic category. This knowledge in turn helps to determine the likelihood that the individual will show deficits on neuropsychological tests. Part of this estimation process includes determining the cognitive, behavioral, and personality characteristics that might predate any illnesses and which might contribute to the appearance of measurable performance deficits on neuropsychological tests. This determination is made by eliciting a patient's history; it is critical to the interpretation of neuropsychological tests because many neuropsychological tests are typically affected by both neuropsychological and nonneuropsychological factors, such as motivation and affect. Performance on any test of cognitive ability (i.e., most neuropsychological tests) is affected by the level of cognitive or premorbid abilities as well as the illnesses that predate the neurological injury or illness. The social and cultural background of a patient can also affect performance on neuropsychological tests. Likewise, performance is affected by various lifestyle characteristics such as nutrition and sleep, and by a variety of nonneurological medical conditions, such as chronic pain or medication effects. Performance can also be affected by personality characteristics such as attitude, motivation, and self-esteem.

If a neuropsychological condition is judged to be very unlikely from a patient's history, this affects how test results are interpreted or used. Conversely, if a condition is judged to be very common from history, this also affects how test results are interpreted or used. For example, an individual with a history of consistently poor academic performance and a vocational history consisting primarily of unskilled labor-based positions might be expected to achieve lower than normal scores on neuropsychological tests that are sensitive to the same factors related to academic performance; such tests include intelligence, vocabulary, and achievement tests. This individual is more likely to show what appear to be neuropsychological deficits than an individual with a history of excellent academic performance and a vocational history consisting of managerial or professional positions. Judgments about the effect of illnesses on brain function would need to be made more conservatively about the former patient than the latter. Ideally these judgments are made adjusted to normative data reflecting these two individuals' differing premorbid achievement levels. We revisit this issue in our discussion of test validity in Chapter 5.

HISTORY GATHERING

History is generally gathered from record review and clinical interviews. The sources for record review are many and varied. When possible, records pertaining to medical history, psychiatric history, education, and vocation should be obtained. Interview information can also come from a variety of sources, including the patient and his or her spouse, parents, siblings, teachers, caregivers, or some combination of these individuals. Because a thorough review of a patient's history is an important part of the assessment process, every effort should be made to obtain relevant history from multiple sources and not from patient report alone. Information obtained from

> **DON'T FORGET**
> ....
> A neuropsychologist's analysis and interpretation of the test results are limited by the history obtained.

significant others and records can corroborate the information obtained from the patient and can supplement those areas that are unfamiliar or unknown to the patient.

The most reliable sources of medical history are usually hospital or treating physician records. In many cases, however, historical information must be gathered from the patient or an informant. The clinician needs to be cognizant of the reliability of these data's sources and must temper any predictions or clinical judgments based on the judged accuracy of the source. Self-report about the conditions causing unconsciousness, for example, may be particularly unreliable, and should always be corroborated carefully. If self-report is the only source of information, the patient's motivation for presenting himself or herself as sick or well must also be considered. Patients and other interested informants may distort medical history to promote a particular perceived outcome of the examination. For example, a patient who is trying to avoid institutionalization or some other loss of independence may not reveal pertinent facts about falls, cardiac disease, or functional problems. Patients involved in litigation may sometimes embellish the facts surrounding the event at issue in the legal proceeding and may not report other illnesses or conditions that could have caused their problems. It is the neuropsychologist's responsibility to judge the accuracy and reliability of any source of medical history and, when possible and necessary, to corroborate the information.

CONTENT OF IMPORTANT HISTORICAL INFORMATION

Multiple items need to be addressed in record review and clinical interview that vary from the mundane like demographic information to the very personal, such as psychiatric history. Every effort should be made to address each of these areas when they are relevant to a particular patient. Within each of the areas to be addressed, multiple questions arise that require answers. Rapid Reference 3.1 provides a summary of the categories of items that should be addressed in record review and clinical interview.

≡*Rapid Reference 3.1*

Important Items to Be Addressed in Record Review and Clinical Interview

- Basic demographic data
- Description of current illness or presenting problem
- Medical history
- Psychiatric history
- Educational history
- Vocational history
- Birth history and early development
- Family background
- Current situation
- Legal history
- Military history

Basic Demographic Information

The questions here focus on name, age, date of birth, race, gender, address, phone number, and handedness. This information forms the basis for scoring of tests according to the correct demographic group and is important for billing purposes as well. An acute confusional state or dementia might be suspected if an adolescent or adult patient is unable to supply this information.

Description of the Current Illness or Presenting Problem

It is important to obtain a detailed account of the patient's current symptoms and complaints, their pervasiveness and severity, and their effect on day-to-day living. The clinician is interested in the subjective characteristics of the illness and the length of time the patient has been affected by the illness. The clinician should find out when the illness or symptoms began and how the disorder began. It is also important to discover any variation in symptoms over time and what medications, treatments, and diagnostic tests the patient has received for the problems. The patient may have already been diagnosed and the current evaluator should also know that information, as well as the functional impact that the illness or injury has had on the patient's life. Rapid Reference 3.2 provides an outline of the areas of focus when delineating the history of the presenting problem.

In many evaluations the referral question may center on an injury incurred as a result of an accident. In this instance it is important to gather information about the accident. In addition to the patient's self-report, records that are particularly helpful include police records of the accident, records from emergency medical technicians or ambulance personnel, emergency room records, and nursing notes following the initial trauma. It also becomes important to gather postinjury records to track the course of the injury. Again, this comes from interviews with the patient (when possible) and from review of medical records. The medical records that need to be examined include reports from independent medical examinations, reports of neurosurgical and neurological examinations and interventions, neuroradiological reports, hospital discharge summaries, and summaries of the examining and treating physicians, as well as previous psychological and neuropsycho-

logical assessment records, including the raw data or recording sheets for tests. Rapid Reference 3.3 summarizes the relevant injury and postinjury records that should be obtained and reviewed for evaluating an injury and its effects.

Rapid Reference 3.2

History of Presenting Problem

- A description of current symptoms and complaints
- The severity of symptoms
- The pervasiveness and duration of symptoms
- Time of onset
- Treatments and their successes
- Medications and doses
- Prior evaluations

Rapid Reference 3.3

Relevant Injury and Postinjury Records

- Police records of the accident
- EMT and ambulance reports
- Emergency room records
- Reports of independent medical examinations
- Neurological, neurosurgical, and neuroradiological records
- Hospital records
- Physician records
- Psychological and neuropsychological assessment records, including raw data

Medical History

This section focuses on the presence of major illnesses, accidental injuries, exposure to toxins, and episodes of loss of consciousness. Of interest are conditions that have some likelihood of affecting neuropsychological test results (e.g., head injury, epilepsy, stroke, and so on), but may include other conditions that present some functional limitation on the individual (e.g., asthma, colitis, and chronic obstructive pulmonary disease). Details are needed in these same categories for current illness, including time of onset, pervasiveness and severity of symptoms, past and current treatments, and the progression of symptoms. In addition, data must be gathered concerning current and past health care providers and past and current medications and doses. Also of interest here are lifestyle variables that can affect physical health such as the use of drugs or alcohol, consumption of caffeine, quality of sleep, and history of nicotine use. Examination of medical history must examine instances of closed head injury; episodes of loss of consciousness, seizures, or epilepsy; cerebrovascular accidents; and other cerebrovascular conditions, such as aneurysm, congenital abnormalities, and so on. Each of these disorders carries a potential risk of longstanding permanent changes in cognitive functioning. Also important are a history of cardiac disease, hypertension, diabetes, and chronic obstructive pulmonary disease, because these disorders are risk factors for ischemic changes in the brain. Infectious diseases, such as encephalitis, meningitis, and brain abscesses; degenerative diseases like multiple sclerosis, Parkinson's disease, and so on; and metabolic disorders such as hypothyroidism, hyperthyroidism, liver disease, and pituitary disease can also affect cognitive function. Examination of medical history must also consider a history of toxic encephalopathies; congenital or developmental diseases or disorders, such as Sturge-Weber, tuberous sclerosis, Williams syndrome, and Klinefelter's syndrome; and pervasive developmental disorders along with dementing disorder such as Alzheimer's disease and Pick's disease. Rapid Reference 3.4 provides a brief list of the many areas of medical history relevant to neuropsychological assessment.

Medical history is also concerned with the details of a patient's alcohol or drug use. Information concerning the drug or drugs of choice, the extent of a patient's use, and known health consequences needs to be obtained. Substance abuse history should focus on estimates of frequency and amount of use, pres-

≡ Rapid Reference 3.4

Medical History Relevant to Neuropsychological Assessment

- Closed head injury
- Episodes of loss of consciousness
- Epilepsy or seizures
- Cerebrovascular accidents and other cerebrovascular abnormalities (e.g., aneurysm)
- Cardiac disease, hypertension, diabetes, chronic obstructive pulmonary disease
- Infectious diseases (e.g., encephalitis, meningitis, brain abscess)
- Degenerative diseases (e.g., multiple sclerosis, Parkinson's disease)
- Metabolic disorders (e.g., hyperthyroidism, hypothyroidism, liver disease)
- Toxic encephalopathy
- Congenital or developmental diseases or disorders (e.g., Sturge-Weber, Tuberous Sclerosis, pervasive developmental disorder)
- Dementing disorders (e.g., Alzheimer's disease, Pick's disease)
- Physical handicaps
- Alcohol or drug use
- Current and past medications and doses
- Past and current health care providers

ence of current or past blackouts, and history of alcohol- and drug-related treatment and legal involvement.

It is also important to know a patient's past and present history of medication use. What medication a patient has been prescribed or is currently taking is important because the side effects of medications can include CNS changes and compromises.

Psychiatric History

Many psychiatric illnesses and their associated symptoms can negatively impact neuropsychological test performance and function. While gathering history, a neuropsychologist must therefore review past and present psychologi-

=Rapid Reference 3.5

Psychiatric History Relevant to Neuropsychological Assessment

- Current symptoms and complaints
- Onset and course of symptoms
- Pervasiveness and severity
- Findings from past and present evaluations
- Hospitalizations
- Past suicide attempts
- Past and present treatment
- Effect of symptoms on day-to-day living

cal and psychiatric symptoms and diagnoses. Details are needed in these same categories for current and past medical illness, including time of onset and the pervasiveness and severity of symptoms. In addition to obtaining information about diagnosis, the clinician should gather details about its effect on daily functioning. Information pertaining to number and length of psychiatric hospitalizations, counseling, and psychotherapy, as well as past and current medications and doses and history of electroconvulsive therapy are also relevant to this category. Additionally, information about past suicide attempts, including the means and subsequent medical consequences (e.g., hypoxia, loss of consciousness) can provide data about possible sources of neuropsychological dysfunction. Rapid Reference 3.5 provides an outline of the areas of focus when obtaining history concerning psychiatric history.

Particular attention should be paid to several classes of disorders because of their association with disorganized thinking, depressive or vegetative symptoms, and anxiety, all of which can disrupt performance on neuropsychological tests in the absence of objective neurological dysfunction. Attention also should be paid to psychiatric disorders that involve somatization or longstanding personality characteristics that may result in motivational issues or poor cooperation. Of particular importance are psychotic disorders, including schizophrenia; affective disorders, such as major depression and bipolar disorder; anxiety disorders, including posttraumatic stress disorder and obsessive-compulsive disorder; somatoform disorders, including conversion disorder and pain disorder; and personality disorders, such as borderline personality disorder or obsessive-compulsive personality disorder. Rapid Reference 3.6 provides a list of the psychiatric conditions relevant to neuropsychological assessment.

≡Rapid Reference 3.6

Psychiatric Conditions Relevant to Neuropsychological Assessment

- Schizophrenia and other psychotic disorders, such as schizoaffective disorder and delusional disorder
- Affective disorders, such as major depression and bipolar disorder
- Anxiety disorders, such as generalized anxiety disorder, posttraumatic stress disorder, and obsessive-compulsive disorder
- Somatoform disorders, such as somatization disorder, pain disorder, and conversion disorder
- Personality disorders, such as borderline personality disorder and obsessive-compulsive personality disorder

Educational History

Educational history is one of several variables that is used to determine premorbid IQ and serves as a baseline against which to compare neuropsychological test results. The information obtained in this category must go beyond simply learning the highest grade attained by the patient. Other important details that should be established include the schools the patient attended, the course or program of study and its difficulty level (e.g., vocational versus college preparatory), pattern of attendance, and grade point average. Information should also be obtained concerning academic strengths and weaknesses, as well as whether the patient has a history of learning disability and special education placements. Other important data include whether the patient has a history of Attention-Deficit/Hyperactivity Disorder (ADHD) or behavioral problems in school resulting in detention, suspension, or expulsion. Rapid Reference 3.7 summarizes the areas on which to focus when obtaining historical information about educational history.

Depending on the age of the subject and the reason for referral, educational history may be gathered through a patient's self-report or by the report of an informant such as a parent. Sometimes, however, the clinician should obtain school records and not rely on the patient's self-report or on the report of an informant. In these instances, school transcripts can clarify the patient's academic performance and may contain other important information such as stan-

≡Rapid Reference 3.7

Relevant Educational History

- Highest grade attended
- Schools attended
- Academic strengths and weaknesses
- Course type and difficulty
- Grade point average
- History of learning disability
- History of Attention-Deficit/Hyperactivity Disorder
- Special education placements
- Transcripts of grades
- Standardized test scores
- Reports from psychoeducational evaluations

dardized test scores. For children, school records will usually contain special education plans and reports from psychoeducational evaluations. Such records should almost always be obtained if the patient is of school (including college) age. In addition to increasing the accuracy of information over self- or informant report, the school records for children and young adults can provide detailed information about the cognitive strengths and weaknesses that may be the focus of the neuropsychological referral in this age group. It is usually less critical (and often very difficult) to obtain educational records for older adults; however, when available, school records may be helpful in determining whether an adult has a longstanding learning disability rather than a problem of new onset that is contributing to their current level of performance.

Vocational History

The historical information relevant to vocation includes the dates and types of occupational positions held, the reasons for leaving a job, job stability, level of attainment, and performance evaluations. By gathering this information, the neuropsychologist can learn much about the consistency of a patient's employment, his or her level of responsibility within a company, and the complexity of a patient's job. Information concerning the areas on which to focus when obtaining historical information about vocational history is provided in Rapid Reference 3.8.

This vocational information has in turn some predictive relationship to premorbid IQ. In particular, in adults born before World War II, vocational history may be a more

> ### ≡ *Rapid Reference 3.8*
>
> **Relevant Vocational History**
>
> - Dates and types of occupational positions held
> - Reasons for leaving a job
> - Job stability
> - Highest level of attainment
> - Job complexity and level of responsibility and independence
> - Performance evaluations

accurate correlate of premorbid IQ than educational level. Many adults born before World War II did not finish high school, and few earned college degrees. A large number completed only six or eight years of education (Matarazzo, 1972) but not necessarily because of limitations in cognitive ability. During and after the Great Depression in the 1930s children were pressured to work and contribute to the economic survival of their families. Many of these adults who left school early went on to have successful vocational histories and relatively high socioeconomic status, thus making academic achievement a poor predictor of occupational success. In these circumstances, vocational history would more accurately predict a higher level of premorbid ability than years of education. After World War II, laws requiring students to be enrolled in school until their sixteenth birthday, a growing expectation that students would complete high school, and open enrollment policies for colleges have made education a critical predictor of premorbid ability for individuals born after World War II. The clinician must examine such cultural factors when making judgments about the accuracy and weight given to the different indicators of premorbid ability.

Birth History and Early Development

In some instances, the source of cognitive difficulties occurs early in life and is related to birth or postnatal trauma; thus, historical information concerning birth and early development is helpful in differential diagnosis. It is important to know about pre-, peri-, and postnatal difficulties. Information should be gathered about prenatal care and complications during pregnancy, labor, and delivery. In addition, age of attainment of early developmental milestones can assist the neuropsychologist in viewing a problem as longstanding versus new. Did the patient learn to walk and talk on time, or were there unusual delays? Information also should be obtained about childhood illnesses or injuries, their treatment, and the child's recovery, as well as information pertaining to behavioral disorders in childhood. Rapid Reference 3.9 provides an overview of the birth and early developmental history relevant to a neuropsychological assessment.

When evaluating a child, the neuropsychologist can usually acquire this information from parents or medical records. Many adults will not know specific

≡ Rapid Reference 3.9

Relevant Birth and Early Development History

- Pregnancy
  - Complications (e.g., anemia, toxemia, maternal diabetes, infections, toxic exposure)
  - Cigarette, alcohol, or drug exposure during pregnancy
  - Length of pregnancy
  - Mother's age at birth
- Birth
  - Length of labor
  - Complications (e.g., cesarean section, forceps, fetal distress, breech, nuchal cord, seizures)
  - Apgar scores
  - Birth weight
  - Neonatal problems
- Early development
  - Age of attainment of milestones
  - Complications (e.g., colic, apnea, failure to thrive, poor feeding)
  - Childhood illnesses and injuries (e.g., ear infections, asthma, scarlet fever, meningitis, febrile seizures, head injuries, allergies)
  - Behavior problems

details about their birth, such as weight at birth, or their early development, but they may be aware of unusual occurrences or abnormalities and be able to share that information.

Family Background

Family history information is also important for analyzing the data obtained in a neuropsychological assessment. Records of family background include information about the age and health status (or cause of death) of parents, siblings, and children. Also relevant is historical

≡Rapid Reference 3.10

Relevant Family Background

- Age and health status or cause of death of parents, siblings, and children
- Educational achievement of parents, siblings, and children
- Occupational achievement of parents, siblings, and children
- Psychiatric history of parents, siblings, and children
- Medical and neurological history of parents, siblings, and children
- Cultural background

information about the educational and occupational achievement, psychiatric history, and medical and neurological history of parents, siblings, and children. Many disorders may be genetically based (e.g., ADHD, learning disability) or associated with sociodemographic factors (e.g., maltreatment or abuse); therefore, family history must be collected to ensure a comprehensive evaluation. Cultural background is also relevant because it may influence family values and development. Rapid Reference 3.10 summarizes the family background information of concern to a neuropsychological assessment.

Current Situation

It is also important to collect details about a patient's current situation. Knowledge of a patient's work, home, and social routines, including a description of a typical day, recreational activities, hobbies, and exercise programs can provide a wealth of information about what a patient's capabilities are. Knowledge about current life stresses, including the recent death or illness of a significant other, distressed interpersonal relationships, recent job changes, and financial worries can inform the examiner about pressures that may be hindering a patient's daily functioning or contributing to emotional upset. In addition,

≡Rapid Reference 3.11

Relevant Current Situation

- Living arrangements
- Work, home, and social routines, including recreational activities, hobbies, and exercise programs
- Current stresses, including family crises, distressed interpersonal relationships, job changes or problems, and financial concerns
- Marital status and marital history

knowledge about a patient's home life is important. Does this child live with his or her parents and siblings, or is the child in a foster home? Is this adult patient married or divorced? Is this patient's spouse healthy, caring, and financially secure? Is this patient satisfied with his or her current relationship, including in the area of sexual intimacy? Rapid Reference 3.11 provides a summary of the areas to be explored when obtaining information about a patient's current living situation.

Legal History

Historical information about a patient's involvement with the legal system may also reveal important facts that affect the interpretation of the test data. In forensic cases a history of frequent litigation may be an important point to consider. In the case of a patient with a behavioral disorder, the severity may be indicated by a history of criminal involvement.

Military History

Obviously this category is not relevant in some cases. For those patients who have served in the military, however, historical information concerning dates of service, assignments, combat status, rank achieved, and discharge status may provide data consistent with or at odds with nonmilitary history and the presenting complaint.

THE CLINICAL INTERVIEW

In addition to giving the neuropsychologist the opportunity to gather information about a patient's medical and social history, the clinical interview is an important source of other information relevant to the interpretation of neuropsychological tests. Like a test measure, the interview provides a sample of behavior from which certain generalizations or inferences may be made. In this way the clinical interview is one of the best sources of information regarding a patient's affect and mood, insight, and motivation for testing. The interview contributes critical samples of behavior relevant to attention, language, and memory functions. The interview may provide information about the organization, focus, and detail of the patient's thinking, as well as the subjective aspects of their presenting problem. From an interview the neuropsychologist may learn that formal testing is impossible. For example, the clinician may learn in the interview that the patient is simply too delusional, confused, or delirious to produce reliable or valid test results. The clinical interview also provides the examiner with an opportunity to explain the testing procedure and to decrease the patient's anxiety.

Interviewing is a skill that develops with practice, experience, and the supervision of a competent teacher. Although this textbook does not allow for a complete course in interviewing, we do discuss the basics of a clinical neuropsychological interview. No hard and fast rules for interviewing exist. Assuming a proper setting and a cooperative patient, the factors that make an interview more productive include establishing rapport, facilitating communication, and using questions effectively.

The interview and assessment should be conducted in a quiet area, free of as many distractions related to noise, visible activity, and environment as possible. Controlling distractions also means discouraging any intrusions or modifications to the environment that make the testing situation substantially different from the environment in which the tests were standardized. The presence of a third-party observer during an evaluation creates a potential confounding factor in the interpretation of test findings. Observers can interfere with testing by serving as a distraction or by altering performance by way of social facilitation effects (McCaffrey, Fisher, Gold, & Lynch, 1996). Observing behavior can influence and change behavior in ways that cannot be known. In addition, having an observer present during testing is inconsistent with testing standards, which demand a distraction-free testing environment (The Standards for Educational and Psychological Testing, APA, 1985). It is also at odds with recent testing manuals (e.g., WAIS-III, WMS-III, and WASI) that state that no observers should be present in the testing room because it is necessary to minimize any potential distractions (Wechsler, 1997). The presence of a

DON'T FORGET

....

Third-party observation and video-taping of interviews and testing sessions create potential sources of interference and diminishes the examiner's ability to rely upon normative data. Third-party observers should be excluded from testing.

third-party observer during an evaluation also potentially decreases the neuropsychologist's ability to rely upon normative data. Neuropsychological tests were standardized in one-on-one conditions with only the examiner and the examinee present. To ensure reliable use of the normative data, administration of neuropsychological tests requires that the same standard set of procedures be followed. In 2000 the National Academy of Neuropsychology set forth an official statement concerning the presence of third-party observers during neuropsychological testing.

It is unethical to audiotape or videotape an interview or encounter with a patient without explicit permission. In addition, audiotaping and videotaping interviews may pose a risk to the integrity of the information obtained. McCaffrey et al. (1996, p. 446) indicate that data suggest that replacing the presence of third-party observers with audiotape or videotape "may not be immune to the effects of social facilitation" because audiotaping and videotaping an interview and test session introduce the same risk of confounding the data.

The setting also plays a role in the interview. A quiet, pleasant office with a testing table and a comfortable chair is preferable for many patients, but in some cases it may be necessary to test the patient at bedside or while the patient is seated in a wheelchair. The neuropsychologist's office should be a professional space. Although it should not be cluttered with too many distracting personal mementos or trophies, it also should not be sterile or void of personal touches. The testing table and any wall hangings should be arranged so that distractions are limited. If possible, the testing table should not allow the patient an opportunity to gaze out the window or be distracted by activities outdoors. Likewise, personal items in the office should be placed out of the patient's view during the test session. Interruptions must be eliminated or kept to a minimum. Phones should be switched to voice mail and a *do not disturb* sign should be placed on the door. Offices should be fairly soundproof. A white noise machine can sometimes add a screen of noise to permit privacy if necessary. Neuropsychological test interpretation is based on the assumption that a patient's performance has been optimized. Any environmental factors that may affect a patient's optimal performance need to be noted and considered in the interpretation of the test results.

Initially, the interviewer should take some time to make the patient comfortable by attempting to establish rapport. Good rapport is necessary for the purposes of interview since a negative or hostile relationship makes interviewing difficult. The establishment of rapport with the patient is a matter of personal style and varies tremendously from clinician to clinician. Some clinicians spend time engaging the client in casual conversation, whereas others may begin testing immediately. Although engaging the patient in so-called small talk sometimes helps the process of establishing rapport, casual conversation usually should be kept to a minimum to maintain professional boundaries. In the beginning, however, conversation about innocuous events may help to break the ice and allow a patient time to adjust to the situation. Interviewer behaviors that can damage rapport include sarcasm, flippant remarks, and boasts about the interviewer's competence. Other behaviors that can damage rapport include allowing mail or notes to become a distraction and lecturing a patient about mistakes they could have avoided. Copious note taking that distracts the interviewer from paying attention to the patient is strongly discouraged.

At the beginning of the interview, the neuropsychologist needs to establish that the patient understands the reason for the evaluation and the basic features of the test session; this informs the patient of what is about to occur, how long the testing takes, and what the patient can expect. It also gives the interviewer a chance to alleviate any anxiety a patient may have about the evaluation, and it gives the patient time to become comfortable with the examiner before commencing the actual testing, which can be threatening to some patients. Many interviewers begin by asking the patient to explain why they are being tested and to describe the problems they may be having. In addition to providing some clues about the potential cause of a patient's complaints and a basis for formulating recommendations addressing perceived problems, these relatively open-ended questions provide the patient with the opportunity to construct an organized narrative with some internal logic and connections. The clinician can then use this opportunity to observe whether the patient can tell the story of the illness or injury with a beginning, middle, and end. The clinician can observe whether a patient is focused, digressive, or tangential and whether his or her language is characterized by appropriate grammar, vocabulary, and prosody. The clinician can also note whether the patient seems appropriately concerned about the impact of his or her problems or whether the patient even recognizes that he or she has a problem. The clinician can observe whether the patient appears inappropriately sad, elated, anxious, or indifferent. With experience, clinicians can learn to recognize whether the patient is able to plan responses, recall the details from the recent and remote past, and focus responses on relevant details.

In terms of communication, the interviewer should follow several guidelines. The interviewer must be sure to talk to the patient in a language that he or she understands and avoid clinical jargon and words outside a patient's background. It is also important to avoid using words that carry one meaning to the clinician and quite another to a layperson. While a clinician might use the word *retarded* to mean an individual with an IQ below 70, the layperson may see this term as pejorative. Effective communication also requires an effective use of silences. Silences must be judged for their meaning within an interview. The interviewer need not feel compelled to fill in silences just to hear him- or herself talk. During silences, patients may be gathering their thoughts or collecting themselves; they may need a brief break before continuing. Effective listening includes hearing silences as part of the communication process.

In an interview, the types of questions used guide the types of responses that are received. Open-ended questions often are more productive than questions calling for briefly worded responses. Open-ended questions do not allow a patient to respond with a simple *yes* or *no*. They allow a patient the opportunity to define what is important and to respond in ways that are more revealing than an affirmation or denial. For example, instead of asking: "Did you find that you were more forgetful after your accident?" it is preferable to ask: "How was your life different after your accident?" or "How did you function differently after your accident?"

When a patient seems to be having difficulty explaining something, the interviewer can aid with comments or questions asking the patient to expand on an issue or requesting the patient to describe a particular aspect of an issue: for instance, how he or she was feeling when the illness or injury manifested itself. Just as is done in the testing situation, the interviewer can ask a patient to be more specific when talking about an issue or ask the patient to provide an example of a particular problem or complaint. Questions can also be used to clarify information or to rephrase a statement made by a patient to be sure that the interviewer has understood a response. Of course, when rapport has been sufficiently established, direct questions may be more useful in allowing a patient to get to the point more quickly.

The interviewer and patient communicate nonverbally as well as verbally during an interview. Both the patient and the interviewer communicate to each other through facial expressions, tone of voice, eye contact, body placement, and gestures. The interviewer should be aware that while he or she is observing the patient's nonverbal behaviors, the patient also might well be reading the interviewer's nonverbal communications.

BEHAVIORAL OBSERVATIONS

Although no norms are available to consult regarding interviews, the observations made during an interview can supplement formal test results, providing examples of behavior that may epitomize the problems determined by standardized measures. In some cases, the observations made in the course of the interview may alter the interpretations of test results. For example, if a patient was observed to have word-finding difficulty, characterized by word-finding pauses, circumlocutions, and even word errors, that patient would be expected to perform poorly on IQ tests requiring expressive language ability and on tests of verbal memory. In other cases, the observations made in the course of the interview may suggest nonneurological explanations for test results (e.g., anxiety, thought disorder). For example, if a patient is exceedingly anxious during testing, slowing or tremulousness may disrupt his or her performance.

Behavioral observations during interview and testing provide a wealth of information to the context in which the test data will be interpreted. Behavioral observations allow the examiner an assessment of motivation and attention. They also permit the examiner to see a patient's limitations in a nontest situation and allow the patient to demonstrate his or her symptoms. Behavioral observations may also give the examiner a chance

---

DON'T FORGET

The means to collect data include
- Record review
- Clinical interview
- Behavioral observation
- Questionnaires
- Neuropsychological evaluation

to glimpse personality characteristics that could influence test performance, suggesting alternative explanations for the test results.

Behavioral observations center on issues such as the patient's appearance, the patient's level of alertness and arousal, and the patient's level of orientation and cooperation. Behavioral observations need to be made concerning use of language, sensorimotor functioning, and interpersonal skills. In addition, behavioral observations focus on a patient's mood, reality testing, and thought control, as well as on issues such as learning and memory, insight, and judgment. The following is a list of issues that can be addressed through observations made in the course of a clinical interview:

1. The interview showcases a patient's level of alertness and arousal and his or her susceptibility to distraction. Is the patient oriented to person, place, and date? The need for frequent repetition and reminders to perform a task, the need for frequent refocusing, responses to stray noises or movement, a sleepy or (on the contrary) hypervigilant appearance may indicate limits in attentional ability that would undermine test performance. These factors may also be indicators of the presence of some forms of brain dysfunction or psychiatric conditions. Also important here is activity, including energy level, motor findings, and speed.

2. The interview also gives the interviewer a chance to observe how cooperative a patient is going to be with an evaluation. Indirectly, this can guide interpretations about the likelihood that test results are a reliable and valid reflection of optimal level of functioning. Although not as accurate as tests of compliance and motivation, it is additional data that can be assimilated into the whole clinical picture.

3. The interview also provides an opportunity to observe the patient's level of hygiene and standard of dress. Attention must be paid to a patient's appearance, including manner of dress, level of grooming, gait and posture, mannerisms, and physical abnormalities. Is the patient appropriately groomed or disheveled and malodorous? A disregard for minimal standards of hygiene and neatness should be noted because it may be related to brain damage and various psychiatric conditions.

4. The interchange that is part of a clinical interview also allows ample opportunity to observe a patient's spontaneous speech in a situation requiring open-ended discourse. Use and comprehension of conversational vocabulary, word-finding difficulties, appropriateness of syntax, and prosody of speech production are all showcased for the examiner in this way. Rapid Reference 3.12 provides a list of the important behavioral observations that can be made during the interview and neuropsychological testing.

5. The interview also allows the neuropsychologist a chance to observe sensorimotor functioning and any abnormalities that may interfere with test performance. Does the patient wear glasses? Does the patient have difficulty in hearing? Does the patient wear a hearing aid? Are there motor abnormalities? Does the patient walk with a cane? Is there evidence of ataxia, spasticity, or muscle weakness? The presence of sensorimotor abnormalities may contribute to the neuropsychologist's understanding of a brain disorder and

≡ Rapid Reference 3.12

Important Behavioral Observations during the Clinical Interview

- Level of arousal and alertness, including energy level, motor findings such as hyperactivity, and speed
- Appearance, including manner of dress, level of grooming, gait and posture, mannerisms, and physical abnormalities
- Level of cooperation, including motivation and effort
- Discourse abilities, including ability to understand and produce conversational speech
- Sensorimotor functioning, including eyesight, hearing, muscle strength, and the use of aids such as glasses, hearing aids, canes, and so forth
- Appropriateness of social skills and level of anxiety
- Speech, including rate, tone, prosody, articulation, fluency, and word choice
- Emotionality, including affect, mood, and appropriateness
- Thought content and processes, including organization and reality testing
- Memory, including retrieval of recent and remote events

may signal limitations in test interpretation because of interfering factors.

6. The interview can provide an optimal opportunity to gather information about a patient's social skills and level of anxiety. Can the patient establish a comfortable interpersonal interaction with the examiner? Is the patient's behavior socially and age appropriate as evidenced by posture, eye contact, mannerisms, and so forth? Behavior that is excessively shy or excessively forward and familiar may be a correlate of some forms of brain damage or different psychiatric conditions. The patient's behavior in the interview situation may parallel his or her behavior outside the interview situation, thus contributing to an understanding of a patient's behavior in real-life social situations.

7. The interview also allows the neuropsychologist to examine a patient's emotionality, including affect, mood, and appropriateness. Depression and anxiety are two nonneurological sources for disruption in neuropsychological test performance. Emotional lability and inappropriateness can also sometimes reflect a reaction to loss as a result of brain damage or organic changes directly related to a brain insult.

8. The clinical interview gives the clinician a chance to gauge a patient's level of insight into his or her deficits and their causes. What is the patient's reaction to the nature and severity of deficits? Is the patient denying any illness, suggesting a possible anosagnosia? Is the patient exaggerating symptoms, suggesting a cry for attention? Does the patient fail to appreciate the significance of physical limitations, suggesting impaired judgment?

9. The interview also provides the examiner with an opportunity to observe the coherence of the patient's expository or narrative language, evidence of how well the patient's thoughts are organized. Is the patient prone to give irrelevant details when telling a story, suggesting circumstantiality? Can the patient stick to a particular train of thought, or is the patient tangential? Is the patient's thinking disorganized, reflecting a possible thought disorder or perhaps impaired reality testing?

10. The interview also allows an informal evaluation of memory abilities. In interview a patient demonstrates his or her ability to recall the details of recent and increasingly remote autobiographical events. Does the patient have difficulty remembering events from yesterday versus a long time ago? Can the patient recall the details of events but not their order or the time frame of autobiographical events? Observations here can provide a basis for hypotheses about what results formal memory testing will provide, and the data can then be examined for consistency.

In Chapter 7 we discuss how to present the information from clinical interview, record review, and behavioral observations in a report and how to integrate it with the results from neuropsychological assessment.

✍ TEST YOURSELF ✍

1. Neuropsychological test results can be interpreted adequately against a backdrop of demographic data alone. True or False?

2. Specificity is the proportion of individuals with brain damage that a test will correctly identify as having brain damage, whereas sensitivity is the proportion of individuals who are healthy, who are correctly identified as healthy. True or False?

3. Determination of the cognitive, behavioral, and personality characteristics that might predate any illnesses and which might contribute to the appearance of measurable performance deficits is critical to the interpretation of neuropsychological tests because many neuropsychological tests are typically affected by both neuropsychological and nonneuropsychological factors, such as motivation and affect. True or False?

4. Which of the following features is one of the most important features regarding the physical arrangements of an interview or test session?

   (a) Privacy
   (b) Reclining chair or couch
   (c) Taking detailed notes
   (d) Videotaping

(continued)

5. **What is the best practice regarding the use of clinical jargon in an interview?**

   (a) It should be used often, especially with bright patients.

   (b) It should be minimized.

   (c) It must never be used.

   (d) It doesn't matter if it is used or not.

6. **Videotaping eliminates the potential sources of distraction created by third-party observation in a testing situation.** True or False?

Answers: 1. False; 2. False; 3. True; 4. a; 5. b; 6. False

Four

ESSENTIALS OF TEST SELECTION, ADMINISTRATION, AND SCORING

This chapter covers the basic conditions and logistics of the neuropsychological examination. Some of the advice dispensed in this chapter may seem the paragon of common sense to an experienced clinician. Expertise with such issues as optimizing test performance, monitoring of clinical test behavior, recording data, using standard procedures of test administration, and understanding the logic of test selection, however, can mean the difference between valid, clinically useful test results and malpractice. Even experienced clinicians can be taken by surprise by malingering or by patients with somatization disorders or conversion reactions if these phenomena are not part of their typical practice.

OPTIMIZING PERFORMANCE

In most cases the interpretation of neuropsychological tests is based on the central assumption that the performance measured by those tests represents the best effort of the patient delivered under conditions as close to optimal as possible. The exclusion of nonneurological causes is the first logical step in making the decision that a lower than expected test score or the presence of an unusual behavioral symptom is related to dysfunction of the central nervous system. This task may be undermined if the patient is unusually anxious, too hot or cold, or subjected to unusual or unpredictable sights or sounds. For example, it would not be unusual for an otherwise normal adult to perform poorly on a test of attention if during the test voices can be heard arguing, or (as sometimes is the case on a busy hospital ward) patients are being examined, trays are being dropped, and so forth. Patients who are very anxious or ruminative may perform poorly on a number of neuropsychological tests, especially those requiring intense or sustained attention. Although these factors may be

DON'T FORGET

It is the job of the examiner to arrange the testing conditions so that the patient can take advantage of the opportunity to work to potential.

significant in predicting cognitive performance in other situations, they often preclude drawing inferences about brain function. Most patients who are referred for neuropsychological testing want to do their best, particularly if they understand the reasons for the testing and their effort's possible benefits to their treatment, job, or school performance.

Some patients, however, do not give their best effort when tested. This may be because they do not understand the reason for the assessment, have been referred involuntarily, or are involved in a situation in which they may gain or be rewarded for poor performance. It is the task of the neuropsychologist to arrange the testing conditions so that a patient can take advantage of the opportunity to work to potential. In this chapter we discuss issues concerning the optimization of a patient's performance and motivation, as well as the steps required for administration and scoring in neuropsychological assessment.

Appropriate Testing Conditions

Optimally, neuropsychological testing should be undertaken in conditions that are reasonably quiet, with no foot traffic or distracting views. In most cases this environment is an examination room that has sufficient artificial light (without glare and reflection), is kept at a comfortable temperature, and has adequate ventilation. It is usually best to seat the patient facing away from windows and doors from which activity can be seen and to prevent glare. When this is not possible, it may be necessary to keep shades drawn and doors closed, particularly if much visible activity is outside the room. The seating plan should also take into account wall spaces containing distracting pictures. If the external environment is noisy, it may be necessary to use a white noise generator or to take steps to soundproof walls and doors. Many clients are not affected by external distractions, but even healthy adults may find themselves turning toward unusual sounds and conversation that divert their attention, particularly when they are anxious about being tested.

The office should appear welcoming and friendly. It probably should be conservatively decorated, however, reflecting the standards of the community in which the clinician works. As discussed in Chapter 3, the office should be a professional space with minimal personal mementos but should not be sterile and devoid of all personal touches. Comfortable seating should be available to both examiner and patient. When administering the tests, most examiners prefer that patients sit opposite them at a sufficiently large table or desk. In some instances, however, because of particular test materials that require a viewing stand, the examiner may sit at the end of a rectangular table while the patient sits on the side. The examiner should also arrange the room so that test materials are close at hand and available for easy access. However, to limit possible distractions, test materials should not be presented before they are necessary. Organization and readiness of test materials permit a smooth transition from one test to the next, thereby decreasing the overall time in testing. Knowing your materials and being practiced in a particular test also keeps the test session flowing, leaving less time for the patient to become bored or lose interest. In addition, a familiarity with administration rules and scoring allows the examiner to administer tests in an automatic fashion so that more time can be devoted to observing a patient's behavior. Rapid Reference 4.1 summarizes the features important for appropriate testing conditions.

Testing must often be done in less than optimal conditions under which the examiner has little control over environment. For example, a hospitalized patient may have to be tested at bedside on a hospital ward, or an incarcerated individual may have to be tested in whatever space is available at the prison. In these instances, the examiner should orchestrate whatever details possible to ensure the best possible testing environment. The examiner should also keep a record of the conditions under which testing took place and include the information in the test report, particularly when the conditions may have had a direct impact on the performance of a particular task.

> ## ≡ Rapid Reference 4.1
>
> ### Appropriate Testing Conditions
>
> - Quiet, nondistracting environment
> - Well-lit room surfaces without glare
> - Welcoming and friendly (but not overdone) room with comfortable seating
> - Test materials organized and at hand

Establishing Rapport

In order to optimize the patient's performance, the examiner should try to gain the cooperation and trust of the person being tested. As discussed in the previous chapter, the way an examiner establishes rapport is a matter of personal style. You should introduce yourself to the patient and acknowledge adults by their titles and surnames. Some casual conversation may be necessary to break the ice initially, but one of the first issues addressed should be an explanation of the purpose of the testing and a discussion of how the session will progress. Issues of confidentiality should be discussed with adults. All patients, both children and adults, need to know that the tasks they will be doing range from easy to hard and that their job is to do their best.

Patients should be encouraged to try on all test items and in some cases to take a chance by guessing while the examiner remains supportive and encouraging. In order to avoid giving information about the correctness or incorrectness of an answer, praise should be given for effort, not for the answer itself. To avoid discouraging the patient early, the examiner should start with simpler tasks and as tasks become more difficult, acknowledge that an item may have been difficult but that no one gets all the answers right. Also, praise should be given judiciously instead of for every answer; this also helps the patient avoid becoming discouraged.

Structure of the Test Session

The scheduling of a test session depends on the referral question, the nature of the tests being used, and the focus and stamina of the patient. In general, test sessions are limited by the severity of patients' presenting problems, their general health, and their age. In some instances shorter test sessions are needed to achieve reliable samples of optimal cognitive ability. For patients whose symptomatology includes distractibility and for patients whose energy level has been compromised by nonneurological health conditions, it may be unwise to attempt testing in only one day if the goal is to obtain the patient's best performance across many tasks. On the other hand, if the goal is to assess cognition and mental stamina over the course of a day, then administering the tests in a one-day session would be more appropriate than dividing up the tasks over several sessions. Other patients who may be unable to work consistently well in one session include older adults, very young children, and patients who suffer from physical pain that is exacerbated by long periods of sitting.

DON'T FORGET
It is generally preferable to complete the testing session in one day.

In general, the clinician should try to complete the interview and testing in one day. This increases the likelihood that the tests are given under similar circumstances. When test sessions are given on different days, differences in sleep, illness, anxiety, and other situational factors may confound the results and make them difficult to interpret. For example, if in the first session a patient is in a good mood and does well on an intelligence test but at the time of a second session does poorly on memory because the patient is sleepy due to a problem with insomnia, the examiner is limited in the ability to conclude that a deficit in memory is the result of brain damage. When it does become necessary to test on different days, the examiner must always make sure that multiple-part tests are given in a single session when validity is dependent on the test's being administered in a given time frame; information about circumstances that could affect test performance should also be investigated. The latter is usually done by finding out if any events that may be influencing the results have occurred in the interval between test sessions.

The length of a test session varies according to the examiner's skill, the test battery chosen, and patient characteristics. An examiner who knows the tests well and is organized can connect tasks with smooth transitions that facilitate an efficient test session. The more tests administered, the longer the time required for testing. Some patients work quickly whereas others work slowly. Some patients need encouragement and multiple follow-up questions whereas others work efficiently from start to finish.

When tests are given in a single session, the patient should be offered a reasonable number of breaks and time for lunch. Some patients may need few breaks, and others may need many. Breaks should be taken only between, not during, tests or subtests. Any signs of fatigue or variations in efforts should be noted. If a brief break with a moment for a small snack is not enough to restore the patient to sufficient levels of concentration and cooperation to return to testing, then the session may need to be terminated and rescheduled.

Balancing Test Order

Most clinicians who give fixed batteries of tests administer these tests in a fixed order for the majority of patients. In addition, some tasks such as the Wechsler intelligence tests have an inherently fixed order of administration. Even clinicians who give flexible batteries that can vary from patient to patient nevertheless tend to give the tests they choose in a specific order, sometimes by design; for example, the clinician starts with orientation tasks and less threatening tasks and does memory assessment early in the session before fatigue becomes a real possibility. Very often, however, the order of tests reflects a longstanding tradition that has never been critically examined by the clinician. In many instances it may not matter when some tests are administered; for example, it does not appear to matter where in the test battery the Letter-Number Sequencing subtest from the WAIS-III or WMS-III is administered. Tulsky and Zhu (2000) administered the Letter-Number Sequencing subtest at three different times during a test session and found no evidence of fatigue or ordering effects. The examiner may decide to plan test order based on the particular needs of a patient, and to keep the patient interested, the clinician may consider counterbalancing tests by varying the tests' subjects and difficulty levels.

OPTIMIZING MOTIVATION AND ALERTNESS

Most patients referred for neuropsychological testing are motivated to expend sufficient effort to produce reliable test results. Usually, patients' desire to obtain information relevant to their health care or their academic or vocational performance serves as an impetus to attend to instructions and complete the examination. To increase the likelihood of adequate motivation, the examiner should spend some time before beginning formal testing explicitly asking the patient whether he or she understands the reasons for examination and offering an opportunity to ask questions about the session. Many clinicians use a standard introductory speech explaining that:

The purpose of the testing is to assess a wide variety and range of skills and abilities. Because the tests are designed to test such a wide range of abilities, some of the questions will appear very simple, and some may appear very difficult and frustrating. You are not expected to solve every problem or answer every question correctly. The most important thing is to try your best.

In spite of such procedures, some populations of patients may not be motivated to perform optimally for the examination. Patients who are medically ill or physically uncomfortable may find it extremely unpleasant to expend mental effort over long periods of time. Elderly patients and patients with psychiatric illnesses or histories of congenitally impaired intellectual abilities often are found to be inadequately motivated or uncooperative with long neuropsychological examinations. Finally, patients who are tested as part of a forensic examination are frequently reported as not expending optimal effort on neuropsychological examinations. Although poor motivation may be manifested by overt signs of distractibility, excessive slowness or carelessness, direct questions about the usefulness or meaning of the tests, or even expressions of contempt for the testing or for the examiner, it is sometimes difficult to determine through simple observation whether patients are applying adequate effort to the tasks at hand. Some circumstances cause certain patients to be motivated actually to perform poorly. These patients do indeed obtain unexpectedly low scores on tests and produce errors that either are extremely rare or not characteristic of patients with objective evidence of brain pathology. The examiner should never assume that the patient is motivated to expend optimal effort and should be alert to the fact that motivation can vary during the course of an examination. A patient's motivation must be monitored and assessed for the duration of the session. When it is suspected that a patient may have motivation to perform poorly, it is a good idea to administer formal tests of malingering or dissimulation. These tests, which are relatively new to the tool chest of the neuropsychologist, have been validated by comparing the performances of patients with brain damage to those of subjects who have been asked to simulate the behavior of patients with brain damage. Many tests of malingering have been validated by comparing patients who have brain injuries and are involved in litigation to similarly injured patients who are not involved in litigation. In a typical test, the performance of simulators is shown to be more impaired than that of patients with documented brain injuries. We return to a discussion of the issue of malingering in Chapter 6.

Patients who repeatedly question the reason for the examination may do so because they are extremely anxious about their performance. This behavior may be most prevalent in patients who are in a confusional state or delirium or suffering from other significant cognitive limitations accompanied by mood swings or agitation. Patients suffering from affective or anxiety disorders may also be distracted. In these cases a reasonable effort must be made to allay any anxieties and make the patient comfortable. No universal rules delineate how to deal with these situations, but excessive anxiety can significantly compromise the reliability of the examination and should not be ignored. Frequently, an acknowledgment of the patient's anxiety helps to initiate a discussion of the issue. The patient can be assured that some of the tasks are easy and some hard, but that he or she is not expected to get all the answers right; the patient's best effort is the most important issue. The examiner should acknowledge the patient's reaction and explain that test items may be difficult.

The clinician needs to balance the efficiency and time constraints of the overall examination with the need to ensure a reliable and valid performance. At some point it may not be possible to help a patient focus on the examination or give a reasonable and consistent level of effort. Under these circumstances, the clinician may choose to terminate the session because the examination is unlikely to produce data that can reliably support clinical neuropsychological inferences. If such a decision is made, the clinician should carefully document and report the behaviors that led to this decision.

BEHAVIORAL OBSERVATIONS

The state of the patient's motivation and degree of effort are just a few of the many inferences that are made on the basis of observable behavior during the course of a clinical session. Observations about a patient's dress, hygiene, posture, language, and behavior may be used to modify or support the results of clinical neuropsychological tests. Rapid Reference 4.2 provides a list of the behavioral observations important in an assessment.

The clinician should observe many factors about a patient during the evaluation. One of these factors is the patient's appearance. Is the patient appropriately dressed? Is the patient well-groomed? A formerly tidy individual who presents in a disheveled, malodorous state may be communicating information about his ability for self-care. The examiner should observe a patient's level of cooperation, effort, and attention to the testing. Does the patient listen when test directions are given, or do the test directions require repetition? Does the patient give up easily or, on the other hand, refuse to quit a task? Does the patient appear interested and invested in testing?

The examiner should also ob-

≡*Rapid Reference 4.2*

Behavioral Observations

- Appearance (dress, hygiene, posture)
- Arousal and alertness
- Attitude toward examiner
- Attitude toward tests
- Level of cooperation, effort, and attention
- Work habits
- Speech and language
- Behavior (motivation, anxiety, affective state)

serve how easily a patient adapts to the testing situation and the patient's adjustment or attitude toward the examiner and the tests. Does the patient appear highly anxious and frightened or relaxed and comfortable? Does the patient engage in nervous laughter or stammering? Is the patient overly eager or noncompliant? Does the patient frequently check on the accuracy of the responses? How does the patient react to successes or failures? What is the patient's attitude toward self? Is the patient confident, boastful, or self-derogatory?

The clinician must also make observations about the patient's work habits during testing. Does he or she work too quickly, sacrificing accuracy for speed, or does the patient work slowly and deliberately? What about the patient's behavior? Is he or she calm or overactive, fidgety, and distractible? Does the patient lack self-control? Observations also must focus on level of arousal and alertness. Is the patient sleepy or hyperaroused? Is the patient oriented to person, place, and date, or does he or she appear confused?

Another area that may be used to supplement formal testing is careful use of observations regarding speech and language. The examiner should develop a sensitivity to normal variations in speech rate, word finding latencies (i.e., how long someone takes to find an average vocabulary word or to initiate a sentence), use of pronouns versus specifying nouns (e.g., *he* vs. *John; I read it* vs. *I read the book*), use of circumlocutions (e.g., *the paper thing with the words* vs. *the book*). Again, no norms exist for evaluating such naturalistic observations, but extreme deviations from the examiner's experience with typical native speakers of English may serve as clues to the presence of language difficulties. In addition, the examiner should note whether the patient's language is fluent and normal in rate and volume, and whether there is a loss of words conveying grammatical structure (i.e., articles, conjunctions, prepositions), word endings (e.g., *ed, ing,* pluralization), or normal word order. In addition to rate and volume, the examiner should mark other prosodic elements of the patient's speech, such as overall pitch and whether changes in pitch and volume are used appropriately to punctuate clauses and sentence endings. Observations about language should focus on whether a patient's speech is fluent versus nonfluent or exact versus imprecise. Observations should also be made about the content and responsiveness of a patient's speech. Is the patient's language bizarre or immature? Is the patient unable to stop talking or reticent?

As noted in the previous chapter, behavioral observations are a primary source of information about the patient's motivation, anxiety level, and affective state. The clinician should note the amount of motor activity and fidgeting displayed by the patient in addition to deviations in eye contact and posture. Does the patient move around excessively in the seat, play with his or her hands, or inappropriately pick up and handle small objects that might be in reach on the examination table? Does the patient seem unusually still or quiet with a fixed posture and little movement? Does the patient's facial expression show observable variation? Are these expressions appropriate in direction and degree to the affect associated with the situation? Does the patient cry when discussing something only slightly negative or frequently laugh in situations that are not humorous? Do the patient's facial muscles seem stiff and fixed? The examiner should also note signs of asymmetry in facial muscles when observing the patient's speech or emotional expression because some neurological conditions produce asymmetries during one and not the other.

Observations must also concentrate on motor behavior during testing. Is the patient awkward or graceful? Coordinated or uncoordinated? Does the patient consistently use one hand for writing and drawing tasks and the other hand to aid in tasks that require bilateral hand movements? Is the patient constantly moving or abnormally still? Does the patient react too quickly or too slowly? In addition, behavioral observations must be made concerning sensorimotor functioning. Does the patient use a cane to assist with ambulation? Does the patient have a hearing aid or wear glasses? Sensorimotor abnormalities may compromise test performance and also help delineate brain dysfunction.

The clinician must carefully consider a patient's cultural and social background when making clinical judgments based on testing behavior, but at the same time must be careful not to be biased by misleading stereotypes of the patient's particular cohort or community. The neuropsychologist must try to decide whether behaviors observed during a session represent a change for the individual patient or whether these behaviors are appropriate for the age or cultural cohort. For example, in most Western cultures a certain amount of eye contact is anticipated during a typical conversation. Although it is hard to quantify what constitutes so-called normal eye contact, most adults find themselves uncomfortable carrying on a conversation with someone who rarely looks at them during the interaction or who studiously avoids eye contact. A patient who looks at the floor or away from the examiner for the majority of the examination may be displaying behavior indicative of extreme social anxiety. This may not be the case in all cultures, however. In some cultures, excessive eye contact is considered rude, particularly when a patient interacts with an older adult in a professional role. It is not possible to accurately apply the internal norms of social behavior for every culture. As a clinician, the neuropsychologist should try to document any behavior that seems unusual or rare within his or her own typical experience, and then decide whether this information is relevant to clinical decision making. In many cases, unusual deviations from implicit social norms and the examiner's own expectations are also deviations from the expectations of the patient's own culture. If these behaviors represent a change for the patient, they may be clues to the status of the patient's cognitive and emotional behavior and ultimately may help the clinician to make inferences about the status of brain function.

The details and interpretation of all the possible categories of behavioral observations relevant to neuropsychology are beyond the scope of this book, but as a rule the clinician should observe and note both typical and unusual behaviors dur-

DON'T FORGET

Take a person's culture into account when making clinical judgments about testing behavior.

ing testing, even when the meaning of these observations is not completely clear.

RECORD KEEPING AND NOTE TAKING

The rules for keeping records and note taking are relatively straightforward: The clinician should keep a written record of any material used to support the answer to a clinical referral question. This material includes notes about patient history from record review or interview, behavioral observations, test responses, and test result data. It is not necessary to keep every scrap of paper associated with the examination (e.g., an appointment slip), but the clinician should keep sufficient records to document anything stated in a written or oral report. In essence, the examiner's notes should allow the testing session to be reconstructed from the record at a later time. This habit is important because the clinician may forget important information in the time between collecting and reporting the data or may confuse information from two similar patients. The examination offers potential for collecting an enormous amount of data. The significance of a behavioral observation or piece of historical data might not be clear until reviewed as a whole when the examination is complete.

The clinician should be careful to write clearly, using consistent common abbreviations, especially when collecting data used to derive formal test scores. Rapid Reference 4.3 provides a list of common abbreviations that can be used in record keeping. The examiner should record responses legibly and immediately in the appropriate places on a test form or test booklet. Illegible writing can lead to scoring errors. Behavioral observations, including the patient's style of response and spontaneous remarks, can be noted in the margins of test forms or on a separate sheet of paper. Many tests used in contemporary neuropsychological assessment like the Wechsler Memory Scale and the Wechsler Adult Intelligence Scales require scoring narrative responses using fairly detailed and complex criteria. It is virtually impossible to score the responses to such tests without verbatim notes. Responses should be scored as they are given, so the examiner must be familiar with scoring criteria and careful to avoid disclosing scores to the examinee. The use of a clipboard held at an angle or a test man-

CAUTION

Keep sufficient records to document anything said by a patient in a written or oral report.

≡Rapid Reference 4.3

Common Abbreviations to Standardize Recordkeeping

- @   at
- a/t   anything
- CPT   correct past time
- Cld   could
- e/o   everyone
- F   failed item
- IDK or DK   I don't know
- IDR   I don't remember
- ll   looks like
- OT   overtime
- P   passed item
- PC   pointed correctly
- Prmt   prompt
- PX   pointed incorrectly
- Q or ?   examiner queried the response or questioned
- R   item repeated
- N   nothing
- NR   no response
- SHN   shake head no
- Shld   should
- s/t   something
- w/   with
- w/o   without
- Wld   would
- X   times

ual to block the patient's view can help prevent the patient from seeing a score and becoming discouraged or overly confident.

Without verbatim records, it becomes impossible to check the accuracy and reliability of the examiner's testing and scoring. Even highly skilled clinicians make errors in scoring. Without sufficient documentation of results through notes and response entries, it becomes impossible to determine whether a

DON'T FORGET

....

Record a patient's responses verbatim.

scoring error is the source of a discrepancy between different measures of a similar function or between measures administered by different clinicians at different times. An inaccurate test score undermines a valid analysis of neuropsychological data and may significantly affect the health and life of the patient.

Clinicians should be skilled in note taking so that they do not appear so immersed in their notes that they are unable to observe the patient or appear disinterested in the patient. Note taking is only one of the examiner's many responsibilities during an examination. Carefully recording responses must coexist with administering the test, keeping test materials ready, observing the patient's behavior, and scoring the patient's responses. Clinicians should not bury their heads in their notes, their clipboards, or test manuals.

In recent years, raw data and clinical records have become an important part of the forensic arena and civil litigation. In these cases neuropsychological data may have important legal or economic implications for both client and examiner. Ethical standards of the APA (1992) require that clinical records be stored in a secure location where patient confidentiality can be maintained. In practice, this means keeping records in a locked filing cabinet that is accessible only to authorized individuals. Similarly, computer files must be stored in a way that does not allow unauthorized individuals access to sensitive patient information. In the course of patient care, it sometimes is necessary to release raw data to other individuals. No records or reports can be released without specific permission from the patient or client. In most cases, these raw data should not be released to anyone not professionally qualified to interpret such data. In practice, test reports are sent to the referring professional and may upon specific request (where appropriate) be sent to the patient or client. Current APA ethical guidelines indicate that raw data should be sent only to other psychologists unless there is a specific legal mandate (e.g., in the case of a court proceeding) to do otherwise.

TEST PROCEDURE AND STANDARDS

Published reliability, validity, and normative data for neuropsychological tests are based on the tests having been administered using a set of repeatable standard procedures and conditions. If you wish to use test norms with confidence, then you must follow standard procedures. Following standard procedures means using the exact wording in the test manual, using the specific materials included with a test, following specific time limits and scoring rules, and using only standard inquiries. Even minor violations of the recom-

---

CAUTION

Using standard procedures means
- Using exact wording of test questions
- Using specific test materials
- Following specific time limits
- Using specific scoring rules
- Making only standard inquiries

---

mended standardized procedures published in the test manual can potentially reduce a test's reliability and validity as a neuropsychological measure. For example, if a test is designed to be given without a break, giving the patient even a brief break can reduce the accuracy of the confidence with which the test norms can be applied. It is also true that some variations in procedure do not affect an examiner's ability to use normative information because the variation falls within the standard error of measurement. Changing even the time limits or the language in which a test is given may invalidate the use of the norms. Unfortunately, it is usually impossible to know whether a particular variation in procedure is innocuous or will lead to inaccurate results.

Some circumstances necessarily require deviations from standard procedures. Materials may have to be adapted for patients with various handicaps or sensorimotor problems. For example, visually impaired individuals may need an examiner to read items aloud that they otherwise would have read themselves. Alternatively, hearing-impaired individuals may need to read materials that would normally be said aloud. When departures from standard procedures are necessary, this information must be indicated in the test report so that the reader is aware that modifications to testing procedures were made and knows that the normative information may have to be interpreted with caution. Clinicians must use their judgment to discern which data is interpretable from tests that have been adapted to meet a patient's special needs.

Some methods of neuropsychological assessment (e.g., Luria Neuropsychological Investigation, Boston Process Approach) call for the clinician to vary test procedures in a quasi-experimental manner to obtain additional information about a patient's abilities by testing limits. Although in the hands of some clinicians, these variations may lead to equally or even more accurate

DON'T FORGET

Testing the limits should occur only after a test has been administered according to standard procedures.

clinical judgments, no data testing the effects of these experimental violations of test sensitivity and specificity are currently available. Although this text does not take an official position on which test system to use, the clinician should be aware of the costs as well as the potential benefits of using nonstandard variations of procedures on standard tests. We can recommend the following: Clinicians should violate standardized procedures only if they can estimate accurately the effects of such violation on the reliability and validity of the tests or if standard procedures are inappropriate because of special circumstances. If testing the limits is desired for the additional information it can provide, it should occur only after a test has been administered according to standard procedures so as not to influence performance on the remaining items on the test.

In terms of standard procedures, we recommend that even skilled examiners reacquaint themselves occasionally with test procedures by rereading the manuals. As one works with a test, one may change its administration or scoring subtly over time. Periodic review of test procedures helps ensure that examiners use exact wording and do not reinvent the rules for scoring. Experienced examiners should also review the test manuals for revised tests in order to be certain that well-known procedures have not been changed.

TEST ADMINISTRATION

An examiner has multiple tasks to carry out during an evaluation. He or she must carefully and correctly administer test items in an organized, smooth, and steady fashion while recording exactly a patient's response, observing the patient's behavior, and scoring the patient's responses—all the while attempting to maintain the patient's cooperation. To ensure that the evaluation goes smoothly, an examiner should be thoroughly familiar with the tests being administered and prepared to proceed in a well-planned, organized fashion. This requires having test materials and the proper supplies ready and on hand so that unnecessary delays are avoided. In addition to the test manuals and stimuli, the examiner's materials should also include sharpened pencils with and without erasers, a pen for the examiner, extra paper, a stopwatch, and a clipboard. Test stimuli, however, should be kept out of sight until they are required and should be taken away as soon as possible after use to minimize the clutter on the tabletop. A small bookshelf on the examiner's side of the table to the examiner's left or right is an appropriate place to store items that should be kept out of the examinee's view. If an examiner is familiar with standard procedures and scoring rules, then moving smoothly from task to task is easier. Rapid Reference 4.4 highlights the steps necessary for test administration.

Test administration requires that test instructions be followed exactly. As part of the standard procedure, general and specific instructions must be phrased exactly as stated in the test manual. Resist the temptation to help the patient by explaining the words in questions unless the manual allows explanations. Resist the temptation to help the patient by adding additional words to the directions or repeating directions unless the manual permits repetition. Inquiries can be made only as instructed in the manual.

Timing should be done carefully but as inconspicuously as possible. The clinician must be careful not to distract the patient with the stopwatch. It is usually not permissible

Rapid Reference 4.4

Steps in Test Administration

- Establish rapport
- Maintain cooperation
- Provide encouragement
- Probe ambiguous responses
- Have test materials accessible
- Use stopwatch inconspicuously
- Observe behavior
- Administer test items in organized, smooth, and steady fashion
- Record responses verbatim
- Score responses as responses occur

DON'T FORGET

Have the following on hand:
- Test manuals and test stimuli
- Pens and sharpened pencils
- Extra paper
- Stopwatch
- Clipboard

CAUTION

State instructions and questions exactly. Resist the temptation to help the patient by explaining the words in questions, adding additional words, or by repeating directions unless specifically permitted in the test manual.

to tell a patient how much time is allotted for a particular test item. It is better when asked about time limits to remind the patient to tell you when the task is complete or to give an answer as soon as possible.

It is also usually not permissible to provide feedback to a patient about the correctness of a response. Feedback and encouragement should be nonspecific to the patient's response. In other words, the examiner should distribute feedback across the test session and not just when a patient is doing poorly and having difficulty. An examiner who responds only to incorrect answers is inadvertently cuing the patient as to the fact that an answer is wrong and might discourage the patient in the process. In addition, giving answers to questions is also unacceptable, even after an item has been completed. In some instances it is necessary to elucidate ambiguous responses from a patient by asking the patient to repeat the response or to be more specific. Probing responses must be done only if explicitly allowed in the test manual and only in the ways specified by the manual. The examiner must never ask leading questions when clarifying a patient's response. Answers should be clarified with neutral probes such as "What do you mean?" or "Tell me more about it."

In some instances it is necessary to encourage a reluctant patient to try a test item. Given that you want the patient's optimal performance, you should not accept initial "I don't know" responses unless you believe the patient is truly incapable of responding. When patients say, "I don't know," they could be indicating a fear of making a mistake. In those instances, ask the patient to try to answer any way he or she can and remind the patient that you are interested in his or her best effort. Sometimes encouragement takes the form of allowing a patient to work briefly past time limits on tasks he or she is close to completing successfully over time. Abruptly taking away a test item just because time has expired may dull a patient's ambition to do well on subsequent items.

TEST SCORING

The examiner must be able to score as the test progresses because on some tests the number of correct and incorrect answers determines when to discontinue a test or subtest. It is also important because some answers are not scorable as is and require inquiry. An examiner thoroughly familiar with scoring criteria is able to score a patient's responses as they are given and thus can ask for clarifications when necessary. When examiners encounter responses that are not easily scored, they should inquire for clarification of the response with neutral probes. If upon later rechecking of the scoring it becomes clear that an inquiry was not necessary, the additional response can be ignored in the scoring.

DON'T FORGET

- Be thoroughly familiar with scoring criteria.
- Score as you go.
- Score according to the test manuals.
- Double-check scoring when done.

When scoring, the clinician should not allow the patient to see the scores because this may affect subsequent responses or distract the patient from the task at hand. Usually a clipboard held at an angle or discreet use of one's hands can serve to shield the scores from the patient's view.

Scoring must always be done according to the test manuals, which often set guidelines concerning prototype answers. The examiner who is thoroughly familiar with the scoring guidelines is best able to discern the score value of a response quickly and accurately and better able to follow standard administration procedures. The manuals never list all possible correct or incorrect responses, however, so understanding the intent of a test or a particular item helps in the scoring of questionable responses.

Even experienced examiners make scoring errors. Reviewing test manuals periodically helps to ensure that an examiner has not inadvertently adopted incorrect scoring standards. Scoring should always be checked and rechecked after examination. This applies to all calculations, including the patient's age, the number of correct and incorrect items, additions, and score transfers from one part of the record to another. It also applies to double-checking the correct conversion of raw scores to scaled or standard scores. The examiner should consult books concerning specific tests to learn about common scoring errors that should be avoided. In *Essentials of WAIS-III Assessment,* for example, Kaufman and Lichtenberger, (1999) point out the common errors in obtaining scaled scores, including miscalculating a sum when adding scores to obtain the raw score or sum of scaled scores, writing illegibly, using the wrong age reference table, and misreading across the rows of the score conversion tables. Computer scoring programs are available from The Psychological Corporation and other test publishers for many tests such as the WAIS-III, WMS-III, Children's

Memory Scale, and NEPSY; these programs can serve to double-check the figures calculated by the examiner.

SPECIAL NEEDS

Input and Output Channels

Most neuropsychological tests are designed with the assumption that basic motor and sensory functions are intact. The examiner must take into account limitations in visual and auditory acuity and physical disabilities affecting the bones, muscles, or peripheral nervous system when administering and interpreting most neuropsychological tests. Any factors affecting the input of information to a patient or any limitation in a patient's output channels must be noted in a test report and used as part of the interpretative process. Limitations in a patient's input or output channels may undermine an examiner's ability to assess particular areas of function. For example, in patients with nonfluent aphasias it may be impossible to assess their ability to understand complex issues of reasoning, simply because there may be no reasonable means by which they can demonstrate their knowledge.

One of the challenges to the field of neuropsychology is the question of how to answer clinical questions posed for patients with significant disabilities in vision, hearing, or the use of the upper limbs. In some cases it may be possible to choose measures that do not require the use of the disabled sensory or motor system. For example, the clinician can use tasks that are primarily auditory for a patient with severe limits in vision or a visual task for a patient with severe limits in hearing. It may also be possible to use tests requiring verbal responses for patients who do not have use of their limbs or manual responses for patients who are severely dysarthric or otherwise unable to speak for reasons unrelated to the central nervous system. In some cases this approach presents significant limitations on the interpretation of test results and may not allow the neuropsychologist to assess the specific neuropsychological functions that may have been altered or diminished. For example, verbal memory may be of interest in a hearing-impaired patient or naming may be of interest in a patient with severe dysarthria, although it may not be possible to assess accurately these skills in these patients.

Many neuropsychologists find themselves tempted to modify existing measures to be more usable in the presence of a disability. For example, it may be possible to substitute a naming-to-definition task instead of a visual confrontation naming task such as the Boston Naming Test (Kaplan, Goodglass, & Weintraub, 1983) to patients who are severely visually impaired and still be able to determine whether they are anomic. Although sometimes inevitable, these modifications must be made only with great caution and only when there are no published alternatives available. When reporting results from such tasks, the examiner should document the origin of the procedure and the reasons for the modifications (e.g., sensory or motor limitations); also, the clinician should describe the procedure in enough detail to allow another clinician to replicate the observations. Even if no standardization or norms exist for the procedure, occasionally the task may be the only means available for documenting change in performance and may allow data useful for clinical purposes. Whenever modifications are considered, the examiner must determine whether other, more suitable measures already exist for a particular special need instead of (or in addition to) administering commonly used tests with adaptations that might confound test result interpretation.

Testing Patients with Visual Impairments

It may be reasonable to administer to blind patients the verbal portions of standardized tests, such as the Wechsler Intelligence and Memory Scales. Assessing nonverbal or visual skills is obviously more difficult. Tests such as the Tactual Performance Test (TPT), which requires spatial manipulation and nonverbal problem solving as well as blindfold use in sighted individuals, may be one alternative. It should be kept in mind, however, that success on tests like the TPT and even some verbal tests might be dependent on prior visual experiences. Sattler (1992) suggests several measures such as the Hays-Binet, Perkins-Binet, and the Blind Learning Aptitude Test that can be used when evaluating blind children.

Testing Patients with Hearing Impairments

Testing a deaf patient is difficult because so many tasks are dependent on verbal abilities and verbal tasks pose a particular obstacle for severely hearing-impaired individuals. If the patient and the examiner know American Sign Language (ASL), then verbal tasks can be administered in this fashion. In some instances written language can be substituted for oral language. Otherwise, verbal tests may have to be omitted entirely. Giving task directions even for nonverbal tasks may be difficult for hearing-impaired individuals. Directions may have to be given in ASL, in writing, and through gesture. Some tasks, such as the Test of Nonverbal Intelligence–Third Edition (TONI-3; Brown, Sherbenou, & Johnson, 1997), the Comprehensive Test of Nonverbal Intelligence (CTONI; Hammill, Pearson, & Wiederholt, 1997), or the Naglieri Nonverbal Ability Test–Individual Assessment (for children and young adults; Naglieri, 2000) may be the most suitable measures of nonverbal reasoning and nonverbal intelligence for the deaf patient because of the language-free format. Response choices are indicated by pointing, and instructions are presented through pantomime. Sattler (1992) offers pantomime instructions for administering the performance subtests from the WISC-R to hearing-impaired children. These instructions can likely be adapted for use with the WISC-III and WAIS-III performance subtests as well. Memory tasks may have to be restricted to nonverbal measures; again, however, the examiner must be sure to provide the patient with sufficient directions through the written word, pantomime, and gesture.

Testing Patients with Aphasia

Establishing that a patient with an acquired language disorder has an adequate output channel is the first challenge when testing such a patient. A patient who has no way of indicating responses cannot be tested. Assessment of the pattern and degree of aphasic symptoms can be accomplished with measures such as the Boston Diagnostic Aphasia Examination (Goodglass, Kaplan, & Barresi, 2000) and the Boston Naming Test (Kaplan et al., 1983). Depending on the severity of the patient's language deficits, assessment (as with hearing-impaired individuals) may have to continue with nonverbal tests and other tests that do not depend on language ability.

Testing Patients with Motor Impairments

Patients with motor disabilities may be at a particular disadvantage on speeded tasks and nonverbal tasks requiring coordinated motor movement. In these instances it may be wise to administer only verbal subtests or motor-free tasks in order to obtain an assessment of overall cognitive ability. In addition, modifications can be made to accommodate motor disabilities although standard normative data may not be available to judge performance relative to other individuals with motor disabilities. Also, remember that motor deficits might give false impressions of cognitive ability. Modifications, for example, can involve reading aloud or indicating test choices in turn for a patient and noting patient agreement when even pointing ability is compromised. Another modification might involve testing without time constraints. Rapid Reference 4.5 provides a summary of possible modifications for testing patients who have limitations in input or output channels.

≡Rapid Reference 4.5

Possible Test Battery Modifications for Individuals with Limitations in Input/Output Channels

Testing Patients with Visual Impairments
- Administer verbal portions of standardized tests.
- Administer nonverbal tests that require spatial manipulation and problem solving but not sight (e.g., TPT).
- Administer the Hays-Binet, Perkins-Binet, and Blind Learning Aptitude Test.

Testing Patients with Hearing Impairments
- Use American Sign Language if possible for verbal tasks.
- Substitute written language for oral language.
- Give directions through pantomime, signing, or gesture.
- Use tests such as TONI-3, CTONI, and the Naglieri Nonverbal Ability Test.

Testing Patients with Aphasia
- Establish that an adequate output channel exists.
- Document aphasic features with tests such as the BDAE or WAB.
- Use nonverbal tests.
- Give directions through pantomime and gesture.

Testing Patients with Motor Impairments
- Assess overall cognitive ability with verbal and motor-free tasks.
- Avoid speeded motor tasks.
- Test motor abilities without time constraints.

TEST SELECTION

When selecting the tests to administer in a neuropsychological assessment, the clinician should pay attention to the referral question, the appropriateness of a test for a given individual, and the comprehensiveness of a test battery. Based upon the reason for referral, the examiner entertains hypotheses about possible deficits and chooses tests that can elicit and measure deficiencies in expected areas. For example, knowing that a patient has had a middle cerebral artery stroke suggests the possibility of acquired language deficits; therefore, the test battery needs to include measures sensitive to aphasic deficits such as the Boston Diagnostic Aphasia Examination (Goodglass et al., 2000). In a case in which damage secondary to hypoxia is suspected, then the focus may be directed more toward an in-depth analysis of memory functions. An important issue is whether the test has validity for the particular application in which it is being considered. The examiner should use tests that are sensitive to dysfunction in the function being examined and be aware of whether particular tests as a sample of function are predictive of behavior in real-life settings.

Tests are also selected based upon whether they are appropriate for the particular patient. Considerations of a patient's age and education play a role in test selection, and in some instances language and cultural history may determine test choice. For each test selected for a test battery, good normative data appropriate against which to compare a patient's performance must be available. Even a mature 15-year-old is too young to take the Wechsler Adult Intelligence Scale–Third Edition (Wechsler, 1997) because the normative data do not exist for a 15-year-old. In another instance, if a patient did not acquire knowledge of the English language until late in life, a test such as the Boston Naming Test (Kaplan et al., 1983) may not provide interpretable data. For patients for whom English is a second language, performance may re-

DON'T FORGET

Select a comprehensive array of tests measuring
- Arousal and attention
- Executive functions
- Intelligence
- Learning and memory
- Language ability
- Visuospatial skills
- Motor skills
- Emotion, behavior, and personality
- Effort and compliance

flect their lack of experience with or exposure to the name of a particular object rather than loss of the ability to name it.

Tests are also selected by their ability to add to the comprehensiveness of a test battery. Many areas need to be assessed in the typical neuropsychological evaluation. The examiner may need to develop data to assess premorbid abilities, and it is almost always necessary to measure intelligence to establish a baseline against which other tests will be compared to confirm discrepancies between skills. A comprehensive test battery contains measures of both higher and lower cognitive domains in order to identify the point of processing at which functions break down. In addition, the clinician must assemble a test battery that permits assessment of the same cognitive domain with multiple measures to explore the reliability of a deficit. A test battery usually needs to include various measures of attention to explore the entire attentional matrix of a patient. A test battery also usually needs to include measures of executive functions such as reasoning, planning, organization, set establishment and maintenance, and measures of verbal and visual leaning and memory. In addition, a test battery generally includes tests to assess language skills and perhaps academic skills, as well as visual, tactile, and motor abilities. In many cases, testing must also address issues of motivation, effort, and emotional function. The number of tests that can be administered is determined in part by time available for testing and by patient stamina. Rapid Reference 4.6 summarizes the factors involved in test selection.

The particular test battery used obviously is the choice of the neuropsychologist and often reflects the examiner's personal preferences. In some cases the neuropsychologist chooses to use a predeveloped or fixed battery of tests such as

---

≡Rapid Reference 4.6

Test Selection

Referral question
- Hypothesis generation
- Established validity for task at hand

Appropriateness
- Age
- Education
- Level of difficulty
- Availability of good normative data

Comprehensiveness
- Assess wide range of functions
- Assess lower and higher domains
- Use multiple measures for the same domain

Fixed versus flexible battery

the Halstead-Reitan Neuropsychological Test Battery, perhaps supplemented by a test of intelligence and another of memory. In other cases the neuropsychologist assembles a flexible battery of tests designed to answer particular questions about cognitive strengths and weaknesses. The tests available for use are varied and too numerous to list here, although we do focus on the different areas of function and discuss some measures for each. For a compilation of neuropsychological tests and commentary and information concerning test administration and norms, the reader is referred to *A Compendium of Neuropsychological Tests* (Spreen & Strauss, 1998) or to *Neuropsychological Assessment* (Lezak, 1995). Rapid Reference 4.7 lists the various resources available for assessment measures.

≡Rapid Reference 4.7

Assessment Resources

• American Guidance Service (AGS)	www.agsnet.com
• Multi-Health Systems (MHS)	www.mhs.com
• National Rehabilitation Services, Inc. (NRS)	1-517-732-3866
• NCS Assessments	http://assessments.ncspearson.com
• NFER-NELSON	Darville House 2 Oxford Road East Windsor, Berkshire SL4 1DF England
• Northern Speech Services (NSS)	1-517-732-3866
• PRO-ED	www.proedinc.com
• The Psychological Corporation	www.PsychCorp.com
• Psychological Assessment Resources (PAR)	www.parinc.com
• Reitan Neuropsychology Lab	1-602-882-2022
• Riverside Publishing	www.riverpub.com
• Western Psychological Services (WPS)	www.wpspublish.com
• Wide Range, Inc. (WR)	www.widerange.com

TEST BATTERIES

Halstead-Reitan Neuropsychological Test Battery (HRB)

Since 1955 the HRB (Reitan & Wolfson, 1993) has allowed computation of the Halstead Impairment Index from seven scores derived from five tests, including the Category Test, the Finger Oscillation Test, the Seashore Rhythm Test, the Speech Sounds Perception Test, and the total time, memory, and localization scores from the Tactual Performance Test. Also routinely included in the HRB, but not part of the Impairment Index, are the Trail Making Test, the Aphasia Screening Test, the Sensory Perceptual Examination, and Grip Strength. The Impairment Index ranges from .0 to 1.0 and indicates the proportion of test scores that are in the range indicative of brain impairment. The Halstead Impairment Index is calculated by dividing the number of scores in the impaired range by the total number of the seven tests given that are part of the Halstead Impairment Index. Patients obtaining scores of .5 or above are classified as brain damaged. The Halstead Impairment Index is used to identify functioning consistent with brain damage, but it does not indicate the level of dysfunction.

Several other summary indexes that assist with this limitation are available for use with HRB and its supplemental tests. The Average Impairment Rating can be used to document the existence of brain damage and to quantify the amount of impairment. The Average Impairment Rating averages the scaled scores (i.e., 0 to 4, where 0 is above average, 1 is average, 2 is one standard deviation below the mean, 3 is two standard deviations below the mean, and 4 is three standard deviations below the mean) from the 12 tests that comprise this index. The 12 tests include the seven measures from the original Halstead Impairment Index along with Trail Making B, WAIS Digit Symbol, Aphasia Screening Test, Spatial Relations Test, and the Perceptual Disorders Test. One other index is the General Neuropsychological Deficit Scale, which is based on 42 different test variables from the subtests of the HRB and is used to indicate the presence of brain damage by evaluating level and pattern of performance, lateralized motor and sensory findings, and particular deficits and pathognomonic signs. The computer program developed by Reitan (1988) can be used to assist with the calculation of the Neuropsychological Deficit Scale for adults. Normative data based on gender, age, and education for adults for the

HRB are also available from Heaton, Grant, and Matthews (1991). Rapid Reference 4.8 provides a description of the HRB, relevant references, and source.

Category Test. This is a complex nonverbal task that assesses concept formation and abstract reasoning. It tests flexible problem solving abilities and the capacity to learn from experience. The original version uses slides, but a booklet version and a short version are available as well from Psychological Assessment Resources (PAR) and Western Psychological Services (WPS), respectively.

≡ Rapid Reference 4.8

Halstead-Reitan Neuropsychological Battery

Tests for Halstead Impairment Index

Category Test
Finger Oscillation Test
Seashore Rhythm Test
Speech Sounds Perception Test
Tactual Performance Test

Ages

Young child (5–8 years)
Intermediate Child (9–14 years)
Adult

Sources

Reitan Neuropsychology Laboratory
2920 S. 4th Ave.
Tucson AZ
1-602-882-2022

Psychological Assessment Resources
1-800-331-8378

Additional Tests

Trail Making Test
Aphasia Screening Test
Sensory Perceptual Examination
Grip Strength

Summary Scores

Halstead Impairment Index
Neuropsychological Deficit Scale
Average Impairment Rating

Relevant Texts

Heaton, R. K., Grant, I., & Matthews, C. G. (1991). *Comprehensive norms for an expanded Halstead-Reitan Battery: Demographic corrections, research findings, and clinical applications.* Odessa, FL: Psychological Assessment Resources.

Reitan, R. M., & Wolfson, D. (1993). *The Halstead-Reitan Neuropsychological Test Battery: Theory and Clinical Interpretation.* Tuscon, AZ: Neuropsychology Press.

Finger Oscillation Test. This task, also called the Finger Tapping Test, measures fine motor speed of the index finger on each hand. It can be helpful in assessing laterality of brain damage. The finger tapping board can be obtained through Reitan Neuropsychology Laboratory and from PAR.

Seashore Rhythm Test. This test requires the patient to discriminate between similar and different musical rhythms. This test was derived from the Seashore Tests of Musical Ability (Seashore et al., 1960) and is dependent on nonspecific functions such as attention.

Speech Sounds Perception Test. This test requires the patient to determine which of four written nonsense words matches a nonsense word said aloud. It is an auditory perception test that is sensitive to attentional problems.

Tactual Performance Test (TPT). This task uses the Seguin-Goddard Formboard to measure the tactual perception and form recognition along with psychomotor problem solving and tactile memory for spatial location and shapes. A portable version of the TPT is available from PAR.

Trail Making Test (TMT). Trail Making Test is a speeded test that measures sustained visual attention, visual scanning, sequencing, and cognitive flexibility. It has two parts, Trail Making A, which requires number sequencing, and Trail Making B, which requires alternation and sequencing between letters and numbers.

Aphasia Screening Test. This is a brief measure of language and nonlanguage skills, such as naming, reading, spelling, writing, identifying body parts, performing arithmetic calculations, drawing shapes, and discriminating left from right.

Sensory Perceptual Examination. This test assesses the patient's ability to perceive tactile, auditory, and visual stimuli on both sides of the body.

Grip Strength. This measure uses a hand dynamometer (available from PAR) to assess the strength of each hand.

Luria–Nebraska Neuropsychological Test Battery (LNNB)

The LNNB (Golden, Purisch, & Hammeke, 1985), like the HRB, is a comprehensive test battery designed to measure neuropsychological functioning. The LNNB provides a global measure of cerebral dysfunction along with lateralization and localization of focal brain impairments. Form I of the battery contains 269 items (Form II has 279 items) from which 11 clinical scales can be derived: motor functions, rhythm, tactile functions, visual functions, receptive speech, expressive speech, writing, reading, arithmetic, memory, and intellectual processes. Form II has an additional clinical scale: intermediate memory. From the clinical scales, five summary scales can be derived: pathognomonic, left hemisphere, right hemisphere, profile elevation, and impairment. In addition, since the battery was first published, eight localization scales have been developed pertaining to the two hemispheres and the frontal, sensorimotor, parietal-occipital, and temporal areas of the brain. The LNNB takes 1.5 to 2.5 hours to administer and can be given in a single session or several brief sessions. It has the advantage of being completely portable and can be given at bedside. The LNNB was designed for patients 15 years and older but can also be used for 13- and 14-year-olds. A child's version of the LNNB (LNNB-C) has been developed for children ages 8 to 12 years old. Scoring and interpretation are complex but can be aided by a computer program. The LNNB and the LNNB-C as well as the computer scoring are available through WPS. Characteristics of the battery, neuropsychological findings, and critical considerations about the LNNB are available in Lezak (1995). Rapid Reference 4.9 provides a description of the LNNB, relevant references, and source.

NEPSY: A Developmental Neuropsychological Assessment

This relatively new test battery (Korkman, Kirk, & Kemp, 1997), when supplemented by an intelligence test, provides a comprehensive assessment of neuropsychological status in children ages 3 to 12. The NEPSY assesses functioning in five core domains: attention and executive functions, language, sensorimotor functions, visuospatial processing, and memory and learning. For each subtest within each domain a scaled score can be derived, and for each domain a summary standard score can be generated. In addition, various supplemental scores are available, including scores for qualitative observations made about a child's behavior. The core battery takes 45 minutes for 3- to 4-year-olds and 65 minutes for older children. The full battery takes an hour for younger children and 2 hours for older children.

Within the attention and executive functions domain, measures are available to assess selective and sustained attention, response inhibition, self-regulation and monitoring, planning, set maintenance and flexibility, and nonverbal flu-

≡ Rapid Reference 4.9

Luria-Nebraska Neuropsychological Test Battery

Tests

Form I (269 items)

Form II (279 items)

Summary Scores

Pathognomonic

Left Hemisphere

Profile Elevation

Right Hemisphere

Impairment

Ages

Child (8–12 years)

Adult (15 years and older)

Relevant Texts

Golden, C. J., Purisch, A. D., & Hammeke, T. A. (1985). *Manual for the Luria-Nebraska Neuropsychological Battery: Forms I and II.* Los Angeles: Western Psychological Services.

Lezak, M. D. (1995). *Neuropsychological Assessment* (3rd ed.). New York: Oxford University Press.

Source

Western Psychological Services

Phone: 1-800-648-8857

---

ency. The language subtests examine phonological processing, verbal fluency, comprehension of instructions, speeded naming, and oromotor ability. Within the sensorimotor domain, measures are available to assess fine motor speed, visuomotor precision, tactile sensory ability, motor sequencing, and the ability to imitate hand positions. The visuospatial processing subtests allow examination of design copying, block construction, and the ability to judge position and directionality. Within the memory and learning domain, the test measures evaluate immediate memory for sentences; immediate and delayed memory for names, faces, and lists; and memory for narrative stories. The NEPSY is avail-

≡ Rapid Reference 4.10

NEPSY: A Developmental Neuropsychological Assessment

Tests

Auditory Attention & Response Set	Visual Attention	Statue
Design Fluency	Knock and Tap	Speeded Naming
Phonological Processing	Verbal Fluency	Oromotor Sequences
Comprehension of Instructions	Fingertip Tapping	Arrows
Repetition of Nonsense Words	Visuomotor Precision	Route Finding
Imitating Hand Positions	Finger Discrimination	Design Copying
Manual Motor Sequences	Block Construction	List Learning
Memory for Faces	Memory for Names	Narrative Memory
Sentence Repetition		

Summary (Core Domain) Scores

Attention and Executive Functions Visuospatial Processing

Language Sensorimotor Functions

Memory and Learning

Ages

Child (3–12 years)

Relevant Texts

Korkman, M., Kirk, U., & Kemp, S. (1997). NEPSY: A developmental neuropsychological assessment. San Antonio, TX: Psychological Corporation.

Kemp, S., Kirk, U., & Korkman, M. (2001). Essentials of NEPSY assessment. New York: Wiley.

Source

The Psychological Corporation
Phone: 1-800-872-1726

able from The Psychological Corporation. Rapid Reference 4.10 provides a description of the NEPSY, relevant references, and source of the test.

PREMORBID ASSESSMENT

Patients are often referred for assessment after an injury or a decline in ability, but in most instances no preinjury test scores are available that allow a specific determination of the level of decline or change. Premorbid function, therefore, has to be estimated based on known demographic variables including educational and vocational achievement, and based on performance on tests resistant to decline from injury and predictive of cognitive ability. Vocabulary, fund of general information, and other skills such as word reading are highly correlated with intelligence and are often the best test means for estimating premorbid mental ability. We describe here several measures that can be used to estimate premorbid cognitive ability. Rapid Reference 4.11 lists the tests, the appropriate age ranges, and the publishers.

National Adult Reading Test–2 (NART-2)

This test was designed to estimate premorbid intellectual ability in adults ages 16 to 70. The NART-2 requires the patient to read aloud 50 irregularly spelled words. The NART-2 was developed in England and first published in 1982 by Nelson; it has been adapted for the United States by Blair and Spreen (1989) as the North American Adult Reading Test (NAART or NART-R).

Shipley Institute of Living Scale

The SILS (Zachary, 1987) is composed of two subtests: a multiple-choice vocabulary test and a measure of abstraction using logical sequencing. Because vocabulary is fairly resistant to decline from brain damage, the vocabulary test

≡Rapid Reference 4.11

Tests for Premorbid Assessment

Test	Ages	Source
NART-2	16–70	NFER-NELSON
NAART	16–70+	Spreen, O., & Strauss, E. (1998). A compendium of neuropsychological tests: Administration, norms, and commentary (2nd ed.). New York: Oxford University Press.
SCOLP	16–65	NSS
SILS	14 and older	WPS
WTAR	16–89	Psych Corp
WRAT3 Reading	5–75	WR

can be used as a measure of premorbid ability and the discrepancy between vocabulary and abstract thinking as a measure of cognitive impairment. Norms are available for individuals ages 14 and up.

The Speed and Capacity of Language Processing Test

The SCOLP (Baddeley, Emslie, & Nimmo-Smith, 1992) is used to detect language processing deficits and to measure rate of language processing. It is designed to discriminate longstanding slow processing from that due to brain damage. The SCOLP is comprised of two tests: the Speed of Comprehension Test and the Spot-the-Word Vocabulary Test. Discrepancies between comprehension speed and vocabulary are then used to rate the probable degree of acquired cognitive impairment. Normative data are available for ages 16 through 65.

Wechsler Test of Adult Reading

The WTAR (2001) is scheduled for release in 2001 by The Psychological Corporation and is designed to estimate the premorbid level of intellectual functioning of individuals ages 16 to 89. The patient is required to read aloud from a list of 50 words with irregular pronunciations. The test is conormed with the WAIS-III and the WMS-III.

Wide Range Achievement Test–Revision 3–Reading (WRAT3; Wilkinson, 1993)

This is a screening measure of word reading ability and was designed as a measure of achievement for individuals ages 5 through 75. It requires the patient to read aloud a series of words that become more and more difficult and are less and less common. In patients without verbal deficits, the Reading subtest can provide information about premorbid cognitive ability.

INTELLIGENCE

Administering a general measure of intelligence or cognitive ability is an important part of the neuropsychological test battery for several reasons. The results of the IQ test set the baseline against which other test results are measured. Patients generally are expected to perform within a normal range of skills variabilities around measured IQ on the broad array of cognitive measures included in a neuropsychological battery. Deviations from this range can signal cognitive impairments. In addition, general intelligence tests are multidimensional instruments that allow the examiner to observe how a patient performs across a wide variety of tasks. A patient's performance on the different subtests provides guidelines for the administration of further tests during the evaluation and can elucidate the pattern of impairments.

Intelligence Screening

In some circumstances it may be necessary because of time constraints, practicality, or the fact that a patient has been tested recently on a full intelligence test to use brief measures to estimate a patient's IQ. Some of the available measures allow measurement of both verbal and nonverbal intelligence, whereas others focus on one skill or the other. Rapid Reference 4.12 lists the tests, the appropriate age ranges, and the publishers.

Comprehensive Test of Nonverbal Intelligence (CTONI)

The CTONI (Hammill et al., 1997) is a nonverbal reasoning test consisting of six subtests: Pictorial Analogies, Pictorial Categories, Pictorial Sequences, Geometric Analogies, Geometric Categories, and Geometric Sequences. The subtests were designed to measure analogical reasoning, categorical classification, and sequential reasoning. From these subtests the CTONI provides three composite scores: Nonverbal Intelligence Quotient, Pictorial Nonverbal Intelligence Quotient, and Geometric Nonverbal Intelligence Quotient. Responses to the test are given by pointing. The test is appropriate for individuals ages 6 through 90.

≡ *Rapid Reference 4.12*

Tests for Intelligence Screening

Test	Ages	Source
CTONI	6–90	PAR
K-BIT	4–90	AGS
TONI-3	6–89	PRO-ED
Raven's Progressive Matrices	5–17	Psych Corp
WASI	6–89	Psych Corp

Kaufman Brief Intelligence Test (K-BIT)

The K-BIT (Kaufman & Kaufman, 1990) contains 2 subtests, Vocabulary (verbal) and Matrices (nonverbal). The Vocabulary subtest measures knowledge of words and their meanings, and the Matrices subtest measures the ability to solve problems concerning the relationships between pictures and abstract designs. The items are presented via easel, and the test can be administered to individuals ranging in age from 4 through 90.

Test of Nonverbal Intelligence–3 (TONI-3)

The TONI-3 (Brown et al., 1997) is a brief measure of nonverbal intelligence based on a matrix reasoning task that measures abstract reasoning and nonverbal problem solving. It is a language-free task and is thus useful with individuals who have difficulty with the English language. The test ages are 6 through 89.

The Raven's Progressive Matrices

The Raven's Progressive Matrices are a series of three sets of matrices designed to assess nonverbal ability. The easiest level is the Coloured Progressive Matrices (Raven, 1947, 1995), which is appropriate for young children (ages 5–11), mentally impaired adolescents, and the elderly. The average level is the Standard Progressive Matrices (Raven, 1938, 1996), which is appropriate for the general population (ages 6–16 and 17+). The most difficult is the Advanced Progressive Matrices (Raven, 1965, 1994), which is intended for the top 20% of the population (ages 12–16 and 17+).

Wechsler Abbreviated Scale of Intelligence (WASI)

The WASI (Wechsler, 1999) was designed as a reliable brief measure of general cognitive functioning. The four-subtest version consists of Vocabulary, Similarities, Block Design, and Matrix Reasoning, which result in a Verbal IQ, Performance IQ, and Full Scale IQ. The two-subtest version consists of Vocabulary and Matrix Reasoning, which result in a Full Scale IQ. The test can be administered to patients ages 6 through 89 and has been nationally standardized with 2,245 cases.

Intelligence Tests

Rapid Reference 4.13 lists the tests of intelligence, the appropriate age ranges, and the publishers.

≡ Rapid Reference 4.13

Tests of Intelligence

Test	Ages	Source
KAIT	11–85+	AGS
SB-IV	2–Adult	Riverside Publishing
WAIS-III	16–89	Psych Corp
WISC-III	6–16	Psych Corp
WPPSI-R	3–7.3	Psych Corp

Kaufman Adolescent and Adult Intelligence Test (KAIT)

The KAIT (Kaufman & Kaufman, 1993a) is a multisubtest intelligence test designed for individuals ages 11 through 85+. From the Core Battery, which consists of six subtests, three scores are obtained: Fluid IQ, Crystallized IQ, and Composite IQ. The Crystallized Scale contains three subtests that measure the ability to solve problems using knowledge: Auditory Comprehension, Double Meanings, and Definitions. The Fluid Scale contains three subtests that measure novel problem solving: Rebus Learning, Mystery Codes, and Logical Steps. The Core Battery can be expanded to four more subtests, which permit comparison of immediate versus delayed memory.

Stanford-Binet Intelligence Scale–Fourth Edition

The SB-IV (Thorndike, Hagen, & Sattler, 1986) consists of 15 tasks measuring four cognitive areas organized within a three-level hierarchical cognitive abilities model. The major organizing factor of the theoretical model is the *g*-factor; the second-level factors consist of Crystallized Abilities, Fluid-Analytic Abilities, and Short-Term Memory. Within this hierarchy the second-level factor of Crystallized Abilities is broken down into third-level factors of Verbal Reasoning and Quantitative Reasoning. Verbal Reasoning includes tests of vocabulary, comprehension, absurdities, and verbal relations. Quantitative Reasoning includes tests of quantitative knowledge, number series, and equation building. The second-level factor of Fluid-Analytic Abilities consists of the third-level factor of Abstract/Visual Reasoning, which includes tests of paper folding and cutting, pattern analysis, copying, and matrices. The third-level factor of Short-Term Memory includes tests of bead memory, sentence memory, digit memory, and object memory. Summary scores consist of Standard Age Scores for each test, Standard Age Scores for each of the four areas, and a composite Standard Age Score. The Fourth Edition of the Stanford-Binet was standardized on more than 5,000 individuals of ages 2 through adult.

The Wechsler Scales

The intelligence scales used most often in the United States are those from David Wechsler. The current adult measure (ages 16–89) is the Wechsler Adult Intelligence Scale–Third Edition (WAIS-III), which was published in 1997 (Wechsler, 1997). For children ages 6 through 16 years, 11 months, the current test, published in 1991 (Wechsler, 1991), is the Wechsler Intelligence Scale for Children–Third Edition (WISC-III). For children ages 3 through 7 years, 3 months, the current test, published in 1989 (Wechsler, 1989), is the Wechsler Preschool and Primary Scale of Intelligence–Revised (WPPSI-R).

The WAIS-III and WISC-III provide IQ, index, and age-scaled subtest scores. The Verbal IQ is comprised of age-scaled scores on subtests of Information, Vocabulary, Similarities, Comprehension, Arithmetic, and Digit Span. The Performance IQ is comprised of age-scaled scores on subtests of Picture Completion, Block Design, Object Assembly (WISC-III) or Matrix Reasoning (WAIS-III), Picture Arrangement, and Digit Symbol-Coding. Also available are the Verbal Comprehension Index, Perceptual Organization Index, Working Memory Index (WAIS-III) or Freedom from Distractibility Index (WISC-III), and Processing Speed Index.

ATTENTION

Assessment of attention means evaluating the multiple facets that make up the attentional matrix. This matrix can be conceptualized as involving span of apprehension; the ability to focus, divide, and sustain attention; mental manipulation; and resistance to distraction or interference. Few attentional tasks, however, can be considered to measure only one of these facets, although each may fit more neatly into one category than another. Since intact attention is a building block on which other cognitive abilities rely, it is necessary to measure how well an individual can deploy and maintain his or her attention. In order to delineate the nature of an attentional problem, multiple tests of attention need to be administered. Rapid Reference 4.14 summarizes the tests, the appropriate age ranges, and the publishers.

≡Rapid Reference 4.14

Tests of Attention

Test	Ages	Source
ACPT	6–11	Psych Corp
BTA	17–84	PAR
Connors' CPT-II	6 and older	MHS
Wechsler Digit Span	6–89	Psych Corp
DVT	20–80	PAR
PASAT	16 and older	Psych Corp
Ruff 2 & 7	16–70	PAR
SDMT	8 and older	WPS
Vigil	6–90	Psych Corp
VSAT	18–60+	PAR

Auditory Continuous Performance Test (ACPT)

The ACPT (Keith, 1994) measures auditory vigilance in children ages 6 through 11 years. The child listens to words said aloud via audiotape and raises his or her thumb upon hearing the target word.

Brief Test of Attention (BTA)

The BTA (Schretlen, 1996) is offered as a test of divided auditory attention for individuals ages 17 through 84. A series of numbers and letters is presented aloud via audiotape. In the first half of the test, the client is to disregard the letters and count the numbers in each series. In the second half, the client is to disregard the numbers and count the letters in each series.

Connors' Continuous Performance Test–Second Edition (CPT-II)

The Connors' CPT-II (2000) is used to identify visual attention problems manifested in impaired vigilance and impulsive responding in children and adults ages 6 and older. The test is presented via computer and provides information concerning measures such as number of omission and commission errors, perceptual sensitivity, and reaction time.

Digit Span

This test is one of the subtests in the WAIS-III and an optional subtest in the WISC-III. In forward digit span the patient repeats digits in the exact order they were presented. Forward digit span is a measure of elementary attention or span of apprehension. In backward digit span the patient recalls the digits presented in the exact reverse order. Backward digit span is a measure of mental manipulation or control and requires working memory.

Digit Vigilance Test (DVT)

The DVT (Lewis, 1995) is a visual cancellation task that is used to measure sustained attention and that requires visual scanning and psychomotor speed. Measures of omission errors and time-to-task completion are available. Normative data are available for the DVT in Heaton, Grant, and Matthews (1991) for ages 20 through 80.

Paced Auditory Serial Addition Test (PASAT)

The PASAT (Gronwall, 1977; Gronwall & Sampson, 1974) was designed to measure sustained and divided attention and speed of information processing. The task requires serial addition of pairs of consecutive numbers at varying interval rates. A computerized version is available from the Psychological Corporation for individuals ages 16 and older.

Ruff 2 & 7 Selective Attention Test

This test (Ruff, Neimann, & Allen, 1992) is used to measure visual search and cancellation in patients ages 16 through 70. Targets (2 & 7) are embedded among either alphabetical letters or other numbers. The test is scored for both speed and accuracy. It can be obtained from Psychological Assessment Resources.

Symbol Digit Modalities Test (SDMT)

The SDMT (Smith, 1991) is a speeded symbol substitution task that requires visual scanning and tracking. With a reference key at hand, the patient pairs specific numbers with specific geometric figures over a 90-second interval. Responses can be both written and oral, allowing a comparison between written and oral responses. The task can be used for individuals 8 years and older.

Vigil Continuous Performance Test

The Vigil (Cegalis, Boroling, & Cegalis, 1996) is used for children and adults ages 6 through 90 to measure sustained attention or vigilance. The test is administered via computer and includes presentations of both verbal and nonverbal targets.

Visual Search and Attention Test (VSAT)

The VSAT (Trenerry et al., 1990) is a visual cancellation task designed to measure speeded visual search and vigilance. It can be used to assess unilateral spatial neglect. Normative data are available for individuals 18 through 60+ years of age.

EXECUTIVE FUNCTIONS

This category refers to the numerous higher-order cognitive functions of establishing, maintaining and changing set; initiation; planning and organization; judgment; reasoning and abstraction; and self-regulation. To capture a patient's abilities and disabilities in the area of executive functions, the tests selected should broadly cover these various processes. Rapid Reference 4.15 provides the test names or acronyms, the appropriate age ranges, and the publishers.

Category Test

Part of the Halstead–Reitan Neuropsychological Battery, the Category Test is a complex nonverbal task assessing concept formation and abstract reasoning. It involves flexible problem solving and the capacity to learn from experience. The original version uses slides, but a Booklet Category Test (BCT; DeFilippis & Mc-Campbell, 1991) is available for adults (15 years and older), and an Intermediate Booklet Category Test (IBCT; Byrd, 1987) for children ages 9 through 15 is

≡Rapid Reference 4.15

Tests of Executive Functions

Test	Ages	Source
Booklet Category Test	15 and older	PAR
Children's Category Test	5–16	PAR
Short Category Test	20 and older	PAR
COWAT	6–95	See Spreen, O., & Strauss, E. (1998). *A compendium of neuropsychological tests: Administration, norms, and commentary* (2nd ed.). New York: Oxford University Press.
RFFT	16–70	PAR
Stroop	7–80	WPS
TMT	8–85	Reitan Neuropsychology Lab
WCST	6.5–89	PAR

available from Psychological Assessment Resources (PAR). Also, a Short Category Test (Wetzel & Boll, 1987) is available from Western Psychological Services (WPS) for adults ages 20 and older. In addition, a Children's Category Test (CCT; Boll, 1993) is available from PAR for children ages 5 through 16.

Controlled Oral Word Association Test

This task is used to measure verbal fluency or the ability to maximally produce words belonging to a particular class. In the FAS–Test, the patient must generate as many words as possible beginning with the letters *F, A,* and *S* in 1-minute intervals. Normative data for ages 6 through 95 are available in Spreen and Strauss (1998). Normative data are also available for the letters *C, L,* and *F.* In a parallel task, Category Fluency, the patient is required to generate as many words as possible belonging to a particular category—for example, animals.

Ruff Figural Fluency Test (RFFT)

The RFFT (Ruff, 1988) is designed as a measure of nonverbal fluency or the ability to maximally produce figural responses. The task requires the patient to draw as many unique designs as possible within 60-second intervals by connecting dots on a grid. It is appropriate for ages 16 through 70.

Stroop Color and Word Test

The Stroop (Golden, 1978) is used to measure cognitive flexibility, resistance to interference from outside stimuli, and the ability to suppress a prepotent verbal response. A patient's performance is compared across three tasks: word reading, color naming, and color word naming. In the latter task the patient must name as quickly as possible the color ink (which is discordant with the color word) in which words are printed rather than reading the word. Normative data are now available for ages 7 through 80.

Trail Making Test (TMT)

The TMT is a speeded test that measures sustained visual attention, visual scanning, sequencing, and cognitive flexibility. It has two parts: Trail Making A, which requires number sequencing, and Trail Making B, which requires alternation and sequencing between letters and numbers. Normative data are available for ages 8 through 85 in Spreen and Strauss (1998).

Wisconsin Card Sorting Test (WCST)

The WCST (Grant & Berg, 1993) is used to measure abstract reasoning, concept generation, and perseverative responding in individuals ages 6.5 through

89. The task requires the patient to sort the cards according to one of three principles of class membership. Available measures include categories achieved, perservative responses, perseverative errors, nonperseverative errors, failure to maintain set, and efficiency of learning.

LEARNING AND MEMORY

Evaluation of memory requires assessment of numerous, seemingly disparate processes in both the verbal and nonverbal modalities. Evaluation of memory means assessing encoding and acquisition of information, retention and retrieval, rate of decay, and susceptibility to interference, as well as recognition memory versus spontaneous recall. Some memory instruments incorporate measures to assess most of these processes, whereas others measure just one aspect. Rapid Reference 4.16 lists the tests, the appropriate age range, and the publisher.

≡ *Rapid Reference 4.16*

Tests of Learning and Memory

Test	Ages	Source
BVRT	8 and older	Psych Corp
Buschke SRT	5–91	Spreen, O., & Strauss, E. (1998). *A compendium of neuropsychological tests: Administration, norms, and commentary* (2nd ed.). New York: Oxford University Press.
CMS	5–16	Psych Corp
CVLT-II	16–89	Psych Corp
CVLT-C	5–16	Psych Corp
MAS	18–90	PAR
RAVLT	7–89	WPS
RBMT	5–96	NSS
RCFT	6–89	PAR
WMS-III	16–89	Psych Corp
WRAML	5–17	WR

Benton Visual Retention Test, Fifth Edition (BVRT)

The BVRT (Sivan, 1992) uses recall of geometric designs to measure visual memory in children and adults ages 8 and older. Three different test forms allow for retesting without the confound of practice effects.

Buschke Selective Reminding Test (SRT)

The SRT (Hannay & Levin, 1985, after Buschke, 1973) uses a multitrial word list learning task to measure verbal memory. Following the first presentation of the list, only the words the patient did not recall are repeated on subsequent trials. See Spreen and Strauss (1998) for normative data for children and adults ages 5 through 91.

California Verbal Learning Test–Second Edition (CVLT-II)

The CVLT-II (Delis, Kramer, Kaplan, & Ober, 2000) is a word list learning task for adults ages 16 through 89 that permits measurement of verbal learning and memory. The CVLT uses a shopping-list format consisting of 16 words from four categories presented over five trials. After the first five trials, an interference list is presented, followed by short-delay recall of the first list and then long-delay recall after 20 minutes. A recognition trial is also available at the end of the test. The CVLT provides information about acquisition, recall, retention, and retrieval of verbal information. It also provides information about strategies used in learning. The CVLT-C (Delis, Kramer, Kaplan, & Ober, 1994) is available for children ages 5 through 16.

Children's Memory Scale (CMS)

The CMS (Cohen, 1997) is a comprehensive memory instrument that measures the dimensions of attention and working memory, verbal and visual memory, short-delay and long-delay memory, recall and recognition, and learning characteristics in children ages 5 through 16. The core subtests result in eight summary scores: Verbal Immediate, Verbal Delayed, Visual Immediate, Visual Delayed, General Memory, Delayed Recognition, Attention and Concentration, and Learning. The core subtests in the auditory (verbal) domain consist of story memory and verbal paired-associate learning. Those in the visual (nonverbal) domain consist of spatial memory and face recognition tasks. Those in the attention and concentration domain consist of digit span and mental control tasks. Available optional memory tasks include word list learning and complex picture memory. The CMS is conormed with the WISC-

III and WPPSI-R, allowing comparisons among intellectual ability, learning, and memory.

Memory Assessment Scales (MAS)

The MAS (Williams, 1991) was designed as a comprehensive battery that assesses short-term, verbal, and visual memory functions. Immediate and delayed memory in both the verbal and visual modalities is assessed through both recall and recognition formats. The memory tasks used include Verbal Span, List Learning, Prose Memory, Visual Recognition, Visual Reproduction, and Names-Faces. Summary scores are available for Short-Term Memory, Verbal Memory, and Visual Memory. A Global Memory Scale score can be derived from the Verbal and Visual Memory summary scores. Normative information is available for adults ages 18 through 90.

Rey Auditory Verbal Learning Test (RAVLT)

Rey (1958) originally developed the RAVLT. It is a superspan list learning task that helps measure verbal learning, memory, proactive and retroactive interference, retention, and encoding and retrieval. The RAVLT requires the patient to learn 15 words over five trials; a second list is then introduced and is followed by short-delay recall, long-delay recall, and recognition of the first list. A handbook (Schmidt, 1996) containing information about administration, scoring, and normative information (ages 7 through 89) for the RAVLT is available from Western Psychological Services.

Rey Complex Figure Test and Recognition Trial (RCFT)

The RCFT (Meyers & Meyers, 1995) uses four trials (copy, immediate recall, delayed recall, and recognition) to measure visuospatial recall and recognition memory, response bias, processing speed, and visuoconstructional ability. The patient copies the original Rey-Osterrieth Complex Figure (Rey, 1941) and three minutes later is asked without warning to reproduce it from memory. After a 30-minute delay, the patient is asked to recall the figure again and perform a recognition trial. The original manual contains normative data for individuals ages 18 through 89. Normative data for children and adolescents ages 6 through 17 are available in the Manual Supplement (Meyers & Meyers, 1996).

The Rivermead Behavioral Memory Test–Revised Edition (RBMT)

The RBMT (Wilson, Cockburn, & Baddeley, 1991) is designed to assess the memory problems encountered by patients in their everyday life. For example, it measures remembering an appointment, a name, and a message to deliver, in addition to story recall, face recognition, picture recognition, and orientation. For the regular version and the children's version normative data are available for ages 5 through 96.

Wechsler Memory Scale–Third Edition (WMS-III)

The WMS-III (Wechsler, 1997) is a comprehensive assessment of memory that is conormed with the Wechsler Adult Intelligence Scale–Third Edition (WAIS-III), allowing measurement of the relationship between intellect and memory in adults ages 16 through 89. The WMS-III provides eight summary scores or Primary Indexes: Auditory Immediate, Visual Immediate, Immediate Memory, Auditory Delayed, Visual Delayed, Auditory Recognition Delayed, General Memory, and Working Memory. The summary scores in the auditory (verbal) memory domain are derived from story memory and verbal paired associate tasks. The summary scores in the visual (nonverbal) domain are derived from complex picture memory and face recognition tasks. In the working memory domain, the primary subtests are a letter-number sequencing task and a measure of spatial span. Also available are a word list learning task, a geometric design memory task, a mental control task, and a measure of information and orientation.

Wide Range Assessment of Memory and Learning (WRAML)

The WRAML (Adams & Sheslow, 1990) was designed to evaluate learning and memory abilities in children ages 5 to 17. Index scores are available for Verbal Memory, Visual Memory, and Learning; from these summary scores a General Memory Index can be derived. Delayed recall and auditory recognition memory tasks are also included. Available subtests include Story Memory, Verbal Learning, Sentence Memory, Design Memory, Picture Memory, Finger Windows (spatial span).

LANGUAGE FUNCTIONS

The clinician can study many aspects of language ability through behavioral observation. Intact auditory comprehension can be evaluated by a patient's ability to follow directions without needing repetitions or explanations. Intact repetition can be seen by observing a patient repeat a phrase or a sentence. Other language functions require specific tests to delineate particular deficits.

Tests may be needed to evaluate vocabulary skills, aphasic features, and naming difficulties. Rapid Reference 4.17 summarizes the tests, the appropriate age ranges, and the publishers.

Boston Diagnostic Aphasia Examination–Third Edition (BDAE-III)

The BDAE-III (Goodglass et al., 2000) is a comprehensive measure of language and language-related abilities that aids in the diagnosis of aphasia syndromes in adults. The test measures in detail spontaneous speech and fluency, auditory comprehension, naming, oral reading, repetition, writing, and reading comprehension. Percentile scores are available to compare the patient's performance with that of a sample of persons with aphasia.

Boston Naming Test (BNT)

The BNT (Kaplan et al., 1983) is used to assess confrontation-naming and word-retrieval deficits. The test evaluates a patient's ability to name pictures of 60 line drawings arranged in order of frequency from high to low. Patients with perceptual problems are allowed categorical or semantic cues; patients with apparent retrieval difficulties are allowed phonemic cues to aid in their production of the object's name. Normative data are available for children and adults ages 5 and older.

≡Rapid Reference 4.17

Tests of Language

Test	Ages	Source
BDAE-III	Adults	Psych Corp
BNT	5+	Psych Corp
EOWPVT-2000	2–18	PAR
EVT	2.5–90+	AGS
K-SEALS	3–6	AGS
PPVT-III	2.5–90+	AGS
ROWPVT-2000	2–18	PAR
Aphasia Screening Test	Adults	Reitan Neuropsychology Lab
WAB	Adolescent+	Psych Corp

Expressive One-Word Picture Vocabulary Test (EOWPVT-2000)

The EOWPVT-2000 (Brownell, 2000) measures vocabulary for English speakers. Children and young adults ages 2 through 18 must name an object or group of objects to confrontation. The test is conormed with the Receptive One-Word Picture Vocabulary Test, thus allowing direct, meaningful comparisons between expressive and receptive vocabulary skills.

Expressive Vocabulary Test (EVT)

The EVT (Williams, 1997) is used as a measure of English expressive vocabulary and word retrieval. This test includes 152 synonym items, as well as 38 labeling items which require the patient to name a picture or body part. For the synonym items the patient is presented with a picture and a word. Then the patient must produce another single word that means the same thing and goes with the picture. The test contains norms for ages 2.5 to 90+ and is conormed with the PPVT-III to allow meaningful comparisons of receptive and expressive vocabulary.

Kaufman Survey of Early Academic and Language Skills (K-SEALS)

The K-SEALS (Kaufman & Kaufman, 1993b) is used as a comprehensive measure of language skills in young children ages 3 through 6. It measures expressive and receptive vocabulary, preacademic skills, and articulation. Summary scale scores are available for Expressive Skills, Receptive Skills, Number Skills, and Letter & Word Skills. Composite scores are available for Early Academic and Language Skills.

Peabody Picture Vocabulary Test–III (PPVT-III)

The PPVT-III (Dunn & Dunn, 1997), called a screening test of verbal ability, is a measure of English hearing vocabulary. The PPVT-III has norms for individuals ages 2.5 to 90+. Patients are required to match one of four pictures on a test page with a word spoken aloud by the examiner.

Receptive One-Word Picture Vocabulary Test (ROWPVT-2000)

The ROWPVT-2000 (Brownell, 2000b) measures English hearing vocabulary. Children and young adults ages 2 through 18 must match an object or concept with its name. The test is conormed with the EOWPVT-2000, thus permitting direct meaningful comparisons of receptive and expressive vocabulary.

Reitan Indiana Aphasia Screening Test

This is a brief measure of language and nonlanguage skills in adults used to supplement the HRB. It screens skills such as naming, reading, spelling, writing, identifying body parts, performing arithmetic calculations, drawing shapes, and discriminating left from right.

Western Aphasia Battery (WAB)

The WAB (Kertesz, 1982) uses four oral language subtests to identify aphasia syndromes and their severity in adolescents and adults. From the five scores that can be derived from these subtests, an Aphasia Quotient (AQ), which marks severity of language impairment, can be calculated. This battery also includes tests of reading, writing, calculation ability, and nonverbal skills. A summary score called the Cortical Quotient (CQ) is derived from all of the cognitive functions measured.

ACHIEVEMENT TESTS

A comprehensive test battery often must include measures of scholastic achievement. Performance on tests of achievement can provide information about the presence and pattern of learning difficulties or disabilities and an individual's academic strengths and weaknesses. Rapid Reference 4.18 lists the tests, the appropriate age ranges, and the publishers.

≡Rapid Reference 4.18

Tests of Achievement

Test	Ages	Source
GORT-4	6–18	PRO-ED
K-ABC	2–6 to 12–5	AGS
K-FAST	15–85+	AGS
K-TEA/NU	6–22	AGS
Nelson-Denny	9–16	Riverside Publishing
WIAT	5–19	Psych Corp
WIAT-II	4–Adult	Psych Corp
WRAT-3	5–Adult	WR
WJ-III	2–90+	Riverside Publishing

Gray Oral Reading Test–Fourth Edition (GORT-4)

The GORT-4 (Wiederholt & Bryant, 2001) is an individually administered measure of oral reading and comprehension. The GORT-4 provides a Fluency Score that combines rate and accuracy and an Oral Reading Comprehension Score based on number of correct responses to comprehension questions. An Oral Reading Quotient is derived from a combination of the Fluency Score and Oral Reading Comprehension Score. The test is designed for children and adolescents ages 6 through 18.

Kaufman Assessment Battery for Children (K-ABC)

The K-ABC (Kaufman & Kaufman, 1983) is used to measure both achievement and intelligence. Intelligence is defined by the K-ABC as a child's ability to use simultaneous and sequential processes to solve problems. In the subtests of Hand Movements, Number Recall, and Word Order, the child arranges the stimuli in sequential or serial order. In the subtests of Magic Window, Face Recognition, Gestalt Closure, Triangles, Matrix Analogies, Spatial Memory, and Photo Series, the child simultaneously integrates and synthesizes information to solve spatial or analogical tasks. The K-ABC also includes measures of achievement or acquired knowledge through the subtests of Expressive Vocabulary, Faces & Places, Arithmetic, Riddles, Reading/Decoding, and Reading/Understanding. The test is appropriate for children ages 2.5 through 12.5.

Kaufman Functional Academic Skills Test (K-FAST)

The K-FAST (Kaufman & Kaufman, 1994) uses two subtests, Reading and Arithmetic, to measure an individual's ability to apply reading and mathematics to everyday situations. The items in the K-FAST reflect daily living situations that occur outside of the classroom. The test is normed for adolescents and adults ages 15 through 85 years.

Kaufman Test of Educational Achievement (K-TEA)

The K-TEA (Kaufman & Kaufman, 1985) is an achievement battery used for measuring reading decoding, reading comprehension, math computation, math application, and spelling skills. The 1998 normative update (K-TEA/NU; Kaufman & Kaufman, 1998) for this task provides norms for ages 6 through 22 and grades 1 through 12.

The Nelson-Denny Reading Test

The Nelson-Denny Reading Test (Brown, Fishco, & Hanna, 1993) is designed to assess student achievement and progress in vocabulary, comprehension, and reading rate. It was developed as a survey test for high school and college students and adults. It is a two-part test that measures vocabulary development, reading comprehension, and reading rate.

Wechsler Individual Achievement Test (WIAT)

The WIAT (Wechsler, 1992) is an achievement battery conormed with the WISC-III, WAIS-III, and WPPSI-R that allows meaningful comparisons between achievement and ability test performance. The WIAT includes eight subtests: Basic Reading, Mathematics Reasoning, Spelling, Reading Comprehension, Numerical Operations, Listening Comprehension, Oral Expression, and Written Expression. The recently released WIAT-II (Wechsler, 2001) includes an expanded age range from ages 4 through adult, including norms for college students.

Wide Range Achievement Test–Third Revision (WRAT-3)

The WRAT-3 (Wilkinson, 1993) measures achievement in the areas of reading, decoding, spelling, and arithmetic. The test is normed for children and adults ages 5 through 75.

Woodcock-Johnson III Tests of Achievement (WJ-III)

The WJ-III (Woodcock, McGrew, & Mather, 2001) is an individually administered test designed to assess academic achievement in reading, mathematics, written language, and general knowledge. Normed for ages 2 to 90+ years old, the test is conormed with the Woodcock-Johnson III Tests of Cognitive Abilities to allow comparisons of achievement versus ability. The Standard Battery includes Letter-Word Identification, Reading Fluency, Passage Comprehension, Spelling, Writing Fluency, Writing Samples, Understanding Directions, Story Recall and Story Recall-Delayed, Calculation, Math Fluency, and Applied Problems. The academic achievement clusters result in summary scores in the areas of Broad Reading, Broad Math, Broad Oral Language, and Broad Written Language. Other Clusters include Academic Knowledge, Phoneme/Grapheme Knowledge, Academic Skills, Academic Fluency, and Academic Application. The Extended Battery includes the tests of Word Attack, Picture Vocabulary, Oral Comprehension, Editing, Reading Vocabulary,

Quantitative Concepts, Academic Knowledge, Spelling of Sounds, Sound Awareness, and Punctuation & Capitalization. The WJ III now features oral language tests, and each Basic Achievement cluster includes a basic skills test, a fluency test, and an application test. In addition, the WJ III also now provides a Total Achievement score.

VISUAL, VISUOSPATIAL, AND VISUOTACTILE FUNCTIONS

A comprehensive assessment battery contains measures designed to evaluate visual perception and visuospatial abilities, such as visual construction and visual integration. It also includes measures examining visuotactile functions and the presence or absence of visual neglect. Rapid Reference 4.19 provides a list of the test names or acronyms, the appropriate age ranges, and the publishers.

≡Rapid Reference 4.19

Tests of Visual, Visuospatial, and Visuotactile Functions

Test	Ages	Source
VMI	3–18+	PAR
Clock Test	65 and older	MHS
VOT	5 and older	WPS
JLO	7–74	PAR
MVPT-R	4–12	PAR
RCFT	6–89	PAR
TPT (Portable)	5–Adult	PAR
TVPS(n-m)-R	4–13	PAR
TVPS(n-m)UL-R	12–17	PAR
Mesulam Cancellation Tests	Adults	Mesulam, M. M. (1985). *Principles of behavioral neurology*. Philadelphia: Davis.
WRAVMA	3–17	WR

Beery-Buktenica Test of Visual-Motor Development (VMI)

The VMI (Beery & Buktenica, 1997) is designed as a measure of visual-motor integration. The patient is required to copy 24 geometric designs that progress from less to more complex. Supplemental measures using the same stimuli as the VMI are available to assess visual perception and motor coordination. The short form test (15 drawings) is normed for ages 3 through 8 years; the long form (24 drawings) is normed for ages 3 through 18 years.

The Clock Test

The Clock Test (Tuokko et al., 1995) assesses visuospatial construction, visual perception, and abstract conceptualization by using the three subtests of Clock Drawing, Clock Setting, and Clock Reading. The task is normed for adults 65 years and older.

Hooper Visual Organization Test (VOT)

The VOT (Hooper, 1958) is a brief screening measure that assesses a patient's mental ability to analyze and integrate visual stimuli. The test stimuli consist of cut-up line drawings of 30 common objects. The test can be administered to both children and adults.

Judgment of Line Orientation

This test measures spatial perception and orientation as well as visuospatial judgment (Benton et al., 1994). The patient is presented with 30 test items, each depicting a different pair of angled lines. The angled lines must be matched to a display card containing multinumber radii forming a semicircle. Normative data are available for individuals ages 7 through 14 and 16 through 74.

Motor-Free Visual Perception Test–Revised (MVPT-R)

The MVPT-R (Colarusso & Hammill, 1996) was designed to assess visual perception in children ages 4 through 11. The test measures five categories of visual perception: spatial relationships, visual closure, visual discrimination, visual memory, and figure ground. The child indicates an answer by pointing to one of four choices on the test plate.

Rey Complex Figure Test and Recognition Trial (RCFT)

The RCFT (Meyers & Meyers, 1995) uses four trials (copy, immediate recall, delayed recall, and recognition) to measure visuospatial recall and recognition memory, response bias, processing speed, and visuoconstructional ability in children and adults ages 6 through 89. The patient copies the original Rey-Osterrieth Complex Figure (Rey, 1941) and three minutes later is asked without warning to reproduce it from memory. After a thirty-minute delay, the patient is asked to recall the figure again and perform a recognition trial.

Tactual Performance Test (TPT)

This task is from the HRB and uses the Seguin-Goddard Formboard to measure tactual perception and form recognition along with psychomotor problem solving and tactile memory for spatial location and shapes. A portable version of the TPT is available from PAR. The test is appropriate for both children and adults.

Test of Visual-Perceptual Skills (non-motor)–Revised

The TVPS-R (Gardner, 1996) is designed to assess visual perceptual skills in children ages 4 through 13 years. The Upper Level can be used with adolescents ages 12 through 17. The subtests of the TVPS-R include Visual Discrimination, Visual-Spatial Relationships, Visual-Sequential Memory, Visual Figure-Ground, Visual Memory, Visual Form-Constancy, and Visual Closure. The test requires only pointing from the child.

Verbal and Nonverbal Cancellation Tests

These tasks (Mesulam, 1985) are used to detect visual neglect or inattention to one side of space or the other in adults. The test consists of four trials varying across the dimensions of target (letter versus symbol) and organization (random versus ordered). The time limit for each trial is 2 minutes.

Wide Range Assessment of Visual Motor Ability

The WRAVMA (Adams & Sheslow, 1995) measures visual-motor integration by assessing visual-motor ability, visuospatial ability, and fine motor ability. The subtest scores available for each of these three areas are combined into the Visual-Motor Integration Composite. The test is applicable for children ages 3 through 17.

MOTOR

The clinician should include tests of motor performance in an assessment battery. These tests can identify motor impairment and can provide possible in-

Rapid Reference 4.20

Motor Tests

Test	Ages	Source
Finger Tapping Test (Tapper)	6–Adult	PAR
Grip Strength (Hand Dynamometer)	6–Adult	PAR
Grooved Pegboard	5–Adult	PAR

formation about lateralized cortical impairment. Rapid Reference 4.20 lists the tests, their appropriate age ranges, and their publishers.

Finger Oscillation Test

This task, also called the Finger Tapping Test and included in the HRB, measures fine motor speed of the index finger on each hand in children and adults. It can be helpful in assessing laterality of brain damage. The finger tapping board is available through Reitan Neuropsychology Laboratory and from PAR.

Grip Strength

This measure uses a hand dynamometer (available from PAR) to assess the strength of each hand. Normative data are available for both children and adults.

Grooved Pegboard

This test measures manual dexterity and requires complex visual-motor coordination. The pegboard (available from PAR) consists of 25 randomly positioned keyholes; the patient must rotate the pegs (keys) to match the holes before the peg can be inserted into the keyhole on the board. Like the Finger Oscillation Test, Grooved Pegboard can be helpful in assessing laterality of brain damage and is used with both children and adults.

MALINGERING

In some populations (e.g., patients involved in forensic cases) the base rate is quite large for patients exaggerating or simulating impairment. Research has shown very clearly that even children can fool seasoned examiners into believing that they have deficits when they do not (Faust, 1988). It is therefore crucial to include measures of compliance and motivation in a test battery. The results from such measures indicate to the examiner how much confidence he or she can have in the reliability and validity of the test findings. Rapid Reference 4.21 summarizes the tests, their appropriate age ranges, and the publishers.

Computerized Assessment of Response Bias

The CARB (Allen, Conder, Green, & Cox, 2000) is a computer-supported assessment used to detect incomplete effort, symptom exaggeration, response

≡Rapid Reference 4.21

Tests of Motivation, Compliance, and Malingering

Test	Ages	Source
CARB	Adults	Psych Corp
DCT	Adults	Lezak, M. D. (1995). *Neuropsychological assessment* (3rd ed.). New York: Oxford University Press.
Recall-Recognition Test	Adults	Brandt, J. (1992). Detecting amnesia's impostors. In L. R. Squire & N. Butters (Eds.), *Neuropsychology of memory* (2nd ed., pp. 156–165). New York: Guilford Press.
RMT	Adults	Spreen, O., & Strauss, E. (1998). *A compendium of neuropsychological tests: Administration, norms, and commentary* (2nd ed.). New York: Oxford University Press.
TOMM	16–84	MHS
VIP	18–69	NCS
VSVT	18 and older	PAR
WMT	18–65	Psych Corp
WRT	Adults	Frederick, R. I. (1997). *Validity Indicator Profile*. Minneapolis, MN: National Computer System.

bias, malingering, and feigning of cognitive deficits. The CARB is based on a forced-choice digit recognition paradigm (e.g., Binder, 1993; Hiscock & Hiscock, 1989) and is self-administered via computer. The results from the CARB are analyzed relative to normative information from adult patients with severe traumatic brain injury and neurological disorders. It can be used in conjunction with the WMT described later in the text.

Dot Counting Test

The DCT (Rey, 1941) is used to assess dissimulation of nonmemory complaints in adults. The patient is presented with 12 cards containing a set of grouped or ungrouped dots and asked to count the dots on each card as quickly as possible. According to Lezak (1983), the ungrouped dots are presented first and the grouped dots second. Results are evaluated according to the difference in time between total time for the grouped versus ungrouped dot counting performances. A performance is considered suspicious for dissimulation when there is little difference between the two times or if the time taken to count the grouped dots exceeds the time taken to count the ungrouped dots.

Recall-Recognition Test

This test (Brandt, 1992) uses a 20-item word list presented for free recall followed by forced-choice recognition to help differentiate true memory impairment from malingered memory impairment in adults. Comparison of patients with amnesia and assumed malingerers on this task indicated that the assumed malingerers performed more poorly on the forced-choice recognition task than the patients with amnesia did.

Rey Memory Test

The RMT (Rey, 1958) is an unsophisticated measure of retrieval that can aid in assessing feigned memory impairment. Adult patients are asked to recall all 15 items presented on a stimulus card for 10 seconds. In the instructions patients are told that there are 15 unique items to be called in just 10 seconds. They are not told that the items can easily be grouped into five easy sets (uppercase letters A, B, C; lowercase letters a, b, c; numbers 1, 2, 3; Roman numerals I, II, III; and three shapes circle, square, and triangle). Results of fewer than three sets recalled or 8 or 9 items recalled are considered suspicious for suboptimal effort or noncompliance. Also suspicious are incomplete rows (with the exception of the row of shapes), reversals, confabulations, or misplaced numbers and letters.

Test of Memory Malingering

The TOMM (Tombaugh, 1996) is a visual recognition memory test used to differentiate between bona fide memory impairment and feigned memory impairment. The TOMM consists of two learning trials containing forced-choice recognition and an optional delayed forced-choice recognition task. Normative data are available from various groups: cognitively intact individuals and patients with neurological disorders, including patients with mild traumatic brain injury. It is appropriate for ages 16 through 84 years.

Validity Indicator Profile

The VIP (Frederick, 1997) is used to assess malingering and response style during testing. The VIP consists of two tasks, matrix reasoning (nonverbal) and vocabulary (verbal), and was constructed using a forced-choice format. The results from a patient can be classified as valid or invalid. Invalid performances are further classified as careless, irrelevant, or malingered. The VIP can be administered to adults ages 18 through 69.

Victoria Symptom Validity Test

The VSVT (Slick, Hopp, Strauss, & Thompson, 1999) is a computerized assessment vehicle used to measure effort on memory tests and the presence of exaggeration or simulation of cognitive impairments. The VSVT is based on the forced-choice digit recognition paradigm popularized by Binder (1993) and Hiscock and Hiscock (1989). It is appropriate for adults ages 18 years and older.

Word Memory Test

The WMT (Green, Allen, & Astner, 2000) is used to test verbal memory and test taking effort and to detect suboptimal effort, response bias, feigning, and symptom exaggeration. The task requires the patient to learn a list of paired associates, half of which have a close semantic relationship and half of which are only subtly linked. Immediate and delayed recognition are assessed along with multiple-choice recognition, a paired associate cued recall task, free recall, and an optional long-delay free recall. Patient performance is compared to normative data obtained from patients with severe traumatic brain injury and other neurological disorders. Normative data are available for adults ages 18 through 65.

Word Recognition Test

The WRT (Rey, 1941) is used to evaluate malingering and suboptimal effort on verbal memory tasks in adults by comparing performance on a recognition memory task to first-trial performance on a free recall word list learning task such as the CVLT or the RAVLT. The patient is asked to learn a 15-item word list presented orally and then provided (either written or orally) with a 30-item list; the patient is then instructed to identify the words from the 15-item list. In general, recognition memory performance should be better than first-trial free recall performance on the CVLT or RAVLT. In addition, fewer than six words recognized or a score of less than five when false positives are subtracted from true positives is indicative of failure on this task (Greiffenstein, Baker, & Gola, 1996).

EMOTIONS, BEHAVIOR, AND PERSONALITY

Neuropsychological test results are often not specific to CNS impairment and can instead reflect nonneurological influences on test performance. It is therefore important to survey a patient's emotional status and mood to determine whether any negative test findings are the result of depression or anxiety. In addition, while most neuropsychological tests can provide information about a patient's cognitive strengths and weaknesses, relatively few neuropsychological tests inform the examiner about how a patient functions in his or her daily environment. When questions arise about a patient's functional capacities (for example, when diagnosing mental retardation), a test battery needs to include measures of adaptive abilities. Rapid Reference 4.22 lists the tests, the appropriate age ranges, and the publishers.

Adaptive Behavior Assessment System

The ABAS (Harrison & Oakland, 2000) was designed to assess the adaptive skills of school-aged to adult individuals (ages 5 through 89) for use in diagnosing and classifying disabilities and disorders, specifying strengths and weaknesses, and monitoring change over time. Parents, teachers, adult informants, and high-functioning adult patients can complete the ABAS. The ten areas surveyed include Communication, Community Use, Functional Academics, School Living, Health and Safety, Leisure, Self-Care, Self-Direction, Social, and Work. The ABAS normative data have been linked to the WISC-III, WAIS-III, and WASI, allowing comparisons of ability to adaptive behavior.

≡Rapid Reference 4.22

Tests of Emotion, Behavior, and Personality

Test	Ages	Source
ABAS	5–89	Psych Corp
ADHDT	3–23	PRO-ED
BAI	17–80	Psych Corp
BDI-II	13–80	Psych Corp
Beck Youth Scales	7–14	Psych Corp
BASC	2.5–18	AGS
CDI	7–17	MHS
CRS-R	3–17	MHS
MMPI-A	14–18	NCS
MMPI-2	18 and older	NCS
NIS	18 and older	WPS
PAI	18 and older	PAR
TSCC	8–16	PAR
TSI	18 and older	PAR
Vineland	0–18 and low-functioning adults	AGS

Attention-Deficit/Hyperactivity Disorder Test

The ADHDT (Gilliam, 1995) is designed to assist clinicians in the diagnosis of ADHD. The test is administered to parents, teachers, and others to assess in children and young adults ages 3 through 23 the presence of symptoms in the areas of hyperactivity, impulsivity, and inattention.

Beck Anxiety Inventory

The BAI (Beck & Steer, 1993) is a face-valid self-report 21-item measure of common symptoms of anxiety and their severity. The BAI is used to discriminate between anxious and nonanxious individuals ages 17 through 80 years.

Beck Depression Inventory–Second Edition

The BDI-II (Beck, Steer, & Brown, 1996) is a face-valid self-report 21-item measure of the common symptoms of depression and the severity of symptoms. The BDI-II can be used to assess the presence and severity of depression in individuals ages 13 through 80.

Beck Youth Inventories

These are five self-report instruments (Beck, Beck, & Jolly, 2001) for children and early adolescents ages 7 through 14. Each inventory contains 20 statements about thoughts, feelings, and behaviors in the areas of depression, anxiety, anger, disruptive behavior, and self-concept.

Behavior Assessment System for Children

The BASC (Reynolds & Kamphaus, 1992) is a set of rating scales and self-report forms for evaluating the behaviors, thoughts, and emotions of children and adolescents ages 2.5 through 18. Parents and teachers and the child or adolescent whose behavior is of concern can complete the BASC. It is designed to help with the differential diagnosis of various emotional and behavioral disorders of children. Composite Scales focus on externalized problems, internalized problems, school problems, other problems, and adaptive skills. A Behavioral Symptoms Index is available from the combination of the scales of Aggression, Hyperactivity, Anxiety, Depression, Somatization, Attention Problems, and Atypicality.

Children's Depression Inventory

The CDI (Kovacs, 1992) is a 27-item self-report scale of depression specifically designed for children ages 7 through 17. The CDI evaluates a range of symptoms in the areas of negative mood, anhedonia, ineffectiveness, negative self-esteem, and interpersonal problems.

Connors' Rating Scales–Revised

The CRS-R (Connors, 1997) includes three scales (parent, teacher, and self-report) used to assess reports of Attention-Deficit/Hyperactivity Disorder symptoms and related problems such as conduct problems, family problems, cognitive problems, anxiety problems, anger problems, and somatic problems. The scales can be used for children and adolescents ages 3 through 17.

Minnesota Multiphasic Personality Inventory–Adolescent

The MMPI-A (Butcher et al., 1992) is a personality inventory designed to measure adolescent psychopathology and help identify personal, social, and behavioral problems in adolescents 14 through 18 years old. The MMPI-A contains several validity scales including Variable Response Consistency, True Response Inconsistency, Infrequency, Lie, Defensiveness, and Cannot Say. It contains the same ten Clinical Scales as in the MMPI-2 (discussed next): Hypochondriasis, Depression, Hysteria, Psychopathic Deviate, Masculinity-

Femininity, Paranoia, Psychasthenia, Schizophrenia, Hypomania, and Social Introversion. In addition, it contains multiple Supplementary Scales, Content Scales, and Subscales to further delineate pathology. Specialized interpretative reports from NCS Assessments are available for the settings of outpatient mental health, inpatient mental health, general medical, school, correctional, and drug/alcohol treatment.

Minnesota Multiphasic Personality Inventory–2

The MMPI-2 (Butcher, Dahlstrom, Graham, Tellegen, & Kaemmer, 1989) is a self-administered personality inventory used to assist with the assessment and screening of psychopathology, the identification of appropriate treatment strategies, and the assessment of major symptoms of social and personal maladjustment in individuals 18 years and older. It consists of multiple validity scales, the three most commonly known as L (Lie), F (Frequency), and K (Defensiveness), along with 10 clinical scales: Hypochondriasis, Depression, Conversion Hysteria, Psychopathic Deviance, Masculinity-Femininity, Paranoia, Psychasthenia, Schizophrenia, Hypomania, and Social Introversion. In addition, several other Clinical Subscales, Content Scales, and Supplementary Scales are available. Specialized interpretative reports are available from NCS Assessments for various settings, including outpatient mental health, inpatient mental health, general medical, chronic pain, correctional, and college counseling. In addition, NCS Assessments can provide reports tailored to specific forensic situations, such as child-custody disputes, competency or commitment hearings, personal injury lawsuits, pretrial criminal evaluations, and general corrections recommendations.

The Neuropsychological Impairment Scale

The NIS (O'Donnell, DeSoto, DeSoto, & Reynolds, 1994) is designed to screen for neuropsychological symptoms through the patient's self-report. Summary scores include a Global Measure of Impairment, Total Items Circled, and Symptom Intensity Measure. The NIS also has validity checks evaluating defensiveness, the influence of affective disturbance, inconsistent responses, and subjective distortion (overreporting of symptoms). Neuropsychological subscales include Cognitive Efficiency, Attention, Memory, Frustration Tolerance, Learning-Verbal, Academic Skills, and Critical Items. The test is appropriate for adults over the age of 17.

Personality Assessment Inventory

The PAI (Morey, 1991) is an objective self-administered personality inventory used to assess clinical syndromes and psychopathology. The PAI is designed for adults 18 years and older. It contains 4 validity scales measuring consistency of report, endorsement of infrequent items, negative impression management, and positive impression management. It contains 11 clinical scales addressing the areas of somatic complaints, anxiety, anxiety-related disorders, depression, mania, paranoia, schizophrenia, borderline features, antisocial features, alcohol problems, and drug problems. It also contains four treatment scales having to do with aggression, suicidal ideation, stress, nonsupport, and treatment rejection. Two interpersonal scales in this inventory assess dominance and warmth.

Trauma Symptom Checklist for Children

The TSCC (Briere, 1996) is a self-report measure of posttraumatic distress and related emotional distress. It is intended for children ages 8 to 16 years old who have been exposed to trauma and who may be at risk for posttraumatic stress.

Trauma Symptom Inventory

The TSI (Briere, 1995) is a self-report measure of posttraumatic distress and other psychological sequelae of traumatic events. It is intended for adults ages 18 years and older. It contains three validity scales assessing the patient's tendency to deny symptoms, to overendorse unusual or bizarre symptoms, and to respond in an inconsistent fashion. It contains 10 clinical scales concerning trauma-related symptoms: Anxious Arousal, Dissociation, Sexual Concerns, Anger and Irritability, Dysfunctional Sexual Behavior, Intrusive Experiences, Defensive Avoidance, Impaired Self-Reference, and Tension Reduction Behavior.

Vineland Adaptive Behavior Scales

The Vineland (Sparrow, Balla, & Cicchetti, 1984) can be used to assess a wide range of adaptive behaviors in the domains of communication, daily living skills, socialization, and motor skills. The Vineland is appropriate for children, adolescents, and low-functioning adults. The Vineland can be administered to a parent or caregiver in semistructured interview format. It also can be administered to a teacher in the form of a questionnaire.

🖎 TEST YOURSELF 🖎

1. **The underlying assumption of neuropsychological testing is that the performances of patients represent their best efforts.** True or False?

2. **Patients may not give their best effort because**

   (a) they are depressed.

   (b) they are involved in litigation.

   (c) they are medically ill.

   (d) all of the above.

3. **Any room is sufficient for testing.** True or False?

4. **It is preferable to complete testing in one day.** True or False?

5. **It is easy to determine through simple observation that a patient is applying adequate effort to the task at hand.** True or False?

6. **Which of the following is not true?**

   (a) Examiners should score as they go.

   (b) Examiners should observe the patient's behavior.

   (c) Examiners should record every statement by a patient.

   (d) Examiners should keep test materials ready.

7. **It is permissible to violate standardized test procedures for the sake of testing the limits.** True or False?

8. **Test administration requires**

   (a) helping patients with explanations of directions.

   (b) following test instructions exactly.

   (c) using a wall clock to time tests.

   (d) informing patients that their answers are correct.

9. **The examiner who is thoroughly familiar with the scoring guidelines is best able to discern the score value of a response quickly and accurately.** True or False?

10. **Pantomime and gesture may have to be used when testing individuals with impairments in**

    (a) hearing.

    (b) vision.

    (c) motor impairments.

    (d) memory.

Answers: 1. True; 2. d; 3. False; 4. True; 5. False; 6. c; 7. False; 8. b; 9. True; 10. a

Five

ESSENTIALS OF INTERPRETATION

W e are now ready to discuss some of the conceptual and logical is-sues and procedures involved in using neuropsychological tests to answer the kinds of referral questions suggested in Chapter 1. Just as psychologists use a variety of approaches to selecting and organizing test measures (i.e., fixed versus flexible batteries), they also use a variety of ap-proaches to make inferences about the brain's influence on test performance and behavior. A review of some of the basic issues of psychometric theory rel-evant to neuropsychological assessment is useful before a discussion of some of the approaches to test interpretation.

TEST VALIDITY

One crucial aspect of psychometrics is whether a test is valid for predicting, measuring, and defining pathology. Correspondingly, each of the various types of validity, including criterion or predictive validity, construct validity, and con-tent validity must be considered.

The most basic task a neuropsychological test must perform is to detect whether a patient's performance is predictive of the presence of an abnormal-ity of the central nervous system. The extent to which a test score successfully allows such a prediction is an example of the concept of test validity, and is, in this case, an example of *criterion* or *predictive validity*. Beyond simply predicting an abnormality of the central nervous system, neuropsychological tests might also be used to predict whether an individual will have adjustment difficulties on the job or in school or even to predict how well an individual will perform in these areas in the future. The ability to predict from neuropsychological test results to real life functioning is often called *ecological validity*.

One also could ask what psychological function or process the test is measuring. Content validity and construct validity refer to the extent to which a test is actually a measure of a function, whether the function is memory, phonological processing, visual perception, or the function of the frontal lobes. Construct validity answers the question: What am I measuring with this test? Content validity answers the question: Is this test a good sample of the construct I am interested in measuring?

The answer to questions of validity may in some cases be directly quantifiable, whereas in other cases the validity of a test is based on a large corpus of data and concepts. Ideally, a test should be able to predict the presence of a disease with perfect certainty, or should be clearly interpretable as defining a psychological construct. Unfortunately, in practice neuropsychological tests are never perfectly valid. No test predicts the presence (or absence) of brain damage with perfect certainty and very few measures can be considered in and of themselves perfect or so-called gold standard measurements of any psychological construct. The different types of validity addressed here are defined in Rapid Reference 5.1.

Criterion Validity

Criterion validity refers to the ability of a test to predict or correlate with other measures that define the function of the test. In neuropsychology, tests are most commonly used as predictors of the presence of brain damage. As we dis-

---

≡ *Rapid Reference 5.1*

The Different Types of Validity Defined

Criterion or predictive validity is the ability of a test to predict or correlate with other measures that define the function of a test. Example: The ability of a test to predict the presence of brain damage.

Construct validity is the extent to which a test measures a theoretically defined construct or function. Example: The extent to which a test is a measure of verbal memory.

Content validity is the extent to which the items on a test are actual samples of the construct being measured. Example: That a test of verbal memory uses words to test the function.

cussed in Chapter 1, some assessment systems such as the Halstead-Reitan Neuropsychological Battery were originally designed with the ability to predict the presence of brain damage as their primary focus. Ward Halstead began the process of forming his initial battery through much trial and error. He primarily used tasks that were not necessarily designed to be sensitive to brain damage (e.g., Seguin-Goddard Form Board; Seashore Musical Aptitude Test), but also used tasks that were considered at the time to be linked to brain function (e.g., Critical Flicker Fusion). His original goal was to develop tests that correctly predicted which patients an independent neurologist clinically classified as having brain damage. In the 1930s when this work began, skull X-rays, neurosurgeons' reports, and in some cases autopsies were available to provide objective evidence of brain damage. In many cases it was the neurological examination that determined whether the patient had brain damage. These criteria provided a very limited and not necessarily accurate view of the actual state of the brain. Skull X-rays could detect only diseases that impacted the bone and were insensitive to the presence of most strokes, brain tumors, degenerative disease, and even the effects of many closed-head injuries. Neurosurgical reports would be available only for those conditions that required the intervention of a neurosurgeon. This might include brain tumors and certain vascular conditions such as aneurysms, but such reports would not be available for many forms of brain damage. A positive neurological examination showing changes in muscle tone, strength, increased briskness of deep tendon reflexes, and reduced sensitivity to touch, pain, or position might indicate the presence of damage to specific structures related to the sensory and motor systems but might not be sensitive to brain damage in other parts of the brain. The presence of classic symptoms of *aphasia* (acquired disorder of language), *agnosia* (loss of apparent knowledge of sensory information not attributable to primary sensory loss), or *apraxia* (loss of the ability to carry out purposeful movement) might signal the presence of brain damage to other areas, but the absence of these symptoms cannot be used to predict the absence of underlying disease. Autopsy reports can give a very accurate picture of the state of the brain at death but do not necessarily reflect the state of the brain when neuropsychological tests are actually administered to the patient. A patient often comes to autopsy months or years after taking a test, in the meantime allowing many intervening changes to occur in the nervous system.

Since Halstead's first attempt to create a valid neuropsychological battery, a number of technological developments in methods have been used to assess directly the integrity of the central nervous system structures important for normal psychological functions. These include the development of electroencephalography (EEG) and the subsequent development of event-related electroencephalography. The latter technique, referred to as the measurement of Event Related Potentials (ERPS), consisted of the mathematical summation of EEG information measured at precise times after an external stimulus has been presented to the subject or patient. Although still primarily a research tool, this technique has allowed for the measurement of specific neurophysiological events related to performance and may ultimately prove useful in the evaluation of clinical measures.

Unquestionably, the most important technological development in the measurement of the state of central nervous system tissue is computerized tomography. Originally developed for use with conventional X-ray in the 1970s, computerized tomography involves the registration of X-ray energy beamed through tissue around a 360° axis. Small differences in density of tissue can then be computed for every point that those two beams cross, allowing the development of a cross-sectional image that provides information about soft tissues. Although the original Computerized Axial Tomography (CAT) scan provided a relatively coarse view of specific neural structures, it was more accurate in determining the presence of many kinds of brain damage in a live person than any other technique. It was also relatively safe and noninvasive. Less than a decade later tomography based on electromagnetic resonance (the energy produced when certain organic molecules are subjected to extremely strong pulsing magnetic waves) allowed for the production of tomographic images of unprecedented detail and sensitivity. Magnetic Resonance Imaging (MRI) also could be used to produce accurate coronal (i.e., from the front) and sagital (i.e., from the side) views of the brain, allowing for remarkably clear views of even tiny neural structures. In the 1990s the advancement in this technology allowed for blood-flow measurement so sensitive it may be used to track extremely subtle localized changes in metabolic rate within populations of neurons. This technique has revolutionized research on cortical function and eventually may prove to be an invaluable tool in diagnosis.

Neuropsychological tests are constantly being revalidated using these increasingly accurate measures as criteria. The irony is of course that as these technologies have become more refined and more economical, the function of neuropsychological tests as predictors of brain damage has become moribund.

If the only purpose of a psychological test is to predict the presence of evidence of disease on a neuroimage and both measures cost a similar amount to administer, why not just use the neuroimage? The answer to this question is straightforward: The presence of brain damage does not necessarily predict a change in function or level of function. Although the size of a lesion may more or less predict the degree of functional compromise, in many cases localization is more important than size of lesion in predicting the kind and severity of functional decline. Localization of a lesion itself, however, is only a modest predictor of function. The presence of a lesion does not guarantee that a specific function is lost, and the loss of a specific function is only a fair predictor of the presence of some kinds of lesions. For example, the presence of aphasia, an acquired disorder of language following brain damage, is usually predictive of a lesion in the territory of the left middle cerebral artery of a right-handed adult. In contrast, the ability to copy drawings or writing is not predictive of a localized lesion in one hemisphere. Although the presence of left hemispatial neglect is usually predictive of the presence of a lesion in the right cerebral hemisphere, that lesion may be in virtually any structure in that side of the brain (McGlinchey et al., 1996). Many classic neuropsychological tests, such as the Tactual Performance Test and the Halstead Category Test from the Halstead-Reitan Neuropsychological Battery, although extremely sensitive to the presence of brain damage, are not valid predictors of the localization of the lesion. Neuropsychological tests not only must predict the presence of brain damage, but also must indicate and (if possible) describe the psychological function (or functions) that has been compromised.

Ecological validity as described by Sbordone (Sbordone & Sauls 2000, p. 178) as "the functional and predictive relationship between an individual's performance on a set of neuropsychological tests and his/her behavior in a variety of real-world settings" can be seen as a subset of predictive validity. Sbordone and Guilmette (1999) caution, however, that no single neuropsychological test can be used at this time to accurately or reliably predict a brain-damaged individual's everyday functioning or ability to work.

Content and Construct Validity

The emphasis on prediction and predictive validity comes from the empiricist tradition that spawned modern clinical neuropsychology in the United States. Although Ward Halstead formulated a concept of *biological intelligence* to describe the fact that the brain is responsible for a range of psychological functions, his holistic leanings caused him to de-emphasize descriptions and theoretical analysis of the specific psychological entities that were being measured. For most of its history the validation of the Halstead-Reitan Neuropsychological Battery and many other neuropsychological tests created before the 1970s subordinated construct validity to predictive validity. As discussed in Chapter 1, a greater emphasis on understanding the specific mental operations measured by tests followed the re-emphasis of cognition as a focus in experimental psychology and the repopularization of localizationist conceptions of brain function in the neurosciences.

The questions of what function a test is measuring and whether the items or tasks are realistic samples of that function are known as *construct validity* and *content validity*, respectively. The current *Standards for Psychological and Educational Tests* (Joint Committee on Standards for Educational and Psychological Testing, 1999) defines a construct as "a theoretical variable inferred from multiple types of evidence, which might include the interrelations of the test scores with other variables, internal test structure, observations of response processes, as well as the content of the test" (p. 174). It goes on to say that, "In current standards, all test scores are viewed as measures of some construct, so the phrase is redundant with validity."

How does a test developer go about establishing the construct validity of a test? In some cases construct validity is operationalized as a kind of criterion validity in which a correlation between a new test and an already established test is demonstrated. This is very common in intelligence tests, in which the test scores from a new test are correlated with the Wechsler Adult Intelligence Scales (as of 1997 the WAIS-III). The Wechsler intelligence scales have been extensively investigated in thousands of studies since they were first published in 1939. The Wechsler intelligence scales perform what most clinicians agree is the function of an intelligence test: They predict academic achievement and performance on jobs in which intellectual abilities are considered important. The test also has been used extensively in studies of neurological and psychiatric diseases and as a result has become the standard for tests of intelligence. A substantial correlation of a new test with a current version of the Wechsler intelligence scales is usually presented as evidence that the new test also measures intelligence. But is this test really a measure of intelligence? In the literature of human abilities, much controversy surrounds the questions of what constitutes human intelligence and whether the Wechsler intelligence scales truly measure what current research considers intelligence to be. An important part of the construct validity of an intelligence test is its relationship to some empirically supported theory of the function it purports to measure. The Wechsler intelligence scales may be excellent predictors of school performance and may even have important roles as neuropsychological tests, but what they measure does not necessarily fit into current theoretical notions of intelligence. The WAIS-III may, in fact, be one of the most commonly used tests in contemporary neuropsychological batteries, yet even experienced clinicians do not interpret its validity as a construct in a consistent manner. This point can be illustrated by an examination of the Picture Arrangement Subtest.

In the construct validity section of the Wechsler Adult Intelligence Scale-Third edition Manual, Picture Arrangement is shown to load on what is known as a *perceptual organization factor* along with the subtests Block Design, Matrix Reasoning, Picture Completion, and Object Assembly. These data confirm that the scores on these tasks covary across individuals, but only scratch the surface of the questions of what the tasks are measuring and how they relate to independently established theories of function. The multitude of functions that Picture Arrangement appears to measure has been compiled in a list by Kaufman and Lichtenberg (1999, p. 105–106) and is available in Rapid Reference 5.2.

Clinicians are often tempted to draw conclusions about the presence of a specific or localized cognitive deficit based on selective impairments detected by such subtests as Picture Arrangement. Apart from the issue of whether such a selective impairment may be used to localize a lesion, the clinician must confront how to describe the impaired function represented by a low score. As the above list suggests, Picture Arrangement is a test of many functions and is itself the subject of research trying to uncover the psychological components that the test measures. This lack of clear construct validity does not permit consensus among clinicians who must provide some interpretation of test scores based on such complex and often not fully understood measures.

The Wechsler intelligence scales and many other tests that have proven valuable as neuropsychological measures were not designed with that purpose in mind and were in most cases not derived from data or theories about how the brain works. In an ideal world neuropsychological tests would be designed to reflect constructs that have been well elaborated and directly related to brain function, minimizing the need to discover what the test is actually measuring

≡ *Rapid Reference 5.2*

Functions Measured with the Picture Arrangement Subtest of the WAIS-III

- Visual perception of meaningful stimuli
- Auditory perception of complex verbal stimuli
- Discrimination between essential and nonessential details
- Perceptual organization
- Crystallized intelligence
- Fluid intelligence
- Integrated brain functioning
- Convergent production and evaluation of semantic stimuli
- Simultaneous processing
- Planning
- Common sense
- Nonverbal reasoning
- Social judgment
- Synthesis of part-whole relationships
- Visual organization
- Visual sequencing

after it already becomes established and popular. Because the construct validity of many neuropsychological measures is not fully established, ideas about the meaning of these measures are constantly evolving. Clinicians must take great care to read the current literature about the tests they are using. The description of a test contained in a manual that is several years old may not reflect current views on the nature of the measure or the neuropsychological function the test purports to measure. The annotated bibliography at the end of this book lists a number of journals and sources that clinicians can use to keep abreast of test measurement developments.

TEST SPECIFICITY

Some tests are good predictors of the presence of brain damage, but sometimes are not good predictors of the absence of brain damage—they incorrectly identify healthy individuals or individuals who perform poorly on tests for reasons other than brain damage as having brain damage. These errors are known as *false-positive* errors. The fact that normal individuals sometimes perform

> # DON'T FORGET
> Because many individual neuropsychological tests are not specific to brain damage, the risk of false-positive errors is large.

poorly on specific neuropsychological tests was recognized early by Ward Halstead. He was one of the first investigators to document formally the poor specificity of individual neuropsychological tests, arguing that it was prudent to create an impairment index based on an individual's performances on multiple measures administered in a battery. In order to minimize the false-positive rates of the tests in the original versions of the Halstead-Reitan Battery, it was necessary for an individual to obtain a score in the impaired range on 6 out of 10 measures.

The problem of false-positive errors may be greater in populations who are at risk for performing poorly on psychological tests for reasons not directly related to structural brain damage. For example, patients with psychiatric disorders and those with histories of congenital mental retardation often perform poorly on neuropsychological tests. It is sometimes argued that these cohorts of patients also suffer from some sort of brain damage. However, if the question is whether a pattern of performance is related to an acquired or newly developed neurological pathology, individuals from these groups may have a greater likelihood of obtaining a score in the impaired range than do individuals with no history of less than normal intelligence or psychiatric disorders. An extremely wide range of normal intelligence and academic ability exists in adults and children referred for neuropsychological testing. General intellectual abilities and educational level influence performance on many, if not most, neuropsychological tests. Individuals with low normal intelligence or low levels of education have a greater probability of performing poorly on neuropsychological tests than do individuals who have greater than average intelligence and higher levels of education. Most modern neuropsychological tests present normative data for individuals across a range of educational levels in order to increase both the sensitivity and the specificity of the measures. Rapid Reference 5.3 summarizes possible sources for false-positive errors.

An individual's cultural background may also be a source of false-positive errors on neuropsychological tests. The most obvious cultural factor in neu-

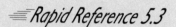

Rapid Reference 5.3

Possible Sources for False-Positive Errors in Predicting Brain Damage

- Psychiatric diseases or disorders
- Mental retardation
- Low normal intelligence
- Low levels of education
- Cultural background
- Nonnative language speaker

ropsychological test performance is, of course, language. Tests not administered in an individual's native language are more likely to yield false-positive errors than those administered in the language in which the individual is fluent. It is possible that even individuals who are fluently bilingual may be disadvantaged on some tasks if their exposure to the language in which the test is administered has been less than that of the native speakers with similar educational backgrounds to whom they will be compared.

The neuropsychological and psychological testing literature is filled with debates on the more controversial claim that subcultural or ethnic differences among individuals who are native monolingual speakers of the language of the test may lead to false-positive errors. This debate has centered on the fact that individuals from some minority ethnic backgrounds consistently score more poorly on psychological tests than the majority white population of European background or certain groups of Asian-Americans. The issues of both the sensitivity and specificity of psychological tests have received the most public attention in the classification of individuals as mentally retarded and in cases in which test scores are used for job advancement or college admissions. One argument holds that the higher rate of false positives (e.g., reduced specificity) of many psychological tests has led to a greater representation of some ethnic minority groups in special education classes, whereas the lower rate of correct identification (e.g., sensitivity) has led to a lower rate of admissions to college and job promotions.

Perhaps because of the expense and time required to obtain test norms, most neuropsychological test publishers release tests with normative data and validity studies conducted on a cross-section of American adults; these data address differences in performance that may occur with age and education. Separate data for groups with psychiatric illnesses, bilingual groups, and different cultural groups are rarely presented in even the most extensive test manuals. This practice is consistent with the standards for test validity in the Standards for Educational and Psychological Tests (1999; see standards 1.2–1.4) published by the American Educational Research Association. Standard 1.4 also includes the explicit warning: "If a test is used in a way that has not been validated, it is incumbent on the user to justify the new use, collecting new evidence if necessary."

Because the sensitivity and specificity of neuropsychological tests have not been used until very recently to gauge the validity of individual measures, the tendency of individual tests to produce false-positive errors tends not be emphasized in test manuals and may be overlooked even by well-trained clinicians. Currently, this situation is extremely problematic for neuropsychologists who frequently must assess individuals from the full range of normal intellectual and educational backgrounds, as well as increasing numbers of individuals from diverse cultural backgrounds and linguistic competencies. This practical exigency may be accompanied by a reduction in the validity of many of the available neuropsychological tests and can result in a high rate of incorrect clinical decision making. In some cases the interpretation of these tests' results forms the basis for decisions in litigation and changes in social policy. The neuropsychologist entering the field needs to be acutely aware of the potential limits of the current technology of measurement because it is not always practical for test publishers to make explicit the limits and cautions that must be considered before a test can be used.

The validity of a test may not only be limited by the tendency of some groups to perform poorly on psychological tests. Test validity may be limited because the measures themselves are not reliable and are sensitive to factors having nothing directly to do with the quantities being measured.

TEST RELIABILITY

The validity of a test can be limited by multiple factors. Sometimes a test score can be affected by influences aside from the entity it was designed to predict or measure. The extent to which a test is a stable and pure measure of some— in this case, psychological—quantity is its test *reliability*. In classical reliability theory (Crocker & Algina, 1986) it is assumed that every score consists of a *true score* (T) and the influences of various sources of error (e). It is assumed that T is a stable quantity from measurement to measurement. Error (e) is considered to be the sum of random influences that might cause an actual measurement to be greater or lesser at any particular time. Reliability is sometimes expressed as a ratio of a hypothetical true score (T) to the true score (T) plus error (e):

$$reliability = \frac{T}{T + e}$$

It is simple to see that as the level of error increases, the level of the test's reliability decreases. If a test is not reliable, it will (under most circumstances) be limited in its ability to make predictions. If each score contains a high percentage of error, the test scores are less likely to be true reflections of the dimensions they are measuring. Consider a ruler made out of a metal that expands and contracts with small variations in temperature. As a result of its instability the ruler would yield a different measurement almost every time it was used. Because of the inconsistency of the measures the ruler yields, its validity as a measure of length would be limited by the amount of variation it showed as a function of the irrelevant dimension of temperature. Sometimes the ruler might predict that an item is 3/4 inches long, sometimes 1 inch long, and sometimes more. The actual physical dimension or the true score of the item being measured is the same, but the ruler produces different results due to error and therefore yields different predictions of what the actual length is.

Most neuropsychological tests, no matter what they are designed to measure or predict, may be influenced by factors contributing to errors of measurement. Sources of error are numerous and can include factors such as the presence or absence of rapport between the patient and the examiner, patient fatigue, the clarity of instructions, the clarity of scoring criteria, and many others.

Reliability can also be viewed as the extent to which test results are internally consistent and the extent to which a given test result may be generalizable to the findings on other occasions when the measure might be administered. These conceptual variations suggest a variety of ways that reliability may be quantitatively estimated. Instead, however, they should be regarded as different ways that error of measurement may be conceptualized. The correlation among individual test items and the correlation between an individual item and the total score are the most typical measures of internal consistency of a test. These measures are important for tests that consist of multiple items and can gauge the extent to which these items are measuring the same factor. Because multiple measurements of the same quantity ideally should increase true scores and decrease error, psychological tests often consist of many trials or questions. If these individual trials are not well selected, they each may be measuring slightly different factors, hence decreasing rather than increasing reliability. The definition of reliability and the different ways to measure it are listed in Rapid Reference 5.4.

Inter-rater and test-retest reliability are the most common ways to assess the generalizability of measures. In these two cases a high correlation of the scores obtained from two different test times suggests that the test scores are stable or generalizable over some time period. Test-retest reliability is in many ways the most intuitive kind of reliability measurement. It would seem that one could not trust a measurement of the same true score that varies from time to time. Imagine the havoc that would occur in the construction industry if tape measures yielded different measurements each day.

In practice, however, tests that appear stable for healthy individuals frequently may not provide stable scores across time for patients with brain damage or for some non–brain-damaged populations such as the elderly, young children, or individuals with psychiatric disorders. In these cases the underlying true scores may themselves vary, leading to poor or modest estimates of test-retest reliability. Furthermore, internal consistency measures may be limited because some patients' performances can vary within a session. In some cases increased susceptibility to fatigue and distractibility paradoxically reduce the relative reliability of longer tests and in turn distort estimates of internal consistency.

≡ Rapid Reference 5.4

Definition and Types of Reliability

Reliability is the extent to which a test is a stable and pure measure of some quantity. Reliability means consistency.

- *Internal consistency:* the correlation among individual test items or the correlation of individual items and total score
- *Test-retest reliability:* the correlation of scores obtained from two different test times
- *Inter-rater reliability:* the correlation between test scores obtained by different examiners

Inter-rater reliability (the correlation between test scores obtained by different examiners) is critical for test items that require the judgement of an examiner for scoring. Examples of such tests include the Wechsler Memory Scale–Third Edition and many of the subtests of the Wechsler Adult Intelligence Scale–Third Edition. Note that a test that has good inter-rater reliability may not be internally consistent and may not necessarily have good test-retest reliability.

In the medical literature a different approach to inter-rater reliability is sometimes used; this approach is known as the reproducibility of diagnosis. Rather than referring to ranges of test scores, as does the concept of inter-rater reliability, reproducibility refers to the agreement among diagnoses given by different raters for the same patient. Instead of calculating a Pearson's r, or correlation coefficient, as is used to depict inter-rater reliability across a range of test scores, a kappa or K coefficient is used to depict agreement among raters, giving a positive or negative diagnosis ranging from 0 to 100%. The idea of reproducibility of diagnosis is not often used to evaluate how neuropsychological tests are used to make diagnostic decisions but has some advantages over the mere report of a typical inter-rater reliability coefficient (Kraemer, 1992). The coefficient of reproducibility provides a metric of the actual reproducibility of a clinical decision, which in many cases is the most important function to be evaluated by the test. Even if the test yields the same score for two different raters, it may not yield the same diagnostic decision. Reproducibility of diagnosis depends in large part on an agreement of what constitutes a true diagnosis or the actual presence of the condition that is being diagnosed. This is more an issue of validity, or more specifically establishing a standard criterion against which the test will be evaluated. Perhaps the idea of reproducibility of diagnosis may not have yet entered the field of neuropsychology because many open issues having to do with diagnostic or predictive criteria themselves still exist. We return to some of the issues surrounding test validation in a moment.

The *Standards for Educational and Psychological Testing* (1999) suggests that test publishers provide information about the reliability of a test measure and should include the kind of reliability being reported (test-retest, internal consistency, etc.). The clinician needs to evaluate this data carefully and must judge whether the kind of reliability reported is relevant to how the test will be used. Reported reliability estimates based on normal controls should only with extreme caution be extrapolated to any other population. A test that has been shown to be reliable for normal individuals may have limited reliability in other populations, including patient populations.

BASE RATES

Test validity is not calculated in a vacuum. The accuracy of predictions about the presence or absence of a condition varies depending on the occurrence of the condition in the population tested. Although the issue of how base rates will affect the efficiency or accuracy of decisions based on tests is now well known among writers on medical diagnosis (e.g., Kraemer 1992), no analysis of this issue is still more eloquent than that in the classic 1955 article in the journal *Psychological Bulletin* by Paul Meehl and Albert Rosen entitled "Antecedent probability and the efficiency of psychometric signs, patterns or cutting scores." Consider the following example adapted with slight modernizing adjustments directly from Meehl and Rosen (1955) to illustrate the problem of base rates for the neuropsychologist:

A neuropsychologist is asked to decide whether the patients who have been referred for admission to a rehabilitation hospital have actual deficits related to a head injury or are malingering (i.e., simulating or exaggerating deficits for secondary gain). The screen must be inexpensive and will be used to decide whether patients should be referred for expensive confirmatory radiological testing. In reviewing the literature the neuropsychologist finds a study that describes a test that will correctly identify 70% of individuals asked to simulate the symptoms of a brain injury (this group will henceforth be called malingerers) who obtain a certain critical score on the test. The test will also correctly identify 70% of individuals with confirmed brain injuries on MRI (henceforth called brain injured). Assuming that 90% of all the patients referred to the rehabilitation hospital actually have brain injuries that will ultimately be confirmed by radiological evidence, how much confidence should the neuropsychologist have in the candidate test? As Meehl points out, based on the base rates and with or without the test, if the neuropsy-

> ### CAUTION
> The accuracy of predictions about the presence or absence of a condition varies depending on the occurrence or base rate of the condition in the population tested.

chologist simply adopted the strategy of predicting that every patient referred to the rehabilitation hospital has a brain injury, the prediction would be correct 90% of the time.

As can be seen from Table 5.1, Part A, 7 of 10 malingerers admitted to the rehabilitation hospital receive a malingering score on the test, while 63 of 90 brain injured patients receive a brain injured score. If every patient with a malingering score is predicted to be a malingerer, then only 7 of 34 or 21% will be identified correctly. The test is, of course, much better at predicting patients who will be in the brain injured group because 63 of 66 brain injured patients received a brain injured score.

Now consider a different situation. The neuropsychologist in our example is now asked to consult for a state prison hospital with the same question. Prison hospital officials are also interested in screening individuals for additional expensive radiological procedures, but their base rates are quite different: 90% of the patients referred to the prison hospital are malingering and end up having no evidence of brain injury, while only 10% are found to have actual brain injury. As can be seen from the scores in Table 5.1, Part B, the same test

Table 5.1 Patients Classified as Malingerers or Brain Injured by a Test that Correctly Identifies 70% of Brain Injured and Malingerers

Prediction by the Neuropsychological Test	Actual Diagnosis		Total Classified by the Test
	Malingerer	Brain injured	
Part A: Rehabilitation hospital admission base rates (90% brain injured, 10% malingerers)			
Malingering score	7	27	34
Brain injured score	3	63	66
Total diagnosed	10	90	100
Part B: Prison hospital base rates (90% malingerers, 10% brain injured)			
Malingering score	63	3	66
Brain injured score	27	7	34
Total diagnosed	90	10	100

now seems to be a better predictor of malingering because a positive malingering score correctly classifies 63 of 66 or 95% of actual malingerers.

In addition to reflecting the actual probabilities of a diagnosis in a specific setting, the concept of base rates can be used to adjust predictions based on the specific historical facts of an individual patient's life. Patients with a known history of stroke or loss of consciousness are more likely to have a brain injury than individuals with no such history. Unfortunately, in many cases specific data about the base rates of various underlying conditions may not be available. It is therefore critical that the neuropsychologist understand how a test was validated, what the base rates of different conditions were in the validating study, and, if possible, what the prevalence (i.e., actual cases) of the condition is in the population in general and in his or her referral population in particular.

USING TEST NORMS

Normative data is used to answer the first question confronting a neuropsychologist: Is the observed test performance evidence of a healthy or normal individual or evidence of an individual with some form of compromise of brain function? To answer this question the neuropsychologist must also consider the importance of what norms to choose. Most contemporary neuropsychological tests contain published normative data showing the range of performance on the test for healthy individuals and in most cases for individuals who have been diagnosed with a disease or disorder of the central nervous system. In some cases norms are also provided for individuals with psychiatric disorders or other nonneurological medical illnesses that may affect test performance. As we have discussed, an individual's age and education may affect performance on any psychological test and most neuropsychological tests. Norms that are stratified by age and education are preferable to norms that simply give scores for patients with brain damage and those with normal brain functioning. Some test publishers go further and publish norms stratified by sex, ethnic group, region, and other common demographic variables used by the United States Census. For most purposes, however, age and education are the most critical variables. Ethnic norms may be important in certain settings as well.

The specific advantage of age- and education-based norms is that they allow a more precise determination of what is normal for the individual as opposed to what is normal for the general population. Age- and education-based norms help to control for IQ and level of cognitive ability. A person with above-average cognitive abilities who scores in the average or normal range on tasks normed according to age and education is performing at expected levels. An example can help to illustrate this point. Consider a 65-year-old male of above-average cognitive ability and 16 years of education who requires 68 seconds to complete Trail Making B. Compared to that of other males aged 65 to 69 and with 16 to 17 years of education (Heaton, Grant, & Matthews, 1991), his performance is average at the 62nd percentile but compared to other males aged 65 to 69 and with 12 years of education his performance is above average at the 79th percentile.

The reliability and stability of normative data also are affected by the sample size used. In general, larger samples yield more generalizable and reliable data than smaller samples. In some cases the test is published with minimal normative data with little stratification but with additional data collected later by investigators. Norms are frequently updated to reflect changes in culture or to extend the data to new populations. It is the responsibility of the neuropsychologist to review consistently the literature relevant to the tests and the settings in which the tests are used to ensure that the norms being used are the most up-to-date and specific to the patients being evaluated.

What Is Normal?

The question of what is normal performance on a neuropsychological test is really the question: What is normal for the individual being tested? Because the natural variations in genetics and environment (rather than disease) result in a great range of normal variation in ability, the question of what is normal for an individual needs to be considered carefully.

Although it may not provide a complete answer to the question of what is normal for the individual, a comparison to test data drawn from a population that is demographically similar to the patient is usually the first step. In most cases test norms use a statistical definition of normality based on the assumption that the underlying distribution of scores in a normal population is a normal (or bell-shaped) distribution. The normal distribution is a continuous probability distribution in which the mean, median, and mode are the same and that shows a gradual decrease in the percentage of cases having scores greater or lesser than the mean. In addition to the mean (M), the shape or dispersion of the normal distribution can be described using a statistic called the standard deviation (SD; σ) or:

$$\sigma = \sqrt{\sum_i \frac{(x_i - M)}{N}}$$

where σ (the symbol for SD) equals the square root of the sum of the differences between the individual scores (x_i) and the mean divided by the number of scores (N). In general, scores within one standard deviation from the mean are considered normal. In a true normal distribution, 68.26% of all scores falls within 1 SD of the mean, and an additional 24% (or 92% total) falls within 2 SDs of the mean. The range of scores within a normal distribution can be presented in several standardized forms allowing for comparisons of the relative position of performance on different tests. One form of standardization involves converting raw scores into z-scores or:

$$z = \frac{x - M}{\sigma}$$

Hence, a score is converted into a z-score by computing the difference between the score and the mean of the distribution divided by SD. The score may then be expressed in terms of standard deviation units with a $z = 0$ being the mean, and $z = 1$ being one standard deviation greater than the mean.

It is very common to present raw scores as percentiles of the normal distribution with the 1st percentile being somewhere between 2 and 3 standard deviations below the mean and the 99th percentile being somewhere between 2 and 3 standard deviations above the mean. In terms of percentiles the normal range of performance falls between the 16th and 84th percentiles (equivalent to ±1 SD).

There are many other ways of standardizing scores that have been found to be convenient in expressing relative differences across measures. This includes the Wechsler intelligence scales, (standardized based on a mean of 100 and a standard deviation of 15), the Wechsler subtest scaled scores (based on a mean of 10 and standard deviation of 3), and the T score (based on a mean of 50 and standard deviation of 10). All these methods produce scores that refer to the shape of the normal distribution and can be used to understand the relative standing of an individual's performance on a test compared to that of other similar individuals.

The normative position of a test score serves as a predictor of whether a score is representative of normal brain functioning or representative of brain damage. The accuracy of the score as a predictor of brain damage depends on the factors just discussed, including the reliability of the test, the likelihood that a deviant score is specific to brain damage, the base rate of brain damage in the population from which the patient comes, and the score the person would have received if that person did not have brain damage. This naturally brings us to the topic of the estimation of *premorbid* ability.

PREMORBID CAPACITY

Because normal human abilities are so widely distributed, even well-stratified norms may not provide an accurate picture of what mental abilities a patient would have brought to a task before suffering brain damage. Although thousands of tests have been published identifying various human abilities, the IQ is by far the best documented and most extensively used measure of premorbid ability. Consider that the normal IQ (i.e., within 1 SD of the mean) ranges from 85 to 115. This range contains individuals with dramatically different expectations of academic and vocational achievement. The relationship between IQ, education, vocational achievement, and other demographic variables such as sex, ethnicity, and geographic origin was recognized by the publication of the Wechsler Adult Intelligence Scale, a test based on a sample that was carefully stratified by these demographic variables. Wilson et al. (1978; Wilson, Rosenbaum, & Brown, 1979) used this data to create equations using demographics to predict IQ. These formulas were updated in 1984 for the WAIS–R by Barona, Reynolds, and Chastain and again in 1996 by Paolo, Ryan, and Troster. Cross-validation studies of these formulas show that demographics are only modestly successful at predicting IQ, with accuracy rates ranging from approximately 60–70%.

Such demographic formulas work best for young and middle-aged individuals and less well for children and the elderly. It is not surprising that demographic formulas for children should be less accurate because education is compulsory for most children under sixteen, allowing for a wide range of abilities to be represented in each grade until the 10th or 11th grades. Demographic variables also do not predict IQ accurately for older adults. This may be due in part to cultural differences in the current cohort of adults older than 65 or 70. As noted earlier, adults who were of school age before World War II often did not complete high school. In fact, because the first compulsory education laws were not put into effect until 1918 many adults born before 1920 stopped their formal education after eighth or ninth grade, in many cases for economic reasons. Adults with a wide range of abilities received an education that today would be unlikely. After World War II the 1944 GI Bill gave many veterans the opportunity to complete high school and college, increasing the likelihood that adults capable of higher levels of educational achievement could afford to fulfill this potential. These legal landmarks and the underlying cultural changes they reflect are likely to affect the relationship between education and IQ for older adults born in the first thirty years of the twentieth century compared to adults born after WWII. It remains to be seen whether education will improve as a predictor of premorbid ability for adults born after WWII.

Comparisons between tests thought to be less sensitive to impairment to tests more sensitive to impairment have a long history as a method for estimating the changes wrought by brain damages for an individual. A comparison among the so-called *hold* and *don't hold* tests of the WAIS was suggested as a way to calculate a *deterioration quotient* by Wechsler. It was argued that such tests as Vocabulary, Information and others were relatively insensitive to deterioration (specifically the effects of aging), whereas such subtests as the Digit Symbol were relatively more sensitive to the effects of conditions expected to produce a deterioration in IQ (such as brain damage and aging). This method is extremely limited because various forms of brain damage may affect hold tests more than some don't hold tests. For example, patients with aphasia, which form a class of acquired language disorders typically as a result of damage to the left cerebral hemisphere of right-handed adults, are likely to perform more poorly on all language tasks, including Vocabulary, than nonverbal tasks. This is an extreme example, but the general problem is that one has to know what subtests are being affected by the condition in question to calculate a deterioration index, leading to potential circularities when trying to decide what is acquired impairment and what is representative of preserved premorbid functions.

A task that has received much attention in recent years as a potential measure of premorbid IQ is the reading of irregular words. Tests such as the National Adult Reading Test (NART; Nelson & McKenna, 1975) have been extensively investigated as measures of premorbid ability, particularly in older adults with suspected dementia. As a lifelong, overlearned skill, reading appears to be a more stable hold task than such WAIS subtests as Vocabulary (O'Carroll, Baikie, & Whittick, 1987) in the face of such dementing illnesses as Alzheimer's disease, but may still be affected by specific brain lesions that cause reading and language deficits. Irregular word reading tasks are also dependent on education and may lead to an underestimate of IQ (and therefore an underestimate of impairment) in poorly educated elderly patients.

To estimate premorbid potential, the clinician should use a combination of methods that includes demographics and performance measures. Methods for estimating premorbid intelligence are outlined in Rapid Reference 5.5.

In many cases, the details of the patient's educational and occupational experience will help with the task of estimating premorbid capacity, though the empirical basis for using such data has not been well studied. However, information like school grades, achievement test scores (e.g., SAT, Iowa Tests of Basic Skills), and an analysis of vocational responsibilities (e.g., level and complexity of a job) can be used to make inferences about premorbid ability. Two adults with similar levels of education, such as completion of high school, may have had very different grades, curricula, and achievement scores. Sometimes estimates of premorbid ability are especially critical; then it may be particularly necessary to ob-

≡ *Rapid Reference 5.5*

Methods for Estimating Premorbid Intelligence

- Hold vs. *don't hold* tests (e.g., Vocabulary vs. Similarities)
- Demographic formula (e.g., see Barona et al., 1984)
- Known educational and occupational attainment (e.g., high school education vs. college; laborer vs. college professor)
- Reading of irregular words (e.g., NART or WTAR)

tain school records and other documentation of premorbid ability and not to rely on a patient's or an informant's self-report alone. Such cases would include those in which the patient has been functioning at a high level of performance with test scores not consistent with this history, cases in which the patient's deficits are subtle, or cases in which no historical reasons can be found for the presence of observed cognitive deficits.

A caution is relevant here. Premorbid estimates of general cognitive ability or IQ may not necessarily generalize to all of the cognitive functions measured by neuropsychological tests. Some measures that may be sensitive to impaired performance in brain-damaged patients may not have the same range and distribution as IQ. So, for example, such measures such as the Wisconsin Card Sorting Test and the Rey-Osterrieth Complex Figure may have ceilings (i.e., topmost scores) that are far lower than IQ. This means that while these tests may be able to identify low scorers as impaired, they may not accurately reflect above-average abilities. In addition, it must be kept in mind that IQ may not be a predictor of all the abilities that are measured by tests sensitive to brain damage. In other words, a person with a superior IQ may have only average attentional abilities; this does not mean, however, that he or she has an impairment in attentional abilities. The relationship between the various cognitive functions of interest in a neuropsychological examination is not yet well studied and until this information is available, great caution should be used in drawing inferences about performance across cognitive measures based on IQ.

QUALITATIVE VERSUS QUANTITATIVE DATA

The availability of tests that have been carefully normed is the scientific cornerstone of clinical neuropsychology. Most instruments that have become well accepted provide estimates of the relative standing of an individual to a normal reference population and can thereby predict whether brain function has been compromised. As we have also discussed, some systems combine multiple measures that meet this basic criterion into a battery that is consistently administered to all patients. The use of such batteries may help increase the specificity of neuropsychological predictions and has the advantage of providing a comparable set of measures to be compared from population to population and from individual to individual. It could safely be said that such *fixed battery approaches* are the culmination of the empiricist tradition and the most straightforward method for quantifying the effects of brain damage on behavior. The two best known examples of quantitative fixed batteries are the Halstead-Reitan Neuropsychological Battery and the Luria-Nebraska Neuropsychological Battery.

Not all neuropsychologists agree, however, that the emphasis on normative data collected within a fixed battery is the optimal method for characterizing the effects of brain damage. As we have noted, many tests, although useful as predictors of the presence of brain damage, were not derived from theories of brain-behavior relationships and are often accompanied by limited or confusing data on construct validity. Several neuropsychology laboratories have advocated assessment techniques that are more like the work of an experimental psychologist applied to an individual. The goal of these approaches is to isolate the specific psychological function or functions that are affected by brain damage. Alexander Luria, who ran a famous neuropsychology laboratory in Moscow for several decades until his death in 1977, wrote several books describing the methods he used to define the effects of brain damage in individual patients. Luria would use some standard materials consisting of pictures, written sentences and words, and objects to create sets of procedures that were designed to isolate various components of more complex functions like reading, speaking, writing, memory, and many more. Many of his observations were organized according to his theory of brain organization, the basic premise of which was that complex behaviors consisted of sets of more basic functions. He also argued that the brain worked by combining the simpler functions, which were independently localized, into more complex integrated patterns to solve the problems of cognition. Luria's approach may be considered the prototype of what is now sometimes called the *qualitative approach* to neuropsychological assessment.

Luria's examinations consisted of sequences of observations organized into various decision trees reflecting the function that was being analyzed. For example, if he observed a patient who had problems writing, he would ask whether the source of the problem was the loss of the recognition of letters as symbols, the loss of the associated sound patterns to the letters, the loss of the rules of sequencing the letters, or the loss of some other component of the writing process. With each task he attempted to demonstrate whether the patient could perform these various components isolated in this case from writing itself, eventually eliminating as many explanations of the deficit as possible.

He might, for example, try to see if the patient could spell a word out loud or copy nonorthographic figures. He then went on to deduce what lesion might have caused the specific deficit that remained. Luria's methods were very difficult to duplicate and were learned by only a small number of students who were able to work with him. This situation limited the extent to which his claims and observations were tested by independent neuropsychological laboratories and the difficulty of his approach prevented his methods from being popularly adopted. However, Luria's approach well fits the emergence of cognitive psychology in the United States and used a framework that augured the main framework of modern neurosciences. Charles Golden used many of the tasks described by Luria in a fixed battery of tasks he called the Luria-Nebraska Neuropsychological Battery (LNNB). The LNNB, however, consists of scales representing either functions (such as writing and reading) or potential lesion locations (such as left versus right hemisphere) and is normed based on the scales or combinations of these scales in much the same way as the Halstead-Reitan Neuropsychological Battery. Although the manual contains some suggestions for noting qualitative performance of the patient, the LNNB should be considered a fixed-battery method that is primarily quantitative.

The Boston Process Approach, developed by Edith Kaplan and her colleagues at the Boston VA in the early 1970s, was inspired by a combination of Heinz Werner's theories of cognitive development and the strong influence of cognitive neuropsychology research that was burgeoning at the Boston VA Hospital at that time. The VA Hospital in Boston attracted some of the pioneers of the field such as Harold Goodglass, Norman Geschwind, Nelson Butters, Laird Cermak, Edgar Zurif, and many others. Although these investigators studied such diverse problems as language, memory, and perception, their work had in common the experimental analysis of cognition into basic components that might be localized in neural structures. Dr. Kaplan joined the VA as a research assistant while a graduate student of Werner at Clark University. She was a keen observer of behavior and was immersed in the pioneering research being conducted around her. Werner's central concept was that the achievement or success at solving a problem may be based on a variety of different cognitive approaches or processes that change as a child develops. Kaplan applied this distinction of *process and achievement* to uncover the basic cognitive functions that were impaired when brain-damaged patients were asked to solve the problems on standard neuropsychological tests.

Over two decades Dr. Kaplan collected a trove of observations and anecdotes about patients' performances on such tasks as the Wechsler Adult Intelligence Scale, (WAIS), the Wechsler Memory Scale (WMS), and other tests that are commonly used in neuropsychological batteries. Using her knowledge of cognitive neuropsychology, Dr. Kaplan developed modifications of these tasks, such as adding delayed recall and recognition memory trials to the WMS; these modifications ultimately became standard components of the revised WMS and other memory batteries. Her observations of how patients approach such tasks as the Block Design subtest of the WAIS helped lead to a critical organizing construct for describing differences between the cerebral hemispheres—the distinction between global and local processing of information (e.g., Robertson, 1995). Many of her techniques were incorporated into a special edition of the WAIS called the WAIS as a Neuropsychological Instrument (WAIS-NI; Kaplan et al., 1991). In addition, she has helped develop a number of important instruments such as the Boston Diagnostic Aphasia Examination, Boston Naming Test, and the California Verbal Learning Test (CVLT), all of which contain elements of her observations. Although not a prolific writer herself, she influenced the practice of many students and practicing neuropsychologists in many countries who consider themselves acolytes of the approach labeled the Boston Process Approach.

Because Dr. Kaplan advocated the use of a core set of tasks including the WAIS, WMS, and so on with the addition of other tasks based on hypotheses developed from the core, the Boston Process Approach should be considered a flexible battery approach. Dr. Kaplan's emphasis on process makes this approach mainly qualitative, although norms may also be used to determine the presence of impairments. In addition, work is being done to quantify the qualitative aspects through new measurement instruments such as the WISC-III as a Neuropsychological Instrument.

Although Dr. Kaplan's work has certainly had a major influence on the practice of neuropsychology by helping to bring the elements of modern cognitive psychology into the world of psychometric testing, great caution must be used in applying this approach to patients. Although intellectually and intuitively appealing with its emphasis on breaking performance down into elements with potential relevance to rehabilitation and education, the empirical basis of the process approach is not sufficiently well developed to allow for scientifically supportable clinical predictions by all clinicians. Without precise norms and a clearly spelled-out blueprint of how and when these procedures should be used, tremendous variations are likely to occur in the skill and accuracy with which this approach is applied. Unlike Luria, who trained only a few students and was not generally avail-

> **CAUTION**
>
> The empirical basis of the process approach is not sufficiently well developed to allow for scientifically supportable clinical predictions by all clinicians.

able for training workshops outside of Russia, Dr. Kaplan, an inspiring lecturer, has trained many students, and still actively presents workshops and seminars effectively exposing a large number of clinicians to her teachings. However, Dr. Kaplan's mastery and the mastery of some students of her techniques do not guarantee that everyone using this approach can be equally successful.

Many of the techniques that comprise the Boston Process Approach have simply not been validated independently of the practitioners who claim expertise in them. Well-normed tests like the WAIS-III, WMS-III, NEPSY, CVLT-2, and others that have been influenced by this approach, should certainly be considered and deserve a place among the best techniques available to contemporary neuropsychologists. The wholesale adoption of many of the fascinating observational procedures of the Boston Process Approach, however, should not be entertained without specific training in a setting in which the validity of one's clinical expertise can be evaluated.

Appendix A outlines the steps that need to be taken in neuropsychological assessment. This outline considers the assessment process from the point of patient referral through selecting, administering, and scoring tests; interpreting the results of the tests; and finally reporting these results.

1. **What principle should guide the clinical neuropsychologist in the choice of assessment tools to predict brain damage?**

    (a) Frequency of use

    (b) Availability

    (c) Empirical validation

    (d) Ease of administration

2. **Which type of validity is involved when one is interested in predicting future behavior from test scores?**

    (a) Concurrent validity

    (b) Predictive validity

    (c) Content validity

    (d) Construct validity

3. **Content validity refers to the extent to which**

    (a) test items adequately cover various aspects of the variable that is being studied.

    (b) test items relate to one another.

    (c) test items predict future behavior.

    (d) test items are clear and understandable.

4. **Which type of validity concerns how well the test score relates to other measures or behaviors in a theoretically expected fashion?**

    (a) Criterion validity

    (b) Predictive validity

    (c) Content validity

    (d) Construct validity

5. **If one subtest of a neuropsychological test measuring memory correlates highly with the total score of the same test, that test has been shown to have**

    (a) internal consistency.

    (b) internal validity.

    (c) test-retest reliability.

    (d) inter-rater reliability.

6. **One of the problems about base rates in prediction is the fact that**

    (a) most measures lack adequate reliability.

    (b) high-frequency events are hard to predict.

    (c) low-frequency events are hard to predict.

    (d) most measures lack adequate validity.

Answers: 1. c; 2. b; 3. a; 4. d; 5. a; 6. c

Six

SPECIAL ISSUES IN NEUROPSYCHOLOGICAL ASSESSMENT

An almost sure sign of the maturity of neuropsychology as a discipline is the emergence of an increasing number of clinical subspecialties reflecting the variety of settings in which practitioners find themselves based. Although undoubtedly many neuropsychologists would still consider themselves generalists, an increasing number of clinicians have established narrowly focused niches requiring specialized knowledge and skills. Whereas pediatric and geriatric neuropsychology and forensic neuropsychology are emerging as bona fide subspecialties, clinicians who work primarily in psychiatric settings, cross-cultural or bilingual settings, or settings with patients who suffer from significant primary or sensory disabilities must develop expertise in resolving problems that have the potential to severely limit the validity of the available array of testing instruments. In this chapter we present some of the issues and concerns a clinician needs to address when asked to assess some of these specialty populations.

ASSESSMENT OF CHILDREN

A number of issues are critical in the neuropsychological assessment of children. Rapid Reference 6.1 summarizes the factors that complicate the interpretation of neuropsychological test results in children. First and foremost, the assessment of children is complicated by the fact that children are evolving in their physical and emotional development and in their knowledge structures needed to perform the cognitive functions that must be assessed. Such abilities as attention, language, memory, self-control, and even motor skills rapidly change from birth to adolescence, reflecting the process of neural development occurring in those years. Although certainly normal developmental trends have been documented, the rates of cognitive development may vary

Rapid Reference 6.1

Complicating Factors in the Neuropsychological Assessment of Children

- Children are evolving in their physical and emotional development and in their knowledge structures needed to perform the cognitive functions that must be assessed.
- Children differ in their exposure to environments that allow opportunities to acquire new information and skills.
- The database of lesion-based studies for children is far more limited than that available for adults.
- The presence of a deficit in a child is not necessarily associated with the same lesions producing the same deficit in an adult.
- The rate of physiological verification in most clinical settings is low for developmental or academic difficulties in children.
- Parents may not be accurate informants about their child's academic performance.
- On average, children may have greater difficulties than adults sitting through lengthy evaluations because of age-dependent distractibility and fidgety behavior.

widely, particularly in the first five or six years of life. In some cases a few months or even weeks can make the difference in the emergence of a function or ability such as a motor skill or language. While undergoing biological development, children are exposed to environments that present the opportunity to acquire new information and skills. Such exposure may also vary tremendously across individuals. Adult neuropsychological tests are designed to use a standard range of exposure to common facts and information. For example, verbal memory tasks are often designed using words that are controlled for frequency of appearance in written materials and degree of interrelationship or associative strength. The statistics used to compute these variables known to affect memory performance are based on reading materials available to adults and may not represent similar levels of difficulty to a child. Basic skills (e.g., reading, writing, following instructions, and sitting still for an interview) that are usually developed during the elementary school years may not be established in younger children. For these reasons, in most cases it is not sufficient to collect norms for children using the materials developed for an adult test. A test with items that allows for valid neuropsychological predictions and good sensitivity in a teenager or young adult is often inappropriate for use even with older children. A test that is sensitive and specific to the effects of brain damage in older, verbally mature children is usually of no use in the assessment of brain damage in preverbal children or even preschool children.

Test developers can be very sensitive to these issues and numerous tests are designed specifically for use with developing children. Some developers have attempted to design tests that appear to share content and construct validity with an analogous adult test. The best examples of such tests are again those used to assess IQ, with the Wechsler series the most explicitly designed to provide normative and construct continuity from preschool children to adults.

An even more difficult issue confronting the pediatric neuropsychologist is figuring out how these materials may be used to assess brain functions in children. Although adult neuropsychology—for better or worse—stands on a large accumulated database of lesion-based studies allowing for the development of numerous hypotheses about brain organization in adults, such data are far less available for children. A large literature examines neuropsychological test performance in children with developmental disorders and various forms of acquired brain lesions; however, the diseases and events that most commonly produce the focal lesions whose effects on behavior have been studied in adults are far less common in children. Although it is tempting to draw an analogy between similar behavioral disturbances that may be exhibited by both children and adults during the course of a neuropsychological examination, these behavioral disturbances are not necessarily comparable. A particular test result may reflect interactions between changes in normal biological development, incomplete acquisition of knowledge, and the focal effects of a lesion. Neuropsychological data should not be used to make predic-

CAUTION

Similar behavioral disturbances exhibited by an adult and a child may not mean the same thing. A particular test result may reflect interactions between two or more of the following: changes in normal biological development, incomplete acquisition of knowledge, and the focal effects of a lesion.

tions for children in the same way as for adults unless specific data warrants such predictions. The presence of a change in language, memory, or executive functions in a child is not necessarily associated with the same lesions that produce such deficits in adults.

Although neuropsychologists are often asked to evaluate the effects of documented brain damage in children, the most common referral question for clinicians who assess young patients concerns the evaluation of developmental or academic difficulties when no clear-cut event or disease state can be physiologically verified. In these cases the choice to use neuropsychological test data to make predictions about the presence of a structural focal deficit should be made with great care and conservatism. The data supporting such assertions are in many cases nonexistent and show a very low rate of physiological verification in most clinical settings. The issues surrounding how such data should be used are complex and beyond the scope of the present text. The reader is thus cautioned and advised to consult specialty pediatric neuropsychology texts to learn what scientifically verifiable information can be derived from neuropsychological tests in a pediatric population.

Neuropsychological batteries with children typically include some evaluation of educational achievement, particularly in the domains of reading, spelling, and arithmetic processes. Tests such as the Wide Range Achievement Test–Revision 3 (WRAT3; Wilkinson, 1993), the Wechsler Individual Achievement Test (WIAT; Psychological Corporation, 1992; 2001), the Woodcock Johnson Tests of Achievement–Third Edition (WJ III; Woodcock, McGrew, & Mather, 2001) and the Kaufman Assessment Battery for Children (Kaufman & Kaufman, 1983) or the Kaufman Test of Educational Achievement (Kaufman & Kaufman, 1998) might be included. These tests are described in Chapter 4. The clinician should also have detailed information about the child's academic performance. Note that in many cases parents may not be accurate informants about their child's academic performance. The neuropsychologist should obtain recent school records whenever possible, especially any special education records. When the clinician is asked to sort out the effects of a recent neurological illness and longer-standing abilities, it may be necessary to evaluate the entire school record to plot the overall course of the child's cognitive development.

A very common diagnostic question for which children are increasingly referred for neuropsychological evaluation is the presence of Attention-Deficit/Hyperactivity Disorder (ADHD). Although children who obtain this diagnosis sometimes perform poorly on neuropsychological tests, these measures have not been shown to be useful in making the diagnosis itself because

> **CAUTION**
>
> Neuropsychological tests have not been shown to be useful in making the diagnosis of ADHD. The diagnosis of ADHD at this time is best made based on behavioral description and history using the symptom criteria specified in *DSM-IV-TR*.

of a lack of specificity. The diagnosis of ADHD is currently best made based on behavioral description and history using *DSM-IV-TR* (*Diagnostic and Statistical Manual of Mental Disorders, Fourth Edition Text Revision*) symptom criteria with the goal of observing consistent patterns of behavior across various environments. In the case of ADHD the clinician should obtain appropriate data from the child's parents and teachers about behavior patterns at home, at school, and, if possible, in other relevant settings. Several standardized inventories are designed for such purposes, including the Attention Deficit/Hyperactivity Disorder Test (Gilliam, 1995), the Conners' Rating Scales (Connors, 1997), and the Behavior Assessment System for Children (Reynolds & Kamphaus, 1992). More information about these measures can be found in Chapter 4.

Maintaining cooperation and motivation is particularly important in children, who typically cannot sit and attend to testing as long as most adults. Signs of fatigue, wandering attention, and distractibility must be monitored constantly when children are being tested. Extraneous motor activity and some distractibility may be age appropriate and can potentially undermine the reliability of test performance, even in relatively normal children. In the case of some developmental abnormalities and such conditions as Attention-Deficit/Hyperactivity Disorder, distractibility may undermine a clinician's ability to obtain reliable test results that can be used for any purpose other than confirming the presence of the deficit in maintaining attention. In these cases test sessions may have to be shortened considerably, with the provision of breaks and opportunities to move around before testing is resumed. Rapid Reference 6.2 offers some general considerations necessary for the neuropsychological assessment of children.

Rapid Reference 6.2

General Considerations in the Neuropsychological Assessment of Children

- Select tests appropriate to the child's age and validated for the desired assessment purpose.
- Gather birth, developmental, medical, psychological, social, and family history from the child's parent or caregiver.
- Corroborate history by requesting and reviewing available records.
- Plan the testing session(s) to accommodate the reduced attention span and fidgetiness of some children, and keep distractions to a minimum.
- Work to make the child feel at ease during testing.
- Encourage the child to be as cooperative as possible.
- Provide encouragement and praise for effort.
- Know the tests to be administered in order to allow the session to progress smoothly.
- Remember to be cautious when interpreting the deficits seen in children. The deficits seen in children may not occur for the same reasons they do in adults.

BILINGUALISM AND CULTURAL ISSUES

The vast majority of neuropsychological tests in use today were originally published in English and normed in the United States. Although some tests originated in other languages such as French (e.g., the Rey Auditory Verbal Learning Test; Rey, 1958) and Italian (the Token Test; De Renzi & Vignolo, 1962), these instruments have been translated into English and renormed using an American population to attain widespread use in the United States or Canada. Performance on these tests depends not only on some mastery of the American dialect of English, but also on exposure to experiences and customs that are intrinsic to Western culture. This should not be surprising because the tests are products of the cultural origins and language of their developers. These tests are not necessarily invalid when used outside the cultural and linguistic context in which they are developed. One cannot assume, however, that neuropsychological tests developed in the United States and normed on primarily monolingual English-speaking Americans will retain similar levels of sensitivity and specificity when translated and applied outside this culture. Although an increasing number of neuropsychological tests have been translated and renormed to be used with native speakers in their countries of origin, very little data address the critical issue of using English-based tests on individuals who are bilingual and who live a significant portion of their lives speaking languages other than English. These individuals may appear conversationally fluent in both languages, but they may not have comparable levels of exposure as demographically similar monolinguals to information in either language. The data that exist for these populations are very contradictory and allow little consistent comparison of similar tests across different bilingual groups. Some data do suggest that some Spanish-speaking bilinguals may be disadvantaged in performance on some tests (Navarrete, 1999) and some bilingual Chinese speakers may be advantaged on others (Hsieh & Tori, 1993). Kaufman (1994) presents data that indicate that a large majority of Hispanic children, even those who speak English adequately, show large differences on the WISC-III between their Verbal Scale IQs (VIQs) and Performance Scale IQs (PIQs) in favor of their PIQs. These studies concerning different kinds of bilingual individuals taking different kinds of tests also differ in subject selection procedures so that the range of age, education, and socioeconomic status of subjects cannot even be compared across studies. Tests that are translated into a second language may work appropriately when used among native monolingual speakers of the language, but may not correct the potential inaccuracies that can occur in testing bilingual individuals.

Even when language is not the primary issue, data suggest that an individual's ethnicity may in itself affect performance on neuropsychological tests. Although it is not at all clear why members of some groups score more poorly (or at superior levels) than others, a significant number of studies demonstrate ethnic group differences on IQ, language, and achievement tests, even when individuals tested are monolingual English speakers. These differences can potentially affect both the sensitivity and specificity of the neuropsychological tests that have only been normed on the general majority population. Because of the greater likelihood of false-positive classifications of impairment for individu-

DON'T FORGET

Neuropsychological tests may underestimate language-based cognitive abilities in bilingual children and adults.

DON'T FORGET

....

Neuropsychological test results may not generalize across different cultures.

als who are members of ethnic groups with tests scores lower than the population for whom the norms are obtained, it is becoming increasingly important to obtain separate norms for some of the larger ethnic groups in the United States. The issue of separate norms is particularly important for African-Americans, who constitute a large ethnic minority group in the United States. African-Americans frequently perform more poorly on some neuropsychological tests than the majority population. The reason for this is not clear, but this group difference has evoked a range of responses, including a justifiable sensitivity to the political implications of such differences. Social and political arguments have been made both for and against the development and use of separate norms for African-Americans; however, most admit that at least under current circumstances, separate norms are critical to ensure the accurate interpretation of neuropsychological test results.

GERONEUROPSYCHOLOGY

Adults over 65 are the fastest-growing population requiring neuropsychological assessment. Even 20 years ago tests were rarely published with norms for adults in their seventies. Today many tests are published with norms for adults between 70 and 90 years old. This change reflects the general demographic shift caused by the large swelling in birth rate that occurred after World War II and the slow but continuous increase in life expectancy since that time. Projections indicate that by the year 2010 the United States will have almost 40 million adults over the age of 65, representing over 13% of the total population of the United States (Malmgren, 2000), with nearly 6 million adults over the age of 85. As age increases, so does the presence of diseases that have an impact on cognition. It has been estimated that Alzheimer's disease affects approximately 19.5% of adults ages 75 to 79, with cerebrovascular disease affecting another 8% of adults ages 75 to 84 (Cummings & Coffey, 2000).

As might be expected, neuropsychological assessment of the geriatric patient presents its own issues and challenges; these are summarized in Rapid Reference 6.3. Again, the primary issue is the availability of appropriate norms for tests. The collection of accurate norms for neuropsychological tests in older adults has

≡*Rapid Reference 6.3*

Complicating Factors in the Neuropsychological Assessment of Older Adults

Appropriate norms may not be available:

- Norms gathered through cross-sectional data may be affected by cohort effects, reflecting differences in the experiences of individuals maturing during different historical eras.

- Because elderly normal populations may have nonneurological medical conditions, neuropsychological tests may have less specificity in older than in younger adults.

- Test norms that include data from age-matched individuals with normal brain functioning may include a number of individuals with early signs of dementia, leading to diminished sensitivity as a function of increased age.

- Tests may be hampered by floor effects.

Elderly patients may be less able to tolerate testing:

- They may fatigue more easily than average younger or middle-aged adults.

- They may suffer from uncomfortable chronic medical conditions.

- They may suffer from undiagnosed but common conditions such as mild depression and sleep deprivation.

been hampered by the elusiveness of a clear-cut understanding of what is normal and what is not normal aging. Much of the data that is collected comparing different age groups is cross-sectional—that is, data collected from random samples of individuals who have attained different ages within the same time period. Cross-sectional data tends to exaggerate differences between individuals of different ages because their test-taking abilities may reflect differences in the experiences of individuals maturing during different historical eras. In addition to such *cohort effects,* data are confounded by the greater likelihood that the older sample is affected by the early stages of diseases that become more prevalent with age. Longitudinal studies, although still affected by the development of diseases as individuals age and sampling bias related to attrition of sample sizes, sometimes eliminate or drastically reduce age differences that are apparent with cross-sectional data. It is likely that geriatric assessment could be improved with items that are created to be more age- and cohort-specific, but the major test-publishing houses have not produced such measures.

The problem of what constitutes normal or healthy aging is a serious one for geriatric neuropsychological assessment. The motivation, energy level, and willingness of a geriatric patient to cooperate with the assessment process may be limited by various systemic illnesses, peripheral sensory and motor loss, and the presence of chronic pain. Such conditions as deafness (especially the loss of higher and high-middle-range auditory frequencies), macular degeneration, cataracts, and diabetic retinopathy increase in prevalence with age and have the potential to impair neuropsychological test performance independent of any actual compromise of brain function. For this reason neuropsychological tests may have far less specificity in older than younger adults. If individuals with these disorders are included in greater numbers in the normal sample used for validation, the criterion score for classifying patients as having brain damage may be too conservative and the sensitivity of the test will be compromised. Without general health screening in the process of selecting normal subjects, the point at which individuals are classified as impaired may require a higher score than is optimal.

Also, individuals with undiagnosed illnesses that do affect the brain can sometimes be included in normal samples. Many geriatric neuropsychological tests are designed and validated to detect the presence of Alzheimer's disease, the most prevalent of the degenerative dementing illnesses. Recently, Sliwin-ski, Lipton, Buschke, and Stuart (1996) found that many of the individuals who fell one standard deviation below the mean of a group of subjects classified as normal in a memory test validation study went on to receive the diagnosis of dementia 6 to 12 months later. This result suggests that the test norms for older adults may be too conservative. Furthermore, because the prevalence of Alzheimer's disease itself increases with age, test norms that include data from randomly sampled age-matched normally functioning individuals may be expected to include larger numbers of individuals with the early signs of dementia, leading to diminished sensitivity of these tests as a function of the increased age of the individual.

Finally, recent data suggest that elevations in such cardiovascular risk factors as blood pressure may impair performance on some neuropsychological tests (Brady, Spiro, McGlinchey-Berroth, & Milberg, in press; Pugh, Milberg, & Lipsitz, 2001), particularly those associated with executive functions, even when the affected individual has not received a diagnosis of dementia or cognitive impairment. Many other diseases affecting the central nervous system also increase in prevalence as adults age, including strokes, neoplasm, and other neurodegenerative disease, such as Parkinsonism. Such observations highlight why the health status of the individuals comprising the normal samples should be known and specified in the validity studies of neuropsychological tests used with older adults.

Motivation and cooperation must be continuously monitored with older patients because they may fatigue more easily and have a lower frustration tolerance than the average younger or middle-aged adult. Although healthy older adults may be able to tolerate testing as well as younger adults, the prevalence of potentially uncomfortable chronic conditions (such as arthritis and other orthopedic impairments) increases with age, as does the presence of primary sensory impairments in vision and hearing. Furthermore, typically undiagnosed but common conditions such as mild depression, anxiety, and sleep deprivation also increase in prevalence with age. The presence of these conditions may impact the older patient's stamina and ability to maintain attention to the procedures, reducing the reliability of test scores and the reliability and specificity of neuropsychological tests as measures of brain dysfunction, damage, or disease.

As with young children, it may be necessary to employ shorter test sessions with older adults. In fact, whenever possible the clinician should attempt to find the briefest, most efficient, and most relevant tests when testing older adults. Unfortunately, very few neuropsychological tests have been designed specifically with the geriatric individual in mind. Even well-normed tests that were originally designed for the range of performance for younger adults may not provide a sufficient range of difficulty to capture the typical level of performance in older adults. Because of the interaction of normal aging effects with disease, many tests show a floor effect with adults whose impairments may only be mild relative to their age cohort. If even mildly impaired adults perform at the bottom of the possible range of a test, the measure will not be able to discriminate between mild and more severely impaired patients and will show a high rate of false-positive errors.

The problem of floor effects has plagued such measures as the 16-item California Verbal Learning Test, which has very poor specificity in older adults: It classifies a large number of relatively healthy adults as having memory impairments. For this reason test developers have produced a 9-item *dementia version* that is much more appropriate for this population (Libon et al., 1996). Floor effects hamper even tests such as the WMS-III. A person age 76 who recalls none of the verbal paired associates after a delay will earn a scaled score of 6, placing performance in the low average range. Should this performance be interpreted as an example of the rapid decay that is the hallmark of Alzheimer's Disease, or should it be seen as the expected performance of a 76-year-old with low average premorbid ability? The answer to the question will have to come from other data—perhaps historical data or disease history—because a floor effect prevents the score from being of particular use. To accommodate the growing number of elderly individuals in the population, test revisions and adaptations need to be forthcoming for many of the classic neuropsychological measures that have good sensitivity to neuropsychological deficits in younger adults.

In some cases in which referral and history strongly indicate that the patient is suffering from progressive deterioration of cognitive functions, neuropsychological batteries with elderly patients may include a brief screening battery such as the Mattis Dementia Rating Scale (Mattis, 1988) or the Neurobehavioral Cognitive Status Examination (Kiernan, Mueller, Langston, & VanDyke, 1987) and, in some cases, the Folstein Mini-Mental State Exam (MMSE; Folstein, Folstein, & McHugh, 1975). Great caution should be exercised in using such batteries, however, because they have generally poor sensitivity and specificity and often are unable to provide reliable information about the specific cognitive domains affected (Milberg, 1996). These measures may be useful in cases in which the base rate of the presence of dementia is high and in tracking gross changes in a patient's cognitive status over time.

In those cases of assessment in which an initial diagnosis needs to be made, it is advisable to use a battery consisting of some formal and well-standardized measures of attention, memory, language, executive functions, and perception to target the critical areas for the diagnosis of the most common neuropsychological disorders in the elderly. One such battery that has been shown to have good sensitivity for the diagnosis of Alzheimer's disease is called the CERAD Battery (Consortium to Establish a Registry for Alzheimer's Disease; Welsh et al., 1994). The CERAD consists of a word fluency or word list generation task, Boston Naming Test items, word list memory with immediate, delayed, and recognition trials, and a number of other tests with documented validity in this population. This battery includes the Folstein Mini-Mental State Exam to help compare an individual to other patients with the known diagno-

≡ *Rapid Reference 6.4*

General Considerations in the Neuropsychological Assessment of Elderly Adults

- Obtain a full history from the patient and a family member or caregiver.
- Employ a shorter test session.
- Find the briefest, most efficient, and most relevant tests.
- If suspicious of a progressive deterioration of cognitive function, include a brief screening battery (e.g., Mattis Dementia Rating Scale, DRS; Neurobehavioral Cognitive Screening Examination, NCSE; Mini-Mental State Examination, MMSE).
- When an initial diagnosis must be made, use formal and well-standardized measures of attention, memory, language, executive functions, and perception to target the critical areas that can contribute to diagnosing the most common neuropsychological disorders in the elderly (e.g., CERAD).
- Include a screen for depression.

sis of Alzheimer's disease (McKhann, 1984). In addition, because mild depression is fairly common in older adults, most batteries should include at least a screen for depression such as the Geriatric Depression Scale (Brink et al., 1982; Yesavage et al., 1983). Rapid Reference 6.4 summarizes the general considerations to be made when performing neuropsychological assessments with elderly adults.

PATIENTS WITH PSYCHIATRIC DISORDERS

Many of the problems concerning the testing of children and older adults also affect the interpretation of the neuropsychological test results for patients with significant psychotic or affective disorders. It is well known that patients with schizophrenia, bipolar disorder, severe obsessive compulsive disorder, and many other psychiatric conditions show deficits on neuropsychological tests. Although many of these illnesses may have their origins in abnormalities of brain function, they produce symptoms that have an impact on test performance that is not a direct result of the underlying pathology itself.

Psychiatric patients may perform poorly because they are distracted by auditory hallucinations rather than because of a deficit in a specific cognitive

CAUTION

Many tests that show good specificity in distinguishing brain-damaged from non-brain-damaged individuals show high levels of false-positive errors when used to distinguish brain-damaged from psychiatric patients.

function that may typically be measured by the test. Alternatively, as a result of the neurovegetative signs of depression they may work slowly and without full effort during testing, reducing their scores for reasons other than brain dysfunction. As a general rule, patients show greater cognitive deficits as the severity of their thought disorder and affective symptoms increases. Many tests that show excellent specificity when asked to distinguish brain-damaged from non-brain-damaged individuals show dismaying levels of false-positive errors when asked to distinguish brain-damaged from psychiatric patients.

The most important adaptation of neuropsychological assessment to this population is the inclusion of interview questions and assessment instruments designed to evaluate the nature and severity of the psychiatric illness. Although it may be advisable to at least screen for the presence of psychiatric symptoms in any evaluation of an adult, detailed data on the presence of hallucinations, delusions, severe depression, mania or hypomania, severe anxiety, phobic symptoms, and the presence of obsessive compulsive disorder must be available before any neuropsychological test protocol can be interpreted. In some settings these data may have been collected by other practitioners and may be available in the patient's medical records.

When working in a psychiatric setting or when there is a strong suspicion that an individual has a psychiatric diagnosis by history or because of the referral question, the neuropsychologist should include test instruments such as the Minnesota Multiphasic Personality Inventory–2 (MMPI-2; Butcher, Dahlstrom, Graham, Tellegen, & Koemmer, 1989), the Beck Scales such as the Beck Depression Inventory (Beck et al., 1996) and the Beck Anxiety Inventory (Beck & Steer, 1993), or other personality or symptom inventories relevant to the question at hand. For the individual who has a long history of abuse or who has been exposed to a traumatic event, the Trauma Symptom Inventory (Briere, 1995) is useful for delin-

DON'T FORGET

When psychiatric problems may be an issue, include measures of emotional report and personality in the test battery.

eating posttraumatic symptoms. Tests that can be used for the report of emotional symptoms and personality are described in Chapter 4. Neuropsychological tests may still be used to provide a valid profile of abilities for psychiatric patients, but should be used cautiously to predict the presence of brain damage in this population. In the future, increasing the specificity of neuropsychological tests may be achieved through the use of multiple longitudinal measurements to determine changes in performance over time. Rapid rates of decline may be used to make inferences about the presence of underlying pathology with greater accuracy than a single data point. This approach is suggested only hypothetically and has not received formal scientific support at this time.

As with the other special populations discussed in this chapter, patients with psychiatric problems require careful monitoring for variations in motivation and compliance that can affect test reliability and validity. Like geriatric and pediatric patients, these individuals may require briefer test sessions and frequent reestablishment of attention to the task at hand.

MALINGERING

The vast majority of individuals who are referred for an evaluation by a neuropsychologist can be expected to cooperate with the examination and perform the various tasks comprising a battery of tests to the best of their ability. Although some individuals may fatigue easily, are distractible, or are otherwise limited in their ability to maintain attention to the examination for long periods, they still may be assumed to be expending a reasonable effort to perform well when they are focused on the tasks. This is particularly true in the typical clinical referral, in which patients have little reason to perform poorly. Sometimes, however, individuals who are referred for testing do not try to perform the tests to the best of their abilities or may actually try to perform poorly. Some of these individuals insidiously try to deceive the examiner into concluding that they suffer from deficits or symptoms (or a higher degree of deficits or symptoms) that in reality they do not.

Although included in the *DSM-IV-TR,* malingering is not technically a psychiatric disease. *Malingering* is the intentional or voluntary production or exaggeration of symptoms or deficits or the purposeful suppression of ability for the purposes of secondary gain, such as economic reward in litigation. Malingering is not an all-or-nothing phenomenon; rather, it occurs on various lev-

≡ *Rapid Reference 6.5*

Inconsistencies That Raise the Suspicion of Malingering

- Lack of consistency in the presented deficits
- Lack of consistency between the patient's performances across similar tasks
- Lack of consistency between a patient's verbal report of symptoms and observed behavior
- Lack of consistency between reported symptoms and clinical findings

els. Some individuals have symptoms that they exaggerate, others have had symptoms and maintain them after their resolution, others have had symptoms that predate an event but consciously (incorrectly) attribute them to a later event, and still others actually simulate or produce deficits. Malingering can involve not only the obvious outright production of false symptoms, which is more rare, but also purposeful suboptimal effort and suppression of ability. Evidence of malingering can be gathered by examining performances on tests specifically designed to measure effort and validity, as well as from unusual neuropsychological test findings and especially from inconsistencies in performance. As is evident from Rapid Reference 6.5, the inconsistencies may be seen between test findings and functional status, between test findings and the degree or type of injury, between different tests measuring similar functions, and between examinations.

Malingering is different from somatoform disorders in that the latter involves the involuntary production of symptoms. In somatoform disorders such as conversion disorder, psychological factors are assumed to play a role in the production of symptoms and medical circumstances cannot fully account for a patient's symptoms. Patients adopting a sick or invalid role and emphasizing medical conditions instead of addressing psychological stress may also perform poorly in testing because of decreased effort. Here, however, the patient is not purposely choosing incorrect responses and therefore is less likely to fail specific tests of malingering even if suboptimal effort is evident throughout testing.

The most common situations in which deception or malingering occurs are those in which the individual perceives some actual or secondary gain. Evidence of malingering is most common, for example, among individuals involved in a criminal investigation (especially when pleas of insanity or diminished capacity are involved), civil litigation, or in the course of insurance disability or workman's compensation claims. In rarer instances, the perceived gain may be of a more psychological or emotional nature, such as increased attention from health care providers or family members; in these cases, the disorder is called factitious disorder. Factitious disorder is like malingering in that the production of symptoms is voluntary but different in that the only obvious secondary gain is the attention that appears to come from being treated as a patient. Because litigation by its very nature is accompanied by secondary gain issues, in forensic cases the area that typically must be explored is malingering rather than factitious disorder, which more often would present in a medical setting. Rapid Reference 6.6 sets out the definitions for malingering versus somatoform disorders versus factitious disorder.

Clinicians who work in medicolegal or forensic settings and other situations in which the base rate of malingering is higher must include tests that are sensitive to motivation, effort, and compliance embedded within a standard battery of neuropsychological tests. Even clinicians who work in more typical neuropsychological settings in which such patients are more unusual nevertheless sometimes find themselves shocked and even hurt that an individual with whom they have entered into an implied contract of trust has tried to deceive them. Clinicians who do see such patients may have the tendency to overlook or underplay evidence of malingering or deception because they find it hard to believe. In addition, clinicians, who are accustomed to being hired by a client and assume the role of patient advocate, may feel uncomfortable questioning a patient's motivation and effort. One of the most difficult aspects of

≡ Rapid Reference 6.6

Differential Diagnoses in Motivational Disorders

Malingering—the intentional exaggeration or production of symptoms or willful suboptimal effort or ability for the purpose of secondary gain

Somatoform Disorders—the involuntary production of symptoms in disorders in which psychological factors are assumed to play a role in the production of symptoms and medical circumstances cannot fully account for a patient's symptoms

Factitious Disorder—the intentional production of symptoms motivated by the patient's desire to assume the sick role, rather than by a desire for external rewards

dealing with malingering is how to report these findings in a way that is professional and in keeping with the patient's or client's interests. A direct accusation of malingering to a patient is potentially destructive, so the issue must be handled sensitively. The neuropsychologist must find a way to report this information in a manner that allows the client to receive proper treatment. In medicolegal cases, which require a routine examination of the issue of malingering, the neuropsychologist must report the information in appropriate ways, keeping in mind that some view the label of *malingerer* as the same as *fake*.

In any case it is part of the neuropsychologist's responsibility to sort out the potential reasons for a patient's test performance by assessing the contribution of neurological, psychological, and motivational effects on the data. This information ultimately leads to the most appropriate treatment for the issues presented by the client.

To ensure that neuropsychological tests are interpreted accurately, the clinician should be aware of the need to investigate a referral's legal circumstances and to directly assess effort and motivation when warranted. Assessment of motivation and compliance is also necessary in forensic evaluations, whether the individual was referred by a plaintiff's attorney or by the defense attorney. In any case the collection of information about a client's legal history must be handled cautiously and tactfully, without undermining rapport and the clinical working relationship. Sometimes questions about legal factors are suggested naturally by the history of the illness. Problems following an apparent accident or medical procedure are more likely to be affected by motivational issues than by stroke or dementing illnesses, for example.

Some clinicians include questions about ongoing or anticipated litigation or criminal investigations in standard personal history forms, interspersing these questions among less charged inquiries about academic and general medical history. Screening for litigation might begin with a question on the patient information form asking, "Is there litigation pending with regard to this matter?" Many individuals involved in such circumstances will not volunteer information about ongoing litigation or criminal charges unless directly asked and may only provide sufficient detail to answer the specific question at hand. Reports of what appear to be severe functional incapacities following seemingly innocuous circumstances (e.g., minor bumps on the head with no loss of consciousness), however, or a pattern of increasingly severe symptoms months or years after an event that typically does not result in such progressive declines, are circumstances that require careful investigation even when the patient has not been referred explicitly for an evaluation in the context of a legal investigation. When test performance is unexpectedly poor given the patient's office behavior, recent functional, academic, or work history, or the circumstances of the alleged causal event, the clinician should entertain the possibility of less than optimal effort as an explanation and should include in the battery tests that can specifically measure this possibility.

There are many so-called signs that circulate in the clinical lore as being useful in deciding whether a patient is performing with optimal effort. These signs include the presence of overt suspiciousness or inappropriate anger at the clinician, excessive slowness during otherwise normal test performance, frequent complaints about the difficulty of the examination, requests for observers to be in the room during testing, and even unexpectedly poor performances. These signs have, for the most part, not been validated scientifically and cannot be used in isolation to document the presence of a malingered performance. The presence of such behaviors, however, does raise the suspicion of malingering and should prompt clinicians to employ some objective methods for determining the level of effort and compliance of the client. These measures also can add to the whole clinical picture when integrated with the history, patient's behavior, and test findings.

Because more and more neuropsychologists in private practice are becoming involved in forensic work and neuropsychology is now used frequently in the courtroom, the development of measures that are sensitive to motivation has been the focus of considerable research in recent years. The most common strategy for developing these measures has been to find tasks that are performed more poorly by simulators than by patients with actual brain damage. In some cases these are forced-choice, two-alternative tasks in which results at or below chance indicate purposefully poor effort. Other tests of malingering are designed to appear difficult but are actually so easy that even patients with severe brain injury can succeed. These concepts have been most successfully applied to the detection of malingered memory deficits, one of the most common domains vulnerable to deception or poor effort. A number of measures such as the Portland Digit Recognition Test (Binder, 1993) and the Test of Memory Malingering (Tombaugh, 1996) are based on the observation that even moderately to severely amnesic patients (i.e., patients with functionally incapacitating disorders of new learning) perform at nearly normal levels when given a simple forced-choice, immediate recognition memory task. Individuals who are asked to fake a memory deficit or are at risk for poor effort are more likely to perform such tasks at or near chance or beneath particular criterion levels that distinguish them from patients with bona fide memory impairments.

Multiple tests are now available to help identify suspicious performances; these are described in Chapter 4. Several measures should be used in each case in order to see whether a consistent pattern of findings occurs across tasks. In addition, it is wise to use different types of malingering tasks because patients may choose to fail or give lesser effort only on those tasks that they see as relevant to their primary complaints.

Failures on specific tests of malingering are not the only means of judging the reliability and validity of test findings. One of the hallmarks of malingering is inconsistency: This should be assessed by comparing behavior during testing with behavior outside testing, by comparing consistency of level of deficit with expected level of deficit given known injury or disease, and by comparing consistency of performance across different tasks measuring the same functions. Consistency should also be examined by comparing reported symptoms and clinical findings. In addition, consistency should also be assessed by comparing performances on the same tasks during different examinations. When making these comparisons, however, the neuropsychologist should be sure to allow for changes in mood or medical status that could influence test effort in different situations.

An assessment of malingering requires a thorough examination of medical records and other documents. This independent information can be used to corroborate or discredit the patient's self-report. Sometimes reports by family members, friends, and coworkers can be used for corroboration; however, because these individuals may have reasons to be biased in their reports as well, this information should consequently be viewed cautiously.

The clinical interview can also be used in the assessment of malingering. The way a patient answers interview questions may raise suspicions of malingering. Patients may signal dissimulation by giving approximate answers, vague responses, or bizarre responses. They may try to avoid the interview or examination, approach the examiner with hostility, or resist answering questions. Patients' behavior during testing may also raise suspicions of malingering. Patients too eager to demonstrate their deficits or those who appear to overact and dramatize their presentation maybe signaling dissimulation. Behavior during testing that contradicts reported symptoms, test findings, or both (e.g., a patient who can give a detailed personal history concerning recent events but who has a WMS-III General Memory Index of 58) can also be a sign of malingering.

≡ *Rapid Reference 6.7*

Commonly Used Qualitative Signs and Symptoms of Malingering on Tests of Cognitive Abilities

- Any disability that is disproportionate to the severity of the injury or illness
- Recognition scores that are relatively lower than recall scores on tests such as list learning
- Disproportionately impaired attention relative to learning and memory scores (e.g., WMS-III Working Memory Index lower than Immediate Memory Index)
- Failing easy items and passing more difficult ones (e.g., higher scores on backward versus forward digits; on Trails B versus Trails A; on difficult paired associates versus easy paired associates)
- Unusually high frequency of *I don't know* responses
- Discrepancies between scores on tests measuring similar processes such as verbal or visual learning
- Inconsistencies between memory complaints and behavior observed during the test or outside the testing situation
- Near misses or approximate answers
- Pronounced decrements in delayed recall
- Chance- or near chance-level performance on forced-choice tasks
- Digit span scaled score of ≤4
- Inconsistent pattern between scores on tests and those expected from neurological illness or injury

Source: Test of Memory Malingering, by T. N. Tombaugh, 1996, New York: Multi-Health Systems. Copyright © 1996, Multi-Health Systems Inc. All rights reserved. In the USA, 908 Niagara Falls Blvd., North Tonawanda, NY 14120-2060, 1-800-456-3003. In Canada, 3770 Victoria Park Ave., Toronto, ON M2H 3M6, 1-800-268-6011. Internationally, +1-416-492-2627. Fax, +1-416-492-3343. Reproduced by permission.

The best assessment for malingering is based on multiple sets of patient data. When suspicious of malingering, the neuropsychologist should evaluate historical information and be familiar with expected findings for the particular brain disorder or disease, as well as with the consistency or inconsistency of findings. The neuropsychologist should also evaluate the types of errors made by the patient in evaluation, looking out for errors occurring for the wrong reason or errors discrepant from those seen in patients with documented brain dysfunction.

In addition, the neuropsychologist should evaluate the results of the neuropsychological tests and the specific tests of malingering. Rapid Reference 6.7 summarizes the commonly used signs and symptoms of malingering on tests of cognitive abilities (Tombaugh, 1996).

TEST YOURSELF

1. **A test with items that will allow for valid neuropsychological predictions and good sensitivity in a teenager or young adult will often be inappropriate for use even with older children.** True or False?

2. **A test result obtained from a child may not mean the same thing as the same result obtained from an adult because**

   (a) children are less educated than adults.

   (b) children's abilities change rapidly from birth to adolescence.

   (c) children's brain organization may be different from that of adults.

   (d) all of the above.

3. **Tests used for the verbal child may be used with confidence for the preverbal child.** True or False?

4. **Translation of a test is sufficient to correct potential inaccuracies that can occur in testing bilingual individuals.** True or False?

5. **Cross-sectional data tends to underestimate differences between individuals of different ages.** True or False?

6. **Testing of elderly adults, young children, and patients with psychiatric problems is similar in that these individuals may not be able to tolerate long testing sessions.** True or False?

7. **Malingering, somatoform disorders, and factitious disorders all involve the voluntary production of symptoms.** True or False?

8. **Suboptimal effort is synonymous with malingering.** True or False?

Answers: 1. True; 2. d; 3. False; 4. False; 5. False; 6. True; 7. False; 8. False

Seven

ESSENTIALS OF REPORT WRITING

To complete a neuropsychological assessment, the information gathered and the results obtained must be interpreted and compiled in a report that summarizes and communicates this information. Overall, the final step in the assessment process has multiple purposes, including summarizing and communicating information and helping the reader understand the findings and conclusions. It is important for the neuropsychologist to work on the report as carefully as on the evaluation. The report serves to inform the referral source and other concerned parties about the patient, may be used in remediation and treatment plans, and may influence readers long after it is written. The neuropsychological report needs to contain particular information organized into separate sections. Each report needs to specify identifying information, the reason for referral, and the source or sources of historical information in the report. Background and historical information should be included, as well as a section detailing relevant behavioral observations. The report also needs to contain a complete list of the tests administered and the results obtained by the patient on each test. In addition, each report needs a summary and conclusions section followed by recommendations when necessary.

The most important principle the neuropsychological report writer must follow is that the report should be useful to the client. Reports should be written with the intended recipient in mind; they should be readable, objective, and appropriately comprehensive. Referrals may originate from many sources, including other psychologists, physicians, other health professionals, teachers, lawyers, and, in rare instances, patients. Although reports should always be written using the clearest, most succinct information possible, the use of technical terminology and level of detail should reflect who will be reading the report. In most instances, even when the intended recipient is another psychologist, the use of jargon should be avoided. To communicate effectively reports must be written clearly and in an organized fashion. Reports should contain material relevant to the questions at hand and treat the material objectively. Reports should leave out information that is not pertinent to the referral question and that does not add to understanding the findings. Statements and conclusions in a report should follow clearly from supporting data. Conclusions must follow from interpretation of the test findings in the context of the available historical information and other sources of information such as behavioral observations. The report must address the referral question and include the findings and appropriate recommendations.

The report is not the place to showcase the examiner's depth of knowledge. Reports consisting only of brilliantly justified and exquisitely detailed predictions about lesion localization and offering no usable and specific recommendations may serve either to hasten the rate of deforestation or increase the profit margins of computer disk driver manufacturers, but are unlikely to be appreciated by those responsible for taking care of patients. The data needed to support conclusions and recommendations should be presented in the report, but the level of detail and comprehensiveness of this information should reflect the setting and the referral questions being asked. An extensive report format that includes details about academic history and information about medical conditions that are not necessarily relevant to brain function might be appropriate in certain pediatric and forensic settings, but is often not appreciated in medical settings in which physicians are interested mainly in the consultant's bottom-line conclusions. In some settings the neuropsychologist may have the luxury of time or may be required to organize and present large amounts of data, as is often the case in forensic evaluations. In other cases, however, the

---

CAUTION

General Guidelines for Report Writing

- Avoid jargon and technical terms.
- Refer to the patient by name, not as "the patient."
- Write clearly and concisely.
- Avoid ambiguous terms and words with negative connotations.
- Support your conclusions.
- Use good grammar and sentence structure.
- Be objective.
- Avoid including inappropriate details.

neuropsychologist must judiciously choose to present only the most critical information to allow for rapid and timely feedback.

As we discuss in Chapter 5, the primary function of a neuropsychological assessment no longer is to decide whether an individual has brain damage or whether there is evidence of organic brain dysfunction. Although the neuropsychologist may still be expected to sort out the possible causes for changes in intellectual and other psychological functions, in many settings assessment is expected to provide practical recommendations that may assist in short- and long-term patient management and the planning of programs for rehabilitation or educational remediation.

MAXIMS FOR WRITING A NEUROPSYCHOLOGICAL REPORT

Although little scientific research addresses the topic of effective communication of technical neuropsychological information to nonneuropsychologists (e.g., Ownby, 1990, for a rare exception) the so-called art of report writing is a frequent topic in many contemporary texts concerned with neuropsychological assessment. In this section we present a series of thirteen maxims for writing a neuropsychological test report based on some of the themes that occur frequently in these writings. Rapid Reference 7.1 summarizes each of the thirteen maxims for quick reference.

1. Be sure you clearly understand the procedures for administering and scoring a neuropsychological test before using it and presenting it in a report. A neuropsychological test report that is based on inaccurately scored or interpreted tests is a potential detriment to the client and may be considered malpractice. All data and test results used in a report should be checked and scored carefully before being included in a report.

2. Avoid technical jargon and follow the rules of clear and readable writing. In almost all cases a simple common word and declarative sentence structure are more effective in communicating information accurately than the use of obscure or technical words and overly long sentences. Modifiers of the word *memory* such as *primary, anterograde, implicit, semantic,* and *episodic* have rich and specific meanings to someone with some expertise in modern neuropsy-

Rapid Reference 7.1

Maxims to Keep in Mind for Report Writing

1. Be sure you are reporting properly scored tests and accurate data.
2. Avoid technical words and jargon.
3. Keep the length of the report appropriate to the anticipated reader of the report.
4. Include relevant historical data.
5. Avoid including irrelevant historical data.
6. Describe physical appearance and behavior.
7. Name and describe the test procedures.
8. Include the test scores.
9. Provide the test scores for all tests, not just the impaired test scores.
10. Consider all the evidence when interpreting data, not just test scores.
11. Do not use each test score for lesion localization.
12. Provide useful, specific recommendations.
13. Describe any and all test modifications and their potential impact on interpretation.

chology but are likely to be misleading or meaningless to even bright and well-educated nonpsychologists. If you do not think your reader can define the term the same way you do, you should not use it. If you must use a technical term, be sure it is accompanied by a brief nontechnical definition. Using common medical terminology (e.g., coronary infarction or hypertension) is acceptable when communicating to readers who are likely to understand this language and when this information is being reported from other sources such as medical records.

3. Keep the length appropriate to the audience and purpose of the report. Weigh the advantages of comprehensiveness against the reader's need to access and use quickly the most important information in the report. Brevity is generally appreciated. Some circumstances require a complete presentation of case material, a detailed and explicit analysis of data, and a presentation of the logic used for interpretation. In most settings reports that present con-

clusions that are clear and easy to follow are more likely to be read. A recent survey of report-writing practices among neuropsychologists (Donders, 2001b) indicated that the mean length of reports by those surveyed was approximately 7 pages; a few clinicians routinely prepared reports that were only one page in length and a few routinely prepared reports of 30 pages or more. Clinicians who worked in geriatric settings and in medical settings tended to write significantly shorter reports than clinicians working in private practice or in settings that were primarily forensic or pediatric.

4. Include historical data that are relevant to the conclusions and recommendations you will make. In most cases the neuropsychological report should include descriptions of any medical history relevant to the function of the central nervous system. This includes any medications that may affect central nervous system functioning and nonneurological medical procedures that carry a possible risk of affecting brain function (e.g., cardiac surgery). It should also include any history of serious infections (e.g., pneumonia) and any history of diseases and conditions that clearly impact the central nervous system (e.g., closed head injury, stroke, epilepsy, loss of consciousness, degenerative diseases, exposure to environmental toxins, drug and alcohol use, etc.). Information concerned with establishing patterns of premorbid ability, such as educational level and vocational history, is also critical to most neuropsychological reports. Pediatric and forensic reports tend to require greater detail and documentation of this information than other kinds of reports, but all neuropsychology reports should include information about this topic.

5. Avoid presenting historical and behavioral data that are not relevant to either the referral question or to the conclusions you draw. The client's dental history, spouse's hobbies, and recent vacations, although interesting, are unlikely to be used in formulating neuropsychological interpretations. In some circumstances, however, seemingly irrelevant issues may actually be very relevant. For example, vacation history may be important in a case in which a patient has more capacity for leisure than for work; in this situation, the information may contribute to understanding the test findings.

In addition, indicate missing historical information that might have been helpful but was not available at the time of the test report. If you feel that additional (but unavailable) information might temper or support your conclusions, this should be indicated.

6. Describe physical appearance and behavior during the interview and formal examination; such information might be relevant to the referral question and the interpretation of the tests. This may include interpersonal behavior (e.g., eye contact and sense of rapport with examiner); demeanor; hygiene and physical appearance; range and appropriateness of affect; characteristics of language production and comprehension; level of attentiveness; and motivation and cooperation.

7. Name and describe the procedures to which you refer in your text. Avoid using theoretical terms and jargon as the only reference to tests, even if your audience consists of other neuropsychologists. As we discuss in Chapter 5, the construct validity of many neuropsychological tests is underdetermined or still under investigation. What may be a test of sequencing to psychologist A may be a test of attention to psychologist B or a test of working memory to psychologist C. Always refer to a test by name and by some behavioral description of the procedure (e.g., Digit Span: ability to repeat a sequence of numbers).

8. Provide actual test scores in standard form either in the text of the report or in a summary table. Be sure that you specify which norms you are using to generate the standard scores so that the reader can know the population against which you have compared the test taker. For those tests in which the norms used can vary (e.g., Boston Naming Test), it may be necessary to include the raw score as well. Reporting test scores has come to be a standard practice for neuropsychologists, according to a recent survey of report-writing practices by Donders (2001a, 2001b). Whether you consider yourself to be a traditional Halstead-Reitan expert or an acolyte of the Boston Process Approach, test scores are still the only common referent that may be used by anyone reading a report in the future, regardless of orientation. When test scores (e.g., 50th percentile) rather than labels (e.g., average range) are pro-

vided, more precise information is conveyed to the reader. Remember that the average range refers to the 25th to the 74th percentile. Stating that someone performed in the average range is insufficiently precise in many cases and labels can be subjective. Even though it should not, the description *the high end of the average range* can carry different meanings for different evaluators. Support labels with test scores.

In addition, including test scores allows the next evaluator to measure any change more precisely. *Within normal limits* extends one standard deviation above and below the mean. Consider a situation in which a patient scores at the 74th percentile on a test the first time it is taken, but the evaluator reports only that the patient scored within normal limits (a correct statement). Consider now that the patient is tested again a year or two later and now scores at the 21st percentile on the same test, also a score within normal range but very different from the first. Because the second evaluator has only the description of the patient's prior performance, he or she will not know that a possibly significant downward change may have taken place.

9. Include the scores and some description of all tests in the Test Result section of the report, not just the scores for those tests in which impairment was found. Not all the information presented needs to be repeated in the summary and conclusions.

10. Neuropsychological interpretations should make sense. The neuropsychologist must consider *all* the evidence when interpreting the data. When interpreting test results, you should think first about neuropsychologically plausible conclusions from the test data that are derived independently of other sources of data, then weigh these conclusions or predictions against all the evidence before you. Indicate what the neuropsychological, historical, medical and neuroimaging data each imply and then weigh the consistencies and inconsistencies between these data sources to draw your conclusions. Do not automatically attribute a test finding to an antecedent event or positive neuroimaging finding even if no other known etiology presents itself. The presence of a lesion on MRI or history of a head injury is not automatically causally related to your

test findings. Your evidence should fit together logically and the test results should be consistent with those expected given the assumed source. If the data cannot be plausibly reconciled with the other information, it is important to say so.

11. Test scores cannot guarantee the presence of lesions. There are few single test scores that are good predictors of the presence of a lesion in a specific location. When such predictions can be made it is because a pattern of deficits or scores is consistent with a specific focal lesion and a plausible reason exists for such a lesion to occur (e.g., nonfluent aphasia following a left middle cerebral artery stroke). If all you are doing in your report is listing a series of test scores as evidence of a series of localizations of lesions, you are not likely to be accurate. In addition, you are unlikely to be providing information that is going to help in the diagnosis of the patient and how to manage the disorder. Individuals who fail a series of neuropsychological tests are unlikely to have a series of verifiable lesions corresponding to those test scores.

12. In most cases recommendations are the most important and most neglected part of the neuropsychology report. Good recommendations should provide useful guidance to whoever is going to take care of the patient and should be based directly on the data in the report. Most neuropsychological recommendations concentrate on the cognitive and emotional strengths and weaknesses of the patient, but they may include issues related to social and self-care skills. General principles for helping patients with brain damage such as recommending the *use of structure, verbal mediation,* or a *paper memory* should be illustrated with relevant examples. In addition, these should be specifically tailored to the circumstances of the client (i.e., the classroom, nursing home, job, etc.). Recommendations should be realistic and focus on the actual resources and services that might be available. Do not recommend cognitive rehabilitation when none exists for the particular problems of the patient.

13. Be sure to indicate whether any of the tests had to be modified to accommodate a special issue such as bilingualism or even disabilities that interfered with the standard administration of a task. That

test modifications may limit the interpretation of the data should be stated clearly in the report.

ORGANIZATION OF THE REPORT

No absolutely single report is right for every evaluation, although certain basic information is contained in each report and the report does follow a certain basic outline as summarized in Rapid Reference 7.2.

1. *Identifying Information.* At the beginning of each report the writer should present information that specifically identifies the patient. This usually includes the patient's name, the patient's date of birth, the patient's age, the date(s) of testing, the date of the report, the examiner's name (if different from report writer), and perhaps the referral source.

2. *Reason for Referral.* This section should state clearly why the neuropsychological assessment was conducted and what the specific referral questions are. It may also include a summary of the symptoms and behaviors that prompted the referral. In addition, this

≡Rapid Reference 7.2

Suggested Report Outline

1. Identifying Information
2. Reason for Referral
3. Records Reviewed or Source of Historical Information
4. Relevant History and Background Information
5. Behavioral Observations
6. Tests Administered
7. Test Results
8. Summary and Impressions
9. Recommendations
10. Examiner and Report Writer Signature(s)

section should name the referral source and his or her relationship to the patient. This information establishes some boundaries for the report because it indicates who will read the report and the specific purpose of the evaluation. This information in turn limits the scope of the evaluation and the report. Who referred the patient and why defines the tests and procedures that are administered, the interpretation of the results, and the applications of the results. In this section the writer may also include the patient's chief complaints and concerns. Putting the patient's subjective report here permits a comparison between the information obtained from the referral source and that from the patient.

This section should also indicate whether the patient was informed about who requested the evaluation and the purposes of the evaluation. In addition, if the testing is being done at the request of a third party, such as the court, this section informs the reader whether the patient was instructed about the limits of confidentiality.

3. *Records Reviewed.* In this section the author should list all the sources from which background and historical information was obtained and the relevant dates of the material. It is important that the reader know from where the information in a report has come. The source of information informs the reader of the comprehensiveness and accuracy of the information and (perhaps) any bias. In some instances historical information comes solely from the patient and in other cases information also is available from relatives, caregivers, and the referral source. In forensic reports an inventory of both records reviewed and the sources of this information is especially crucial because any opinions will be based on the available facts.

4. *History and Background Information.* In this section you should report the history taken from record review, clinical interview, and the reports of others. The information reported should be relevant to the questions at hand and should include any information that will be used to support your conclusions. In this section, birth and developmental, educational, vocational, medical, social, and family history should be reported as necessary to establish a good de-

scription of the patient. This section should also include information from prior neuropsychological evaluations. Typically it is sufficient to highlight the primary findings to allow a comparison between earlier test performances and the current one.

5. *Behavioral Observations.* This part of the report should contain the information learned from observing the patient during interview and testing. Important here are observations of interpersonal behavior; demeanor; hygiene and physical appearance; range and appropriateness of affect; characteristics of language production and comprehension; level of attentiveness; and motivation and cooperation.

6. *Tests Administered.* In some form or another (list or paragraph format) all the tests and procedures administered to the patient should be provided in this section of the report. This informs the reader what particular tests were administered and what versions of those tests (e.g., WAIS-III versus WISC-III) were used.

7. *Test Results.* In this section the examiner has the opportunity to provide the specific results obtained during testing by reporting the test scores and the patient's level of performance on each test. A handy way to organize the report is by cognitive function, so that a report from a comprehensive neuropsychological examination might contain subheadings of Intellectual Functions, Attention and Executive Functions, Learning and Memory, Language Functions, and so on. This section should be organized so that the reader can easily find specific information about particular areas being measured by finding the appropriate subheading.

8. *Summary and Impressions.* This section of the report should bring together all the test findings in the context of available history and observations, providing an interpretation of the data. The pattern of strengths and weaknesses should be summarized and discussed here. The interpretation of the findings requires including the information supporting the conclusions.

9. *Recommendations.* This final section should include any treatment and case management recommendations that can be provided to guide patient care. Recommendations should be specific and clearly stated.

10. *Examiner's and Report Writer's Signatures.* This identifies for the reader who administered the tests and wrote the report and their credentials.

SAMPLE REPORT

Neuropsychological Evaluation

Name: Susan Smith   Date of Testing: 06/30/98
DOB: 08/09/63   Date of Report: 07/02/98
Age: 34 years   CONFIDENTIAL

Reason for Referral

Dr. Susan Smith is a 34-year-old, right-handed, single physician referred for neuropsychological assessment by her treating psychologist. An evaluation was requested to investigate whether any cognitive deficits correspond to Dr. Smith's subjective complaints of difficulties affecting her daily functioning in her job as a physician.

As her presenting complaint, Dr. Smith reported that despite her accomplishments, she has difficulty remembering the faces of people she has seen or met. She reported that this is not simply a matter of recognizing someone and not being able to remember a name, but rather not recognizing the face at all. She reported that this happens daily in her medical practice and can occur within an hour or two of having met someone. Dr. Smith indicated that she remembers things about the people that she has seen, including parts of faces, but it is as though she is unable to process the face itself. She also indicated that she has no difficulty recalling details about an individual's medical case, despite not recalling the individual's face. Dr. Smith reported that she is able to recognize people that resemble

---

DON'T FORGET

Information to Include in the Reason for Referral Section of the Report

- The referral source
- The referral questions
- The patient's complaints and concerns

family members and that she does eventually recognize faces after multiple repetitions. She reported having particular trouble remembering undistinguished faces. Dr. Smith reported that as a result she often avoids situations in which problems with not recognizing faces are likely, such as parties. She indicated that she tends to have more intensive one-on-one relationships rather than casual relationships. She indicated that she has no real strategies for dealing with the problem and that she is not sure if she attends well to a person's image beyond identifying characteristics such as moles and other features relevant to medicine.

Historical information in this report came from interview with Dr. Smith and from her referring psychologist. Dr. Smith appeared to be a reliable historian.

Relevant History and Background Information

Dr. Smith reported that she works in internal medicine in the Basic Care Clinic at a local hospital. She indicated that she is almost full time in this position but

DON'T FORGET

Information to Include in the Relevant History and Background Information of the Report

- Age, gender, handedness, ethnic identity
- History of presenting complaint
- Educational history
- Employment or vocational history
- Birth and early development
- Medical history
- Neurological history
- Psychiatric history
- Current and past medication(s)
- Substance abuse history
- Psychosocial history, including stressors
- Family medical, neurological, and psychiatric history
- Other relevant information gathered in interview

that she also does a considerable amount of computer work, managing a website on the Internet. She described herself as a successful investor and indicated that she loves numbers. She reported that prior to coming to her present hospital position she had moonlighted there for two years and that she had been at another local hospital before that for about six months.

Dr. Smith reported that from 4th through 12th grades, she attended a so-called elitist test school where various experimental learning programs were tried. Dr. Smith reported that she graduated from university in 1985 with a B.A. in physics and that she had attended on a full-tuition scholarship. She then earned her M.D. from the Southwest University Medical School in 1989; she did her residency and attended one year in the Emergency Room at an urban hospital in the Southwest. She described going to university as the first real break from her family. Following that, she moved to a large northeast city because she had a close friend living in the area and she began to work at a private city hospital doing home-based primary care. Unhappy with that job, however, she then worked at a large suburban medical clinic and then at the local hospital mentioned previously until she began her present position. Dr. Smith reported that she has always done well academically and she believes she has done well because she worked very hard.

Dr. Smith reported that she spends a lot of time working both at the hospital and on the Internet and that she has very few social activities outside of visiting with her closest friends for dinners and movies on the basis of about once every other month. She reported that she has taken tai chi classes, that she swims every other day, and that she used to play the piano regularly. Dr. Smith reported that her family (mother, father, and three sisters) lives in a dangerous neighborhood in another northeastern city. She reported that of her two eldest sisters, one has never married and one is about to be married. She reported that her oldest sister is a letter carrier and that her second oldest sister is a pediatrician. Her youngest sister suffers from mental retardation and has had behavioral difficulties, at least of late. She indicated that her father is a draftsman who has been unemployed since he was in his fifties because his shop closed. She also reported that he has been diagnosed with lung cancer, which he has refused to treat after receiving radiation treatment. She reported that her mother graduated from high school and worked as a waitress prior to having children. She believes her father went to about eleventh grade in school. She reported that they were very insular as a family and that her mother pushed her academically.

For purposes of confidentiality Dr. Smith's psychiatric history is only summarized briefly. Dr. Smith reported that as a youngster she witnessed considerable abuse within her family and that she has had episodes of suicidal ideation since the mid-1980s as a result. She has never been in a psychiatric hospital and took antidepressants only for a short time many years ago before discontinuing them. Dr. Smith reported her past medical history as basically unremarkable. She denied any history of head injury or loss of consciousness. She denied any known exposure to toxins and she denied any neurological symptoms or history. Dr. Smith also denied any history of alcohol or drug abuse. She does not smoke cigarettes and her consumption of caffeine is minimal. She reported being on no medications at the time of testing.

Behavioral Observations

Dr. Smith presented on time for the evaluation. She was neatly and appropriately dressed in casual attire. She was cooperative during testing and her man-

DON'T FORGET

Information to Include in the Behavioral Observation Section of the Report

- Physical appearance and grooming
- Level of alertness and arousal
- Attention span
- Level of cooperation
- Activity level
- Response to failure or success
- Response to encouragement
- Speech and discourse abilities
- Emotionality
- Appropriateness of social skills
- Sensorimotor functioning
- Thought content and processes
- Unusual habits or mannerisms

ner was pleasant. She was clearly nervous at least initially, as evidenced in some hesitation and embarrassment in discussing her difficulties. As the testing progressed she appeared to grow more comfortable and confident.

At some points during testing, it appeared that Dr. Smith did not concentrate as fully as she could; she herself seemed to note this when, for example, during administration of the K-FAST, she remarked, "Boy I'm not concentrating, am I?" Dr. Smith also reported that she found the tests to be intimidating and tried to instruct herself to relax "a little bit." Also, at some points during testing Dr. Smith appeared to have difficulties primarily because she imposed complexities on simple tasks and as a result made some tasks more difficult than intended. This was notable, for example, on the Wisconsin Card Sorting Test, in which she searched for unusual patterns; the same tendency was probably also present during Animal Naming, in which she attempted to recite animal names in alphabetical order. Dr. Smith indicated that she did not want to learn what her actual IQ was because she believes it is either low average or just average. She believes she attained what she has as a result of her hard work rather than her natural abilities.

Speech was fluent and well-articulated and no instances of word-finding difficulties occurred in spontaneous speech. Dr. Smith had no difficulties understanding test directions or the examiner's language. Because of Dr. Smith's cooperation and behavior during testing, the test findings are considered to be a reliable and valid measurement of her current level of cognitive functioning.

DON'T FORGET

Information to Include in Test Result Section of the Report

- List of tests and procedures used
- Test descriptions
- Test scores
- Test score ratings
- Summary data
- Indication of norms used
- Findings organized by domain or test-by-test basis
- Findings integrated across domains or tests

Test Results

Tests Administered

Dr. Smith was administered the following battery of tests: Wechsler Adult Intellectual Scale–Third Edition (WAIS-III); Mesulam Verbal and Nonverbal Cancellation Tests; Trail Making A & B; Stroop Neuropsychological Screening Test; Wisconsin Card Sorting Test (WCST); Controlled Oral Word Association Test (FAS); Animal Naming; Wechsler Memory Scale–Third Edition (WMS-III); Rey Complex Figure; Boston Naming Test (BNT); Reading and Spelling subtests from the Wide Range Achievement Test–Revision 3 (WRAT3); Kaufman Functional Academic Skills Test (K-FAST); and the Hooper Visual Organization Test (VOT). In addition, Dr. Smith completed the Beck Depression Inventory (BDI).

Intellectual Functions

On the WAIS-III, Dr. Smith earned a Verbal IQ in the very superior range (99th percentile) and a Performance IQ in the average range (42nd percentile). There was a statistically significant discrepancy of 38 points between Dr. Smith's VIQ and PIQ, a discrepancy that was so large as to be unusual in the normative population. As a result the Full Scale IQ that was obtained within the high average range (88th percentile) cannot be considered an accurate summary of Dr. Smith's overall level of intellectual functioning. The large discrepancy between verbal and nonverbal skills suggested uneven development of these skills relative to each other. The large discrepancy between scores in the context of fairly even developed skills within modalities also suggested that this is a longstanding finding. Dr. Smith's IQ, Index, and age-scaled subtest scores on the WAIS-III are available in the following table:

Full Scale IQ 118

Verbal IQ 135	**Performance IQ 97**
Information 17	Picture Completion 8
Vocabulary 17	Block Design 10
Similarities 14	Matrix Reason 13
Verbal Comprehension Index 136	**Perceptual Organization Index 101**
Arithmetic 13	Digit Symbol-Coding 7
Digit Span 15	Picture Arrangement 10

The large discrepancy between Dr. Smith's VIQ and PIQ was paralleled in a nearly equally large discrepancy of 35 points between her Verbal Comprehension Index (99th percentile) and her Perceptual Organization Index (53rd percentile). It should be noted that perceptual organizational skills and performance on nonverbal tests were generally within the average range and not deficient relative to normal, but simply deficient relative to Dr. Smith's very superior verbal abilities. Of Dr. Smith's verbal scaled scores, none was significantly different from her Verbal Mean of 15.17. Of the nonverbal scaled scores, none was significantly different from her Performance Mean of 9.6 with the exception of a particular strength on Matrix Reasoning (above average), a nonverbal reasoning test.

On the verbal subtests of the WAIS-III, Dr. Smith demonstrated a very superior definitional vocabulary knowledge (99th percentile) and very superior fund of general information (99th percentile). She scored in the superior range in terms of verbal abstraction (91st percentile) and in the very superior range in terms of span of apprehension with digits forward at 9 and digits backward at 7. She demonstrated above-average mental calculations (84th percentile).

On the performance subtests of the WAIS-III, Dr. Smith basically scored in the average or low average range with the exception of performance on a nonverbal reasoning test on which performance was above average (84th percentile). Performance on this particular subtest was more similar to the better performances seen on the verbal subtests than it was to the lesser performances obtained on nonverbal subtests. Dr. Smith scored in the average range (50th percentile) when logically organizing temporally-related pictures to tell a story and when constructing abstract designs using blocks. She scored in the low end of the average range (25th percentile) when identifying essential from inessential elements in incomplete pictures. She scored in the low average range (16th percentile) on a psychomotor speed test requiring the transcription of symbols.

Attention and Executive Functions

Dr. Smith was alert and oriented during testing. Performance on the Information and Orientation subtest from the WMS-III was well within normal limits; all questions were answered correctly. As noted earlier, span of apprehension was strong at 9 digits forward and 7 digits backward. Mental control of overlearned sequences, however, was only average (50th percentile). Dr. Smith's speed on this test was inconsistent, and on one instance she lost the sequence when alternating serial 6s and days of the week.

Vigilance on a letter cancellation test was intact with no omissions seen. The test was completed well within time limits, and the progression of search was organized and moved from left to right. This was also true of Dr. Smith's performance on a symbol cancellation test. In contrast, complex tracking on Trail Making A, which requires visual scanning and number sequencing, according to the Heaton et al. (1991) norms, was low within the average range relative to age and education (27th percentile). Dr. Smith made no errors here but worked more slowly than expected. Furthermore, on Trail Making B, a complex tracking test requiring alternation and sequencing between letters and numbers, Dr. Smith scored in the borderline range (5th percentile) relative to age and education. She worked relatively slowly on this task in general and slowed herself further with one error involving loss of set.

On the SNST, a test measuring self-regulatory and inhibitory skills, Dr. Smith scored in the low average range as well (8th–9th percentile) relative to age. Once again, slowed processing was apparent. In addition on the WCST, a card sorting test requiring concept formation and set flexibility, Dr. Smith scored in the low average to average range overall relative to age and education norms. She scored within normal limits in terms of categories completed (6), trials to complete the first category (11), and failures to maintain set (0). Total number of errors (21st percentile), perseverative errors (18th percentile), nonperseverative errors (21st percentile), and percent conceptual level responses (19th percentile), however, were all low average relative to age and education. Dr. Smith's difficulty here may have stemmed from the fact that once she sorted the first two most salient categories, she then attempted unusual combinations and patterns before she finally succeeded in recognizing the third category. Once she had established the correct three categories she then quickly completed the remainder of the test.

Verbal fluency was also low average relative to age and education for phonemic categories (norms in this section are from Spreen & Strauss, 1998). Dr. Smith could name only 31 FAS items in a three-minute interval, scoring at the 9th to 10th percentile. The words presented tended to be those of an articulate person with a good vocabulary but were simply too few in number. Performance actually dropped off here too across the trials with 12 words for the first two letters, but only 7 for the third letter. Performance was also worse than expected for verbal fluency for the semantic category of animals; Dr. Smith named only 16 animals in a one-minute interval. This placed her performance at the low end of the average range (25th percentile) relative to age norms and in the low average range (10th percentile) relative to age and education norms.

Learning and Memory Functions

On the WMS-III, Dr. Smith earned scores on the various Primary Indexes ranging from the borderline range (3rd percentile) to the high end of the average range (70th percentile), with most performances low average or average. Her primary index scores are contained in the following table:

Primary Indexes	Index Score	Percentile
Auditory Immediate	105	63
Visual Immediate	71	3
Immediate Memory	87	19
Auditory Delayed	108	70
Visual Delayed	81	10
Auditory Recognition Delayed	95	37
General Memory	93	32

Upon comparison of these scores to each other, a statistically significant difference is apparent between the Auditory Immediate and Visual Immediate Indexes and between the Auditory Delayed Index and the Visual Delayed Index. Both of these differences were also relatively unusual in the normative sample (4.2% and 7.9%, respectively). The direction and degree of findings parallels that seen on the WAIS-III with verbal immediate and delayed memory significantly better than visual immediate and delayed memory.

Because Dr. Smith's FSIQ is unlikely to be an accurate composite of overall ability, examination of ability versus memory differences must be made according to separate analyses of verbal and visual performances versus VIQ and PIQ, respectively. Verbal learning and memory abilities relative to predicted ability based on VIQ indicated that the difference between Verbal Immediate Index and Verbal Delayed Index and Dr. Smith's VIQ approached significance. Visual learning and memory abilities relative to predicted ability based on PIQ indicated that the differences between Dr. Smith's PIQ and Visual Immediate Index and the difference between Dr. Smith's PIQ and Visual Delayed Index were statistically significant and abnormally large. The data suggest that Dr. Smith was not learning on the WMS-III tasks as expected, especially significantly so in the area of visual learning and memory. The differences were in the direction that would be expected, given Dr. Smith's subjective complaints of difficulty recognizing faces. The problem seems to be more extensive than that, however, as is evident later.

Acquisition of prose passage information was only average (50th percentile) with performance comparable after a delay (50th percentile) and with percent retention of the information average (63rd percentile). Acquisition of verbal paired associates was above average (75th percentile) and good recall of this information was seen after a delay (84th percentile) with full retention. Recognition for auditory information after a delay was in the average range (37th percentile). Dr. Smith had an easier time recognizing word pairs from among foils than she had recognizing prose passage information. Although overall learning in the area of prose passages was less than expected, no decay or loss in memory was apparent over time.

Immediate recognition of faces was low average (16th percentile), while delayed recognition of the same faces was relatively better (37th percentile) because no information was lost over time (100% retention). Of particular note was Dr. Smith's performance on the Family Pictures subtest, in which she is shown briefly four scenes containing different family members and her task is to recall the "who, what, and where" from each scene. On this particular test immediate acquisition of information was in the borderline range (2nd percentile). No decay was seen after a delay (5th percentile), however. Incidental delayed recall of a complex design was also less than expected relative to age (norms as reported in Spreen & Strauss, 1998: 21st percentile). Dr. Smith recalled only the major outline figure and appeared to have forgotten most of the internal details.

Language Functions

As noted earlier, Dr. Smith is an articulate woman with a very good vocabulary. Basic language functions were intact to observation. Confrontation naming as measured by the BNT was within normal limits for age (norms from Spreen & Strauss, 1998: 65th percentile) with 57 of 60 items named correctly and with three additional correct responses to phonemic cues. As noted earlier in this report, however, despite Dr. Smith's good vocabulary, word list generation for words belonging to both phonemic and semantic categories was less than expected.

Reading recognition as measured by the WRAT3 was at expected levels (90th percentile) and at a post–high-school level. Spelling was also at expected levels (96th percentile) and at a post–high-school level. Functional reading skills (those required in day-to-day living) as measured by the K-FAST were very superior (98th percentile), and functional arithmetic skills were above av-

DON'T FORGET

Important Considerations for the Summary and Impressions Section of the Report

- Summarize critical history concisely
- Summarize strengths and weaknesses
- Summarize most important test findings
- Consider all sources of information
- Integrate and interpret the findings
- State or resolve inconsistencies
- Make diagnostic formulations
- Support your conclusions and diagnosis

erage (77th percentile). On this test Dr. Smith made some calculation errors that lowered her score. She herself noted that she was having a difficult time concentrating during this portion of the testing.

Visuospatial Functions

Basic visual perception was intact on object-naming and figure-copying tasks. Ability to integrate objects visually was also intact, as measured by the VOT (norm = 26 ± 5: 62nd percentile) with 27.5 of 30 items named correctly. Ability to integrate and organize visual information was also intact relative to age, as measured by copy of a complex design (norms from Spreen & Strauss, 1998: 90th percentile).

Self-Report of Mood

On the BDI, a face-valid and self-report measure of depressive symptomatology, Dr. Smith scored in the *minimal* range (5). She did not endorse a significant number or degree of depressive symptoms.

Summary and Impressions

Dr. Smith is a 34-year-old, right-handed physician referred for neuropsychological testing by her psychologist because she wished to undergo neuropsychological testing to evaluate her subjective report of difficulty remembering faces. Dr. Smith's description of her complaint suggested that the problem was longstanding and detrimental to her work. Dr. Smith's educational and medical history is unremarkable for problems, whereas her psychiatric history suggested some longstanding emotional issues centered on self-esteem and interpersonal difficulties.

Measurement of intellect at this time indicated very superior verbal skills in contrast to average nonverbal abilities. Although nonverbal abilities were generally average (a strength was apparent in nonverbal abstraction), they were deficient relative to verbal abilities, which were uniformly above average to very superior. This large discrepancy between verbal and nonverbal skills is likely to be longstanding and is probably the source of Dr. Smith's subjective complaint of difficulty remembering faces. Elementary attentional skills were intact and indicated an excellent span of apprehension and good vigilance in terms of visual scanning. In contrast, performance on tests of executive functions suggested slower-than-expected processing and a tendency to make the tests more complicated than they needed to be. Slowed processing was evident on Trail Making B, the SNST, and on verbal fluency tests. Verbal learning and memory tended to be average and mildly beneath what would be expected, given Verbal IQ. Nonverbal learning and memory, however, were clearly discrepant with expected performance at this time relative even to PIQ. While Dr. Smith tended to learn verbal information at average to above average levels, her acquisition of nonverbal information presented as faces and as visual scenes was clearly below average. No decay was seen in memory over time, indicating that what Dr. Smith learned, she retained. Basic language functions were intact, and academic achievement for reading and spelling were at expected levels given educational history. Functional reading skills were also at expected levels while functional arithmetic skills, although above average, showed some effects of inefficient concentration. Basic visual perception was intact, as were visual integrational and visual organizational skills. At the time of testing Dr. Smith did not report an unusual number or degree of depressive symptoms.

The results from Dr. Smith's neuropsychological evaluation indicated an individual with a clear, significantly and abnormally large, and probably longstanding advantage for verbal over nonverbal skills that was evident both on cognitive tests as well as on tests of learning and memory. Although she showed no evidence of impairment in basic visuospatial skills, including visual perception, visual integration, and visual organization, Dr. Smith had difficulties relative to her verbal abilities in processing and using visual detail information. She also had difficulties relative to normal in learning visual information such as faces and visual scene information.

The source of Dr. Smith's relative visual difficulties is unclear, but given that the dysfunction is apparently longstanding, it is likely to be congenital in na-

DON'T FORGET

Important Considerations for the Recommendations Section

- Practicality and viability
- Clear and understandable presentation
- Intervention goals
- Possible treatment and rehabilitation strategies
- Use of strengths and weaknesses in remediation
- Recommendations for follow-up evaluations

ture. This pattern of discrepancy with verbal abilities so much better than nonverbal abilities can be viewed as a nonverbal learning disability, a disability that is often associated with interpersonal difficulties. Such difficulties often appear to stem from difficulties in understanding the visual cues and visual information that occur during interpersonal interaction.

Recommendations

Given the likely longstanding nature of the dysfunction seen in testing, Dr. Smith would do best to develop compensatory strategies to deal with these difficulties. This examiner is not aware of any specific rehabilitation that is available to deal with these problems, but Dr. Smith would likely benefit from social skills training that helps her to understand social interaction and that allows her to be comfortable with social interaction. She might also consider developing strategies for recalling faces and visual scenes. These strategies would include specifically examining people's faces upon meeting them and noting all characteristics that she can then use verbally based mnemonic devices to retrieve. Although this strategy might never fully compensate for failing to recall the visual image, it would help her to have information available to her with which to recognize an individual later. This will require, however, that Dr. Smith actively encode such information. When meeting with a patient she might wish to record this information on her initial history and physical exam sheet, and she might wish to review the information on any subsequent meetings. Dr. Smith would also be wise to allow others to aid her in dealing with her difficulties with recognizing faces. When encountering persons she does not know, she might wish to ask a friend quietly the facts about the individuals in her visual field, thus using others to help her recognize people.

Given the suspected longstanding nature of this problem, further workup does not appear to be necessary. Should Dr. Smith discover that her abilities appear to be declining, a full neurological evaluation with repeat neuropsychological testing and imaging by MRI should be considered.

John Doe, Ph.D.
Board Certified in Clinical Neuropsychology,
American Board of Professional Psychology

🐟 TEST YOURSELF 🐟

1. **Test reports should be written like a scholarly paper with formal citations and bibliography.** True or False?

2. **All neuropsychological reports should contain complete medical histories.** True or False?

3. **The Behavioral Observations section in a report should include all but the following:**
   (a) Observations relevant to the patient's cooperation and motivation
   (b) Observations relevant to the patient's mood and affect
   (c) Observations relevant to the patient's favorite clothing designer
   (d) Observations relevant to the patient's ability to pay attention

4. **As an expert it is important in a report to include the most current theoretical terms used by experimental psychologists to describe test results.** True or False?

5. **In describing test results in a report it is important to do the following:**
   (a) Never include test scores.
   (b) Use jargon and technical terms.
   (c) Present only impaired scores.
   (d) Provide names of the tests that you are describing.

6. **It is not necessary to support your conclusions with data included in the test report.** True or False?

7. **Test reports should reflect the questions asked by the referral source.** True or False?

Answers: 1. False; 2. False; 3. c; 4. False; 5. d; 6. False; 7. True

Appendix A

A General Guide for Neuropsychological Assessment

A. PLANNING THE ASSESSMENT
    1. Obtain information about the referral question and the patient's history from the referral source.
    2. Request and review available historical information and records concerning the patient's medical, social, psychological, educational, and vocational history.
    3. Select neuropsychological tests validated for the assessment purpose. These may form a fixed or flexible battery that is brief or comprehensive or consists of a single targeted test depending on the referral question, the possible diagnosis, and the ability of the patient to cooperate or tolerate testing.

B. THE ASSESSMENT
    1. Interview the patient and, when necessary (e.g., child, patient with severe traumatic brain injury, patient with known or presumed Alzheimer's disease), the accompanying parent or caregiver to gather medical, social, psychological, educational, and vocational history.
    2. Administer the neuropsychological tests following all directions explicitly. Note any deviations from standard protocol. Adjust or revise the tests to be administered based on information obtained through interview or observation.
    3. During interview and test administration, observe and note patient behavior relevant to test interpretation (e.g., effort, anxiety, language difficulties, emotional upset).
    4. Score the tests as testing proceeds to ensure proper inquiries for each test question.

C. SCORING THE ASSESSMENT FINDINGS
    1. Finish scoring any individual responses not completed during the evaluation.

2. Tabulate raw scores and make conversions to scaled scales, standard scores, and other scores such as percentile scores. Calculate any composite scores or impairment indexes as necessary for test battery.

3. Double-check all scores to ensure proper tabulations and conversions.

4. Compare scores across tests as necessary (e.g., WAIS-III IQ scores and WMS-III Primary Index scores).

D. INTERPRETATION OF THE FINDINGS FROM ASSESSMENT

1. *Stage One:* Setting the stage for interpretation—base rates or prevalence of likely conditions.

   a. What was the referral question? What was the purpose of the assessment (e.g., rehabilitation, diagnosis, overall global assessment of functioning)?

   b. What is the likelihood that the patient has cognitive impairment given the referral source and history? Consider the base rate or prevalence of brain dysfunction given the referral source (e.g., acute hospital ward, workmen's compensation, school psychologist) and the patient's history (e.g., cardiovascular accident, closed head injury with no loss of consciousness, severe academic difficulties, native language).

   c. Do the behavioral observations provide information about the possible source of or contribution to any impairment found (e.g., sleepiness, distractibility, suboptimal effort, thought disorder, word finding difficulties, poor comprehension)?

   d. What factors other than brain damage could have impacted the patient's performance (e.g., age, education, motivation, effort, anxiety, cultural background, psychiatric difficulties)?

2. *Stage Two:* Determining premorbid level of function.

   a. What premorbid level of functioning do the patient's educational and vocational achievements suggest?

   b. What premorbid level of function does performance on hold tests (e.g., WAIS-III Vocabulary) suggest?

   c. What premorbid level of function does performance on tests requiring reading of irregular words (e.g., NART or WTAR) suggest?

   d. What premorbid level of function does the Barona et al. IQ demographic formula estimate?

3. *Stage Three:* Determining whether evidence of brain damage or dysfunction is present.
   a. Was the patient sufficiently attentive, cooperative, and effortful so that the test results are likely to be a reliable and a valid reflection of their optimal current performance?
   b. If specific tests of motivation and compliance (e.g., TOMM, VIP) were administered, did the patient's performance suggest suboptimal effort or symptom exaggeration that could diminish the reliability and validity of the test results?
   c. Were any factors such as culture or primary language different from those of the standardized tests used? Could these have affected test performance and reduced the validity of the tests to measure the functions for which they were designed and to predict the presence of the conditions in question?
   d. Was there evidence of a psychiatric disorder that could account for some (or all) of any findings?
   e. Do the test scores fall in a range for normal individuals similar to the patient in terms of age and education?
   f. Are the test scores in the range that would be expected from the patient's specific educational and vocational achievements?
   g. How discrepant are the results from the expected findings? In other words, what do the results suggest about the degree of deficit: mild, moderate, or severe?
   h. Do the results provide consistent evidence of a deficit in one or more cognitive domains?
   i. Are the results consistent in both type and degree with those expected, given the referral question and suspected etiology?
4. *Stage Four:* Making inferences about brain damage or dysfunction.
   a. Does the pattern of deficits suggest that the deficits are relatively isolated with a clear-cut pattern of strengths and weaknesses (e.g., memory versus perception or language)?
   b. Do the deficits fall into one of the classic neurobehavioral categories (e.g., aphasia, agnosia, apraxia, neglect, alexia, or amnesia)?
   c. Do the deficits suggest a generalized pattern of deficits affecting many cognitive domains, including IQ?

    d. Does the history of the symptoms suggest an etiology with focal (e.g., single incident stroke), multifocal (e.g., closed head injury), or diffuse (e.g., toxic and metabolic disease) impact on the brain?

    e. Does the history suggest a slow (e.g., neoplasm) or sudden (e.g., cardiovascular accident) onset or a longstanding problem (e.g., mental retardation)?

    f. Does the progression of symptoms and deficits follow a particular etiology? In other words, was the deterioration gradual and consistent suggesting disorders such as Alzheimer's Disease or Parkinson's Disease, or was the deterioration irregular and inconsistent suggesting disorders such as multiple sclerosis?

E. COMMUNICATING THE FINDINGS FROM THE ASSESSMENT

    1. Write a report that contains the referral information, relevant history, behavioral observations, tests administered, test results, interpretation, and recommendations.

    2. Communicate results to the referral source and, if appropriate, have feedback session with patient.

Appendix B

Essentials of the Neurobehavioral Syndromes

In this brief Appendix we provide the reader with a list of some of the main clinical phenomena that lie at the center of many neuropsychological referrals. An understanding of these and similar syndromes is critical to the development of skills in neuropsychological assessment. Because this text focuses primarily on the procedures and logic of the clinical assessment of brain-behavior relationships, it presents little of the clinical phenomenology of clinical neuropsychology and neurology and does not contain a presentation of anatomy and neuropathology. An even cursory examination of these areas would be far beyond the scope of this volume. In Chapter 2 we review the important areas that form the basis of the clinician's basic material knowledge, and in the annotated bibliography we provide a listing of texts and journals that can be used to access this scientific substance of clinical neuropsychology. Appendix B is provided only to help orient the reader to the kinds of specific syndromes that may occur in isolation as a result of specific brain lesions. Some information about typical causative lesions is provided with many of these examples. Readers should familiarize themselves with basic neuroanatomy to understand the terminology used for this purpose. Where relevant we present the names of the syndromes using the Greek prefix *a* to mean *without* to refer to disorders of specific functions rather than the Latin prefix *dys* meaning *impaired*. Both are used in the literature, but the form used in this book is the form most often used in the United States.

Acalculia. Acalculia refers to a number of different disorders affecting a patient's ability to perform calculations. The problem may be secondary to a loss of comprehension of written symbols (i.e., *alexia* for numerals) or to difficulties using the spatial information needed to align correctly the columns in written arithmetic problems. Acalculia may also be caused by an inability to recall or use arithmetic facts or to a primary loss of conceptual arithmetic knowledge. Acalculia may occur with any lesion of the left cerebral hemisphere that produces aphasia, but is most likely to be associated with lesions of the posterior temporal or parietal region.

Agnosia. Agnosia refers to a series of disorders that cannot be explained by primary sensory loss and that involve the loss of recognition of previously learned information. Agnosia may occur in any sensory modality (e.g., visual or auditory) and may involve specific kinds of material (e.g., prosopagnosia for faces). Agnosia rarely occurs in isolation of other limitations in cognition, but may do so in the presence of highly specific lesions. Agnosia is usually caused by a lesion to the primary sensory area of the affected modality and is more likely to occur with bilateral rather than unilateral lesions.

Agraphia. Agraphia is an acquired disorder of writing. In rare instances agraphia may occur in relative isolation, but it is usually seen as part of a general disorder of language. Patients may lose the mechanics of writing, the ability to spell, or they may not be able to write because of a loss of understanding of the written symbol (i.e., alexia). An agraphia is most likely to occur with a lesion in the left cerebral hemisphere, particularly in the areas of the frontal, parietal, and temporal lobe surrounding the Sylvian fissure.

Alexia. Alexia is an acquired reading disorder that may occur in isolation, but is most commonly seen accompanying symptoms of aphasia. Several subtypes of alexia exist, including pure alexia, where patients can read single letters but not words, and deep dyslexia, in which patients make numerous syntactic and semantic errors. Pure alexia is most likely the result of a lesion in the occipital/temporal area of the left hemisphere, whereas deep dyslexia is most likely the result of a lesion that includes Broca's area of the left hemisphere (see *aphasia*). The term *dyslexia* is typically used to refer to developmental disorders of reading.

Amnesia. This classic acquired disorder of memory is characterized by an inability to retain new information. Patients with amnesia are still alert and may be capable of recalling information that was learned before the onset of the disorder. *Anterograde amnesia* refers to an inability to learn or recall information that has been presented since the injury, and *retrograde amnesia* refers to an inability to recall information that was known before the injury. Some patients have attention or retrieval difficulties that may impact memory performance significantly. These disorders are considered distinct from true amnesia. Many patients with amnesia may show a remarkable ability to learn practiced motor skills and may show evidence of perceptual learning. A lesion affecting the hippocampus or the adjacent structures of the medial temporal lobes is considered critical for the presentation of the disorder, although lesions in such structures as the anterior thalamus, fornix, mammillary bodies, and amygdala may also be important.

Aphasia. Aphasia is an acquired language disorder that is typically characterized by word-finding difficulties and word errors. Some aphasias are characterized by fluent speech lacking meaningful nouns and verbs with varying degrees of word substitution errors or *paraphasias* (e.g., semantic = cat for dog; phonemic = rog for dog). These patients may use stock phrases (e.g., "I'm fine, thank you"), common or overlearned expressions (e.g., "You know how it is"), and circumlocutions (e.g., "The thing you eat with") without being able to express specific ideas with language. *Fluent aphasias* are often accompanied by poor comprehension of written and auditory language. In its mildest form fluent aphasia may appear as word-finding difficulties or *anomia*.

Other aphasias are characterized by effortful, sparse speech emphasizing nouns, pronouns, and some common verbs but lacking in sentence structure. These patients may also make paraphasic errors, typically of the phonemic variety, and may also make gross violations of the conventions of word order and sentence structure (e.g., "There I" for "I went there"). Patients with *nonfluent aphasias* typically appear to have much better comprehension of auditory and written language than patients with fluent aphasias, but may nevertheless misinterpret longer or complex sentences.

Many aphasias affect all language-related response systems, including abilities to repeat, to read, and to write. In some cases these response systems may be selectively impaired or preserved, depending on the specific localization of the causative lesion. Some of the classic syndromes of aphasia include *Broca's aphasia* (nonfluent; poor repetition, reading, and writing, but relatively preserved comprehension), *Wernicke's aphasia* (fluent; empty speech with varying degrees of paraphasic errors and poor comprehension, repetition, reading, and writing). Some patients with aphasias fit into these categories but show relatively preserved repetition ability. These patients are classically referred to as having *transcortical aphasias* and may be fluent or nonfluent. Some patients with aphasia may repeat more poorly than would be suspected from their spontaneous speech. These patients are classically classified as having *conduction aphasia*. Aphasia is most often a disorder of the left cerebral hemisphere (in most right-handed and a significant number of left-handed adults). Patients with nonfluent aphasia tend to suffer from lesions affecting the frontal and sometimes anterior parietal lobes, whereas patients with fluent aphasia tend to suffer from lesions affecting the temporal and inferior parietal lobes. Small variations in lesion location can make a large difference in clinical presentation of aphasia.

Apraxia. Apraxia is loss of the ability to perform previously known movements both voluntarily or to command. Although this term is sometimes used to describe disorders that may reflect attention or sensory problems (e.g., *dressing apraxia, constructional apraxia,* or *optic apraxia*), it is usually considered to be a disorder related to the highest level of motor programming that is not due to primary muscle weakness or spasticity. Classic forms of apraxia include *ideational apraxia,* in which patients have difficulty executing organized sequences of movements (e.g., washing dishes or cooking) and *ideomotor apraxia,* in which patients cannot perform gestures to command (e.g., show me how you comb your hair). Sometimes patients with ideomotor apraxia are able to produce the general limb movement without the detailed hand or finger positioning needed to produce the required gesture correctly (e.g., the patient may use a hand as comb when asked to show how to comb hair). This phenomenon is known as *body part as object.* Motor apraxic symptoms are more likely to be caused by lesions to the left hemisphere and often accompany aphasic symptoms.

Delirium or Confusional State. This is a disturbance of the ability to maintain basic attention and a consistent stream of thought. It may be accompanied by difficulties with wakefulness or in some cases by hypervigilance. Delirium usually reflects a widespread central nervous system impairment that may be caused by an infection, toxic or metabolic disturbance, or any brain disease causing significant disruption of central nervous system functioning. Delirium may have an acute onset and be time limited or may have a slow onset and chronic course, depending on the causative illness (e.g., central nervous system infection versus dementia, respectively).

Dementia. Dementia refers to a set of disorders characterized by a progressive decline in cognitive functions. Patients with dementia usually suffer from a loss of multiple functions that may include language, perception, and executive functions (see Dysexecutive Syndrome), but must also have a disorder of memory to receive the diagnosis. The most common illness producing dementia is *Alzheimer's disease.* Other illnesses such as *vascular dementia* and *Pick's disease* may present initially with difficulties with executive functions or language and then later progress to a memory disorder. Illnesses producing dementia are more prevalent in older adults, becoming increasingly common in the seventh decade of life and later.

Dysexecutive Syndrome. Although not a classical syndrome, disorders of what are termed *executive functions* have been increasingly recognized in recent years. Executive functions refer to a variety of abilities ranging from the mental maintenance and manipulation of information (i.e., working memory) and the initiation and termination or inhibition of behavioral responses to such high-level functions as planning and social judgment. A number of different clinical manifestations of dysexecutive disorders occur, ranging from patients who appear inert with diminished spontaneous behavior, to patients who appear to act out in socially inappropriate manners with sexual or aggressive behavior, and to patients who appear to be sufficiently disorganized with disrupted work and daily activities. Dysexecutive syndromes are often attributed to lesions of the frontal lobe, but they vary considerably depending on the exact localization within this large cortical structure. Clinicians must be particularly cautious in relating dysexecutive behavior to a specific lesion, however, because these disorders may appear as a result of lesions to other cortical and subcortical structures or may be related to psychiatric illness.

Hemianopsia. This is a primary visual disorder affecting one visual field. Hemianopsia or hemianopia usually results from a visual system lesion that occurs in the optic tract beyond the optic chiasm or in the occipital cortex itself. Hemianopsia is equivalent to blindness affecting a visual field rather than an eye.

Hemispatial Neglect. This is an acquired disorder wherein despite normal sensory function, patients fail to acknowledge or respond to information that is present on one side of space. Neglect is considered a disorder of attention rather than sensation and affects the side of space on the side of the patient's body opposite that of the causative lesion. Neglect is most likely to occur and is most severe with a lesion of the right cerebral hemisphere rather than the left cerebral hemisphere. Neglect may result from lesions to many different brain structures, including the frontal and temporal lobes, but is most severe and enduring with lesions in the area of the parietal lobes.

References

Adams, K. M., & Rourke, B. P. (Eds.). (1992). *The TCN guide to professional practice in clinical neuropsychology*. Amsterdam: Swets & Zeitlinger.

Adams, W., & Sheslow, D. (1990). *Wide Range Assessment of Memory and Learning*. Delaware: Wide Range.

Adams, W., & Sheslow, D. (1995). *Wide Range Assessment of Visual Motor Ability*. Delaware: Wide Range.

Allen, L. M., Conder, R. L., Jr., Green, P., & Cox, D. R. (2000). *Computerized Assessment of Response Bias*. Durham, NC: Cognisyst.

American Board of Professional Neuropsychology. (2000). *Goals and objectives of ABPN*. Retrieved September 22, 2000, from www.abpn.net/abpn-goals.htm.

American Psychological Association. (1992). Ethical principles of psychologists and code of conduct. *American Psychologist, 47*(12), 1597–1611.

American Psychiatric Association. (2000). *Diagnostic and Statistical Manual of Mental Disorders, Fourth Edition, Text Revision*. Washington, DC: American Psychiatric Association.

Anderson, J. A. (1995). *An introduction to neural networks*. Cambridge, MA: MIT Press.

Ardila, A., Rosselli, M., & Puente, A. E. (1994). *Neuropsychological evaluation of the Spanish speaker*. New York: Plenum Press.

Baddeley, A., Emslie, H., & Nimmo-Smith, I. (1992). *The Speed and Capacity of Language-Processing Test*. Suffolk, England: Thames Valley Test Company.

Barona, A., Reynolds, C. R., & Chastain, R. (1984). A demographically based index of pre-morbid intelligence for the WAIS-R. *Journal of Consulting and Clinical Psychology, 52,* 885–887.

Beck, A. T., & Steer, R. A. (1993). *Beck Anxiety Inventory*. San Antonio, TX: Psychological Corporation.

Beck, A. T., Steer, R. A., & Brown, G. (1996). *Beck Depression Inventory–II*. San Antonio: Psychological Corporation.

Beck, J. S., Beck, A. T., & Jolly, J. (2001). *Beck Youth Inventories*. San Antonio, TX: Psychological Corporation.

Beery, K. E., & Buktenica, N. A. (1997). *The Beery-Buktenica Developmental Test of Visual-Motor Integration*. Parsippany, NJ: Modern Curriculum Press.

Belar, C. D., & Perry, N. W. (1992). National conference on scientist-practitioner education and training for the professional practice of psychology. *American Psychologist, 44,* 60–65.

Benton, A., & Adams, K. M. (2000). *Exploring the history of neuropsychology: Selected papers*. New York: Oxford University Press.

Benton, A. L., Sivan, A. B., deS. Hamsher, K., Varney, N. R., & Spreen O. (1994). *Contributions to neuropsychological assessment* (2nd ed.). New York: Oxford University Press.

Binder, L. M. (1993). An abbreviated version of the Portland Digit Recognition Test. *The Clinical Neuropsychologist, 7,* 104–107.

Bihrle, A. M., Bellugi, U., Delis, D., & Marks, S. (1989). Seeing either the forest or the trees: Dissociation in visuospatial processing. *Brain and Cognition, 11*(1), 37–49.

Blair, J. R., & Spreen, O. (1989). Predicting premorbid IQ: A revision of the National Adult Reading Test. *The Clinical Neuropsychologist, 3,* 129–136.

Boll, T. (1993). *Children's Category Test.* San Antonio, TX: Psychological Corporation.

Brady, C. B., Spiro, A., McGlinchey-Berroth, R., Milberg, W., & Gaziano, M. (2001). Stroke risk predicts verbal fluency decline in healthy older men: Evidence from the Normative Aging Study. *Journal of Gerontology: Psychological Sciences, 56B,* 340–346.

Brandt, J. (1992). Detecting amnesia's impostors. In L. R. Squire & N. Butters (Eds.), *Neuropsychology of memory* (2nd ed., pp. 156–165). New York: Guilford Press.

Briere, J. (1995). *Trauma Symptom Inventory: Professional Manual.* Odessa, FL: Psychological Assessment Resources.

Briere, J. (1996). *Trauma Symptom Checklist for Children: Professional Manual.* Odessa, FL: Psychological Assessment Resources.

Brink, T. L., Yesavage, J. A., Lum, O., Heersema, P. H., Adey, M., & Rose, T. L. (1982). Screening tests for geriatric depression. *Clinical Gerontologist, 1,* 37–43.

Brown, J. I., Fishco, V. V., & Hanna, G. S. (1993). *Nelson-Denny Reading Test.* Itasca, IL: Riverside.

Brown, L., Sherbenou, R. J., & Johnson, S. K. (1997). *Test of Nonverbal Intelligence–III.* Austin, Texas: PRO-ED.

Brownell, R. (2000a). *Expressive One-Word Picture Vocabulary Test.* Novato, CA: Academic Therapy.

Brownell, R. (2000b). *Receptive One-Word Picture Vocabulary Test.* Novato, CA: Academic Therapy.

Buschke, H. (1973). Selective reminding for analysis of memory and learning. *Journal of Verbal Learning and Verbal Behavior, 12,* 543–550.

Butcher, J. N., Dahlstrom, W. G., Graham, J. R., Tellegen, A. M., & Kaemmer, B. (1989). *MMPI-2: Manual for administration and scoring.* Minneapolis, MN: University of Minnesota Press.

Butcher, J. N., Williams, C. L., Graham, J. R., Archer, R. P., Tellegen, A., Ben-Porath, Y. S., & Kaemmer, B. (1992). *MMPI-A: Manual for administration, scoring, and interpretation.* Minneapolis, MN: University of Minnesota Press.

Byrd, P. B. (1987). *Intermediate Booklet Category Test.* Odessa, FL: Psychological Assessment Resources.

Cegalis, J. A., Bowlen, J., & Cegalis, S. (1996). *Vigil Continuous Performance Test.* San Antonio, TX: Psychological Corporation.

Churchland, P. M. (1989). *A neurocomputational perspective.* Cambridge, MA: MIT Press.

Cohen, M. (1997). *Children's Memory Scale.* San Antonio, TX: Psychological Corporation.

Colarusso, R. P., & Hammill, D. D. (1996). *Motor-Free Visual Perception Test–Revised.* Novato, CA: Academic Therapy.

Connors, C. K. (1997). *Connors' Rating Scales–Revised: Technical Manual.* Toronto, Canada: Multi-Health Systems.

Connors, C. K., & Multi-Health Systems Staff. (2000). *Connors' Continuous Performance Test II*. Toronto, Canada: Multi-Health Systems.

Cripe, L. I. (2000). Listing of training programs in clinical neuropsychology, 2000. *The Clinical Neuropsychologist, 14*(3), 357–448.

Crocker, L., & Algina, J. (1986). *Introduction to classical and modern test theory*. Fort Worth, TX: Holt, Rinehart and Winston.

Cummings, J. L., & Coffey, C. E. (2000). Geriatric neuropsychiatry. In C. E. Coffey & J. L. Cummings (Eds.), *Textbook of geriatric neuropsychiatry* (2nd ed., pp. 3–15). Washington, DC: APA Press.

Damasio, A. R. (1995). *Descartes' error: Emotion, reason, and the human brain*. New York: Avon Books.

Dana, R. H. (1993). *Multicultural assessment perspectives for professional psychology*. Boston: Allyn and Bacon.

DeFilippis, N. A., & McCampbell, E. (1991). *Manual for the Booklet Category Test*. Odessa, FL: Psychological Assessment Resources.

Delis, D. C., Filoteo, J. V., Massman, P. J., Kaplan, E., & Kramer, J. H. (1994). The clinical assessment of memory disorders. In L. S. Cermak (Ed.), *Neuropsychological explorations of memory and cognition: Essays in honor of Nelson Butters* (pp. 223–239). New York: Plenum Press.

Delis, D. C., Kramer, J. H., Kaplan, E., & Ober, B. A. (1987). *California Verbal Learning Test–Adult Version*. San Antonio, TX: Psychological Corporation.

Delis, D. C., Kramer, J. H., Kaplan, E., & Ober, B. A. (1994). *California Verbal Learning Test–Children's Version*. San Antonio, TX: Psychological Corporation.

Delis, D. C., Kramer, J. H., Kaplan, E., & Ober, B. A. (2000). *California Verbal Learning Test–Second Edition*. San Antonio, TX: Psychological Corporation.

De Renzi, E., & Vignolo, L. (1962). The Token Test: A sensitive test to detect receptive disturbances in aphasics. *Brain, 85,* 665–678.

Division 40. (1989). Definition of a clinical neuropsychologist. *The Clinical Neuropsychologist, 3*(1), 22.

Donders, J. (2001a). A survey of report writing by neuropsychologists: I. General characteristics and content. *The Clinical Neuropsychologist, 15*(2), 137–149.

Donders, J. (2001b). A survey of report writing by neuropsychologists: II. Test data, report format, and document length. *The Clinical Neuropsychologist, 15*(2), 150–161.

Dunn, L. M., & Dunn, E. S. (1997). *Peabody Picture Vocabulary Test–Third Edition*. Circle Pines, MN: Academic Guidance Service.

Faust, D., Hart, K., & Guilmette, T. J. (1988). Pediatric malingering: The capacity of children to fake believable deficits on neuropsychological testing. *Journal of Consulting and Clinical Psychology, 56,* 578–582.

Finger, S., & Stein, D. G. (1982). *Brain damage and recovery: Research and clinical perspectives*. New York: Academic Press.

Flourens, P. (1960). Recherches Expérimentales sur les Propriétés et les Fonction du Système Nerveux dans les Animaux Vertébrés. Paris: Crevot. Translated and reprinted in G. von Bonin (Ed.), *Some papers on the cerebral cortex*. Springfield, IL: Thomas. (Original work published 1824)

Fodor, J. A. (1983). *The modularity of mind: An essay on faculty psychology*. Cambridge, MA: MIT Press.

Folstein, M. F., Folstein, S. E., & McHugh, P. R. (1975). "Mini-mental State": A practical method for grading the cognitive state of patients for the clinician. *Journal of Psychiatric Research, 12,* 189–198.

Frederick, R. I. (1997). *Validity Indicator Profile.* Minneapolis, MN: National Computer Systems.

Freedman, M., Leach, L., Kaplan, E., Winocur, G., Shulman, K. I., & Delis, D. C. (1994). *Clock drawing: A neuropsychological analysis.* New York: Oxford University Press.

Gall, F. (1835). *On the functions of the brain and each of its parts: With observations on determining the instincts, propensities, and talents, or the moral and intellectual dispositions of men and animals, by the configuration of the brain and head* (Vol. 3; W. Lewis Jr., Trans.). Boston: Marsh, Capen and Lyon.

Gardner, M. F. (1996). *Test of Visual-Perceptual Skills (Non-motor): Revised.* Burlingame, CA: Psychological and Educational Publications.

Gilliam, J. E. (1995). *Attention-Deficit/Hyperactivity Disorder Test: Examiner's manual.* Austin, TX: PRO-ED.

Golden, C. J. (1978). *Stroop Color and Word Test.* Chicago, IL: Stoelting.

Golden, C. J., Hammeke, T. A., & Purisch, A. D. (1978). Diagnostic validity of a standardized neuropsychological battery derived from Luria's neuropsychological tests. *Journal of Consulting and Clinical Psychology, 46,* 1258–1265.

Golden, C. J., Purisch, A. D., & Hammeke, T. A. (1985). *Manual for the Luria-Nebraska Neuropsychological Battery: Forms I and II.* Los Angeles: Western Psychological Services.

Goldstein, K. (1939). *The organism.* New York: American Book Company.

Goodglass, H., & Kaplan, E. (1983). *The assessment of aphasia and related disorders* (2nd ed.). Philadelphia: Lea & Febiger.

Goodglass, H., Kaplan, E., & Barresi, B. (2000). *Boston Diagnostic Aphasia Examination* (3rd ed.). Philadelphia: Lea & Febiger.

Grant, D. A., & Berg, E. A. (1993). *Wisconsin Card Sorting Test.* Odessa, FL: Psychological Assessment Resources.

Green, P., Allen, L. M., & Astner, K. (2000). *Word Memory Test.* Durham, NC: Cognisyst.

Greiffenstein, M. F., Baker, W. J., & Gola, T. (1996). Comparison of multiple scoring methods for Rey's malingered amnesia measures. *Archives of Clinical Neuropsychology, 11,* 283–293.

Gronwall, D. M. A. (1977). Paced Auditory Serial-Addition Task: A measure of recovery from concussion. *Perceptual and Motor Skills, 44,* 367–373.

Gronwall, D. M. A., & Sampson, H. (1974). *The psychological effects of concussion.* New Zealand: Auckland University Press.

Groth-Marnat, G. (Ed.). (2000). *Neuropsychological assessment in clinical practice: A guide to test interpretation and integration.* New York: Wiley.

Halstead, W. C. (1947). *Brain and intelligence.* Chicago: University of Chicago Press.

Hammill, D. D., Pearson, N. A., & Wiederholt, J. L. (1997). *Comprehensive Test of Nonverbal Intelligence.* Austin, TX: PRO-ED.

Hannay, H. J., Bieliauskas, L., Crosson, B. A., Hammeke, T. A., deS. Hamsher, K., & Koffler, S. (Eds.). (1998). Proceedings of the Houston Conference on Specialty Training in Clinical Neuropsychology, September 3–7, 1997. *Archives of Clinical Neuropsychology, 13*(2), 157–249.

Hannay, H. J., & Levin, H. S. (1985). Selective reminding: An examination of the equivalence of four forms. *Journal of Clinical and Experimental Neuropsychology, 7,* 251–263.

Harrison, P. L., & Oakland, T. (2000). *Adaptive Behavior Assessment System: Manual.* San Antonio, TX: Psychological Corporation.

Heaton, R. K., Grant, I., & Matthews, C. G. (1991). *Comprehensive norms for an Expanded Halstead-Reitan Battery: Demographic corrections, research findings, and clinical applications.* Odessa, FL: Psychological Assessment Resources.

Hiscock, M., & Hiscock, C. K. (1989). Refining the forced-choice method for the detection of malingering. *Journal of Clinical and Experimental Neuropsychology, 11,* 967–974.

Hooper, H. E. (1958). *The Hooper Visual Organization Test.* Beverly Hills, CA: Western Psychological Services.

Hsieh, S. L. J., & Tori, C. D. (1993). Neuropsychological and cognitive effects of Chinese-language instruction. *Perceptual and Motor Skills, 77,* 1071–1081.

Ivnik, R. J., Haaland, K. Y., & Bieliauskas, L. A. (2000). The American Board of Clinical Neuropsychology (ABCN), 2000 update. *The Clinical Neuropsychologist, 14*(3), 261–268.

Jackson, J. H. (1894). The factors of insanities. *Medical Press and Circular, 2,* 615–619.

Joint Committee on Standards for Educational and Psychological Testing of the American Educational Research Association, the American Psychological Association, and the National Council on Measurement in Education. (1999). *Standards for educational and psychological testing.* Washington, DC: American Educational Research Association.

Joy, S., Fein, D., Kaplan, E., & Morris, F. (2001). Quantifying qualitative features of Block Design performance among healthy older adults. *Archives of Clinical Neuropsychology, 16*(2), 157–170.

Kaplan, E., Fein, D., Morris, R., & Delis, D. C. (1991). *WAIS-R NI for use with WAIS-R manual.* San Antonio, TX: Psychological Corporation.

Kaplan, E. F., Goodglass, H., & Weintraub, S. (1983). *The Boston Naming Test–Second Edition.* Philadelphia: Lea & Febiger.

Kaufman, A. S. (1994). *Intelligent testing with the WISC-III.* New York: Wiley.

Kaufman, A. S., & Kaufman, N. L. (1983). *Kaufman Assessment Battery for Children.* Circle Pines, MN: American Guidance Service.

Kaufman, A. S., & Kaufman, N. L. (1985). *Kaufman Test of Educational Achievement.* Circle Pines, MN: American Guidance Service.

Kaufman, A. S., & Kaufman, N. L. (1990). *Kaufman Brief Intelligence Test.* Circle Pines, MN: American Guidance Service.

Kaufman, A. S., & Kaufman, N. L. (1993a). *Kaufman Adolescent and Adult Intelligence Test.* Circle Pines, MN: American Guidance Service.

Kaufman, A. S., & Kaufman, N. L. (1993b). *Kaufman Survey of Early Academic and Language Skills.* Circle Pines, MN: American Guidance Service.

Kaufman, A. S., & Kaufman, N. L. (1994). *Kaufman Functional Academic Skills Test.* Circle Pines, MN: American Guidance Service.

Kaufman, A. S., & Kaufman, N. L. (1998). *Kaufman Test of Educational Achievement–Normative Update.* Circle Pines, MN: American Guidance Service.

Kaufman, A. S., & Lichtenberger, E. O. (1999). *Essentials of WAIS-III Assessment.* New York: Wiley.

Kaufman, A. S., & Lichtenberger, E. O. (2000). *Essentials of WISC-III and WPPSI-R Assessment*. New York: Wiley.

Keith, R. W. (1994). *Examiner's manual for the auditory Continuous Performance Test*. San Antonio, TX: Psychological Corporation.

Kemp, S., Kirk, U., & Korkman, M. (2001). *Essentials of NEPSY Assessment*. New York: Wiley.

Kertesz, A. (1982). *Western Aphasia Battery*. San Antonio, TX: Psychological Corporation.

Kiernan, R. J., Mueller, J., Langston, J. W., & Van Dyke, C. (1987). The Neurobehavioral Cognitive Status Examination: A brief but differentiated approach to cognitive assessment. *Annals of Internal Medicine, 107,* 481–485.

Korkman, M., Kirk, U., & Kemp, S. (1997). *NEPSY: A developmental neuropsychological assessment*. San Antonio, TX: Psychological Corporation.

Kovacs, M. (1992). *Children's Depression Inventory: Manual*. New York: Multi-Health Systems.

Kraemer, H. C. (1992). *Evaluating medical tests: Objective and quantitative guidelines*. Newbury Park, CA: Sage.

Lashley, K. S. (1929). *Brain mechanisms and intelligence*. Chicago: University of Chicago Press.

Lewis, R. F. (1995). *Professional user's guide for the Digit Vigilance Test*. Odessa, FL: Professional Assessment Resources.

Lezak, M. D. (1983). *Neuropsychological assessment*. New York: Oxford University Press.

Lezak, M. D. (1995). *Neuropsychological assessment* (3rd ed.). New York: Oxford University Press.

Libon, D. J., Mattson, R. E., Glosser, G., Kaplan, E., Malamut, B. M., Sands, L. P., Swenson, R., & Cloud, B. (1996). A nine-word dementia version of the California Verbal Learning Test. *The Clinical Neuropsychologist, 10,* 237–244.

Luria, A. R. (1973). *The working brain: An introduction to neuropsychology*. New York: Basic Books.

Luria, A. R. (1966). *Higher cortical functions in man*. New York: Basic Books.

Malmgren, R. (2000). Epidemiology of aging. In C. E. Coffey & J. L. Cummings (Eds.), *Textbook of geriatric neuropsychiatry* (2nd ed., 17–31). Washington, DC: APA Press.

Matarazzo, J. D. (1972). *Wechsler's measurement and appraisal of adult intelligence* (5th ed.). Baltimore: Williams & Wilkins.

Mattis, S. (1988). *Dementia Rating Scale: Professional manual*. Odessa, FL: Psychological Assessment Resources.

McCaffrey, R. J., Fisher, J. M., Gold, B. A., & Lynch, J. K. (1996). Presence of third parties during neuropsychological evaluations: Who is evaluating whom? *The Clinical Neuropsychologist, 10*(4), 435–449.

McCaffrey, R. J., Williams, A. D., Fisher, J. M., & Laing, L. C. (1997). *The practice of forensic neuropsychology: Meeting challenges in the courtroom*. New York: Plenum Press.

McKhann, G. (1984). Criteria for the clinical diagnosis of Alzheimer's disease: Excerpts from the NINCDS-ADRDA work group report. *Neurology, 34,* 939.

McGlinchey-Berroth, R., Bullis D. P., Milberg, W. P., Verfaellie, M., Alexander, M., & D'Esposito, M. (1996). Assessment of neglect reveals dissociable behavioral but not neuroanatomical subtypes. *Journal of the International Neuropsychological Society, 2,* 441–451.

Meehl, P. E., & Rosen, A. (1955). Antecedent probability and the efficiency of psychometric signs, patterns, or cutting scores. In D. N. Jackson & S. Messick (Eds.), *Problems in human assessment* (pp. 392–412). New York: McGraw-Hill.

Meier, M. J. (1998). On the emergence of clinical neuropsychology as a specialty. *Division 40 Newsletter 4* (spring), 7–8.

Mesulam, M. M. (1985). *Principles of behavioral neurology.* Philadelphia: Davis.

Meyers, J. E., & Meyers, K. R. (1995). *Rey Complex Figure Test and Recognition Trial.* Odessa, FL: Psychological Assessment Resources.

Meyers, J. E., & Meyers, K. R. (1996). *Rey Complex Figure Test and Recognition Trial. Manual Supplement.* Odessa, FL: Psychological Assessment Resources.

Milberg, W. P. (1996). Issues in the assessment of cognitive function in dementia. *Brain and Cognition, 31,* 114–132.

Milberg, W. P., Hebben, N., & Kaplan, E. (1996). The Boston process approach to neuropsychological assessment. In I. Grant & K. M. Adams (Eds.), *Neuropsychological assessment of neuropsychiatric disorders* (2nd ed., pp. 58–80). New York: Oxford University Press.

Morey, L. C. (1991). *Personality Assessment Inventory: Professional manual.* Odessa, FL: Psychological Assessment Resources.

Naglieri, J. A. (2000). *Naglieri Nonverbal Ability Test–Individual Administration.* San Antonio, TX: Psychological Corporation.

NAN Policy and Planning Committee. (2000). Presence of third party observers during neuropsychological testing: Official statement of the National Academy of Neuropsychology. *Archives of Clinical Neuropsychology, 15*(5), 379–380.

Navarrette, M. G. (1999). Verbal and nonverbal memory differences in bilingual children. *Dissertation Abstracts International 60,* 1013A.

Nelson, H. E. (1982). *National Adult Reading Test (NART): Test manual.* Windsor, United Kingdom: NFER Nelson.

Nelson, H. E., & McKenna, P. (1975). The use of current reading ability in the assessment of dementia. *British Journal of Social and Clinical Psychology, 14,* 259–267.

O'Carroll, R. E., Baikie, E. M., & Whittick, J. E. (1987). Does the National Adult Reading Test hold in dementia? *British Journal of Clinical Psychology, 26,* 315–316.

O'Donnell, W. E., DeSoto, C. B., DeSoto, J. L., & Reynolds, D. McQ. (1994). *The Neuropsychological Impairment Scale.* Los Angeles, CA: Western Psychological Services.

Ownby, R. L. (1990). A study of the expository process model in mental health settings. *Journal of Clinical Psychology, 46,* 366–371.

Paolo, A. M., Ryan, J. J., & Troster, A. I. (1996). Demographically based regression equations to estimate WAIS-R subtest scaled scores. *The Clinical Neuropsychologist, 10,* 130–140.

Parsons, O. A., Vega, A., & Burn, J. (1969). Different psychological effects of lateralized brain-damage. *Journal of Clinical and Consulting Psychology, 33,* 551–557.

Penrose, R. (1997). *The large, the small and the human mind.* Cambridge, United Kingdom: Cambridge University Press.

Poeck, K. (1986). The clinical examination for motor apraxia. *Neuropsychologia, 24,* 129–134.

Poreh, A. M. (2000). The quantified process approach: An emerging methodology to neuropsychological assessment. *The Clinical Neuropsychologist, 14*(2), 212–222.

Puente, A. E., & Marcotte, A. C. (2000). A history of Division 40 (Clinical Neuropsychology). In D. A. Dewsbury (Ed.), *Unification through division: Histories of the divisions of the American Psychological Association, Volume V* (pp. 137–160). Washington, DC: American Psychological Association.

Pugh, K. G., Milberg, W. P., & Lipsitz, L. A. (2001). Frontal executive dysfunction in community dwelling elderly persons with preserved memory [Abstract]. *Journal of the American Geriatrics Society, 49*(4), 77–78.

Raven, J. C. (1994). *Advanced Progressive Matrices Sets I and II.* Oxford: Oxford Psychologists Press. (Original work published 1965)

Raven, J. C. (1995). *Coloured Progressive Matrices Sets A, Ab, B.* Oxford, United Kingdom: Oxford Psychologists Press. (Original work published 1947)

Raven, J. C. (1996). *Progressive Matrices: A Perceptual Test of Intelligence.* Oxford, United Kingdom: Oxford Psychologists Press. (Original work published 1938)

Reitan, R. M. (1955). The distribution according to age of a psychological measure dependent upon organic brain functions. *Journal of Gerontology, 10,* 338.

Reitan, R. M., & Davison, L. A. (Eds.). (1974). *Clinical neuropsychology: Current status and applications.* New York: Wiley.

Reitan, R. M., & Wolfson, D. (1988). *Traumatic brain injury: Recovery and rehabilitation* (Vol. 2). Tucson, AZ: Neuropsychology Press.

Reitan, R. M., & Wolfson, D. (1993). *The Halstead-Reitan Neuropsychological Test Battery: Theory and clinical interpretation.* Tucson, AZ: Neuropsychology Press.

Reitan, R. M., & Wolfson, D. (1996). Theoretical, methodological and validated bases of the Halstead-Reitan neuropsychological test battery. In I. Grant & K. M. Adams (Eds.), *Neuropsychological assessment of neuropsychiatric disorders* (2nd ed., pp. 3–42). New York: Oxford University Press.

Rey, A. (1941). L'examen psychologie dans les cas d'encephalopathie traumatique. *Archives de Psychologie, 28,* 286–340.

Rey, A. (1958). *L'examen clinque en psychologie.* Paris: Presse Universitaire de France.

Reynolds, C. R. (Ed.). (1998). *Detection of malingering during head injury litigation.* New York: Plenum Press.

Reynolds, C. R., & Kamphaus, R. W. (1992). *Behavior assessment system for children: Manual.* Circle Pines, MN: American Guidance Service.

Robertson, L. C. (1995). Hemispheric specialization and cooperation in processing complex visual patterns. In F. L. Kitterle (Ed.), *Hemispheric communication: Mechanisms and models* (pp. 301–318). Hillsdale, NJ: Erlbaum.

Rogers, R. (Ed.). (1997). *Clinical assessment of malingering and deception* (2nd ed.). New York: Guilford Press.

Rourke, B. P., & Murji, S. (2000). A history of the International Neuropsychological Society: The early years (1965–1985). *Journal of the International Neuropsychological Society, 6,* 491–509.

Ruff, R. M. (1988). *Ruff Figural Fluency Test professional manual.* Odessa, FL: Psychological Assessment Resources.

Ruff, R. M., Neimann, H., Allen, C. C., Farrow, C. E., & Wylie, T. (1992). The Ruff 2 and 7 Selective Attention Test: A neuropsychological application. *Perceptual and Motor Skills, 75,* 1311–1319.

Saetveit, J. G., Lewis, D., & Seashore, C. E. (1940). *Revision of the Seashore Measure of Musical Talents* (University of Iowa No. 5). Iowa City: University of Iowa Press.

Sattler, J. M. (1992). *Assessment of children* (3rd ed.). San Diego: Sattler.

Sbordone, R. J. (1996). Ecological validity: Some critical issues for the neuropsychologist. In R. J. Sbordone & C. J. Long (Eds.), *Ecological validity of neuropsychological testing* (pp. 15–41). Orlando, FL: St. Lucie Press.

Sbordone, R. J., & Guilmette, T. J. (1999). Ecological validity: Prediction of everyday and vocational functioning from neuropsychological test data. In J. J. Sweet (Ed.), *Forensic neuropsychology: Fundamentals and practice* (p. 227–254). Lisse, Netherlands: Swets & Zeitlinger.

Sbordone, R. J., & Saul, R. E. (2000). *Neuropsychology for health care professionals and attorneys* (2nd ed.). Boca Raton, Florida: CRC Press.

Schmidt, M. (1996). *Rey Auditory Verbal Learning Test: A handbook.* Los Angeles: Western Psychological Services.

Schretlen, D. (1996). *Professional manual for the Brief Test of Attention.* Odessa, FL: Professional Assessment Resources.

Seashore, C. E., Lewis, D., & Saetveit, D. L. (1960). *Seashore Measures of Musical Talents* (Rev. ed.). New York: Psychological Corporation.

Seguin, E. (1907). *Idiocy: Its treatment by the physiological method.* New York: Bureau of Publications, Teachers College, Columbia University. (Original work published 1866)

Sivan, A. B. (1992). *Benton Visual Retention Test* (5th ed.). San Antonio, TX: Psychological Corporation.

Slick, D., Hopp, G., Strauss, E., & Thompson, G. B. (1999). *Victoria Symptom Validity Test (VSVT) for Windows.* Odessa, FL: Psychological Assessment Resources.

Sliwinski, M., Lipton, R. B., Buschke, H., & Stewart, W. (1996). The effects of preclinical dementia on estimates of normal cognitive functioning in aging. *Journal of Gerontology: Psychological Sciences and Social Sciences, 51,* 217–225.

Smith, A. (1991). *Symbol Digit Modalities Test.* Los Angeles: Western Psychological Services.

Sparrow, S. S., Balla, D. A., & Cicchetti, D. V. (1984). *Vineland Adaptive Behavior Scales: Interview Edition, Survey Form Manual.* Circle Pines, MN: American Guidance Service.

Spreen, O., & Strauss, E. (1998). *A compendium of neuropsychological tests: Administration, norms, and commentary* (2nd ed.). New York: Oxford University Press.

Thorndike, R. L., Hagen, E. P., & Sattler, J. M. (1986). *Stanford-Binet Intelligence Scale: Fourth edition.* Chicago: Riverside.

Tombaugh, T. N. (1996). *Test of Memory Malingering.* New York: Multi-Health Systems.

Trenerry, M. R., Crosson, B., DeBoe, J., & Leber, W. R. (1990). *Visual Search and Attention Test.* Odessa, FL: Psychological Assessment Resources.

Tulsky, D. S., & Zhu, J. (2000). Could test length or order affect scores on Letter Number Sequencing of the WAIS-III and WMS-III? Ruling out effects of fatigue. *The Clinical Neuropsychologist, 14*(4), 474–478.

Tuokko, H., Hadjistavropoulos, T., Miller, J. A., Horton, A., & Beattle, B. L. (1995). *The Clock Test.* Toronto, Canada: Multi-Health Systems.

Vanderploeg, R. D. (2000). *Clinician's guide to neuropsychological assessment* (2nd ed.). Mahwah, NJ: Erlbaum.

Wechsler, D. (1955). *Manual for the Wechsler Adult Intelligence Scale.* New York: Psychological Corporation.

Wechsler, D. (1989). *Manual for the Wechsler Preschool and Primary Scale of Intelligence–Revised.* New York: Psychological Corporation.

Wechsler, D. (1991). *Manual for the Wechsler Intelligence Scale for Children–Third Edition*. San Antonio, TX: Harcourt-Brace Jovanovich.

Wechsler, D. (1992). *Wechsler Individual Achievement Test*. San Antonio, TX: Psychological Corporation.

Wechsler, D. (1997a). *Administration and Scoring Manual for the Wechsler Adult Intelligence Scale–Third Edition*. San Antonio, TX: Harcourt Brace.

Wechsler, D. (1997b). *Administration and Scoring Manual for the Wechsler Memory Scale–Third Edition*. San Antonio, TX: Harcourt Brace.

Wechsler, D. (1999). *Manual for the Wechsler Abbreviated Scale of Intelligence*. San Antonio, TX: Harcourt Brace.

Wechsler, D. (2001). *Wechsler Individual Achievement Test–Second Edition*. San Antonio, TX: Psychological Corporation.

Wechsler, D. (2001). *Wechsler Test of Adult Reading*. San Antonio, TX: Psychological Corporation.

Wecker, N. S., Kramer, J. H., Wisniewski, A., Delis, D. C., & Kaplan, E. (2000). Age effects on executive ability. *Neuropsychology, 14*(3), 409–414.

Weinstein, C. (2001). For your information: Definition of a clinical neuropsychologist—Official position of the National Academy of Neuropsychology (Draft). *Massachusetts Neuropsychological Society Newsletter, 11*(2), 9.

Welsh, K. A., Butters, N., Mohs, R. C., Beekly, D., Edlands, S., Fillenbaum, G., and Heyman, A. (1994). The consortium to establish a registry for Alzheimer's disease (CERAD) .5. A normative study of the neuropsychological battery. *Neurology, 44*(4), 609–614.

Wetzel, L., & Boll, T. J. (1987). *Short Category Test, Booklet Format*. Los Angeles: Western Psychological Services.

Wiederholt, J. L., & Bryant, B. R. (2001). *Gray Oral Reading Test–Fourth Edition*. Austin, TX: PRO-ED.

Wilkinson, G. S. (1993). *Wide Range Achievement Test–Revision 3*. Delaware: Wide Range.

Williams, J. M. (1991). *Memory Assessment Scales*. Odessa, FL: Psychological Assessment Resources.

Williams, K. T. (1997). *Expressive Vocabulary Test*. Circle Pines, MN: Academic Guidance Service.

Wilson, B., Cockburn, J., & Baddeley, A. (1991). *The Rivermead Behavioural Memory Test, Revised Edition*. Suffolk, England: Thames Valley Test Company.

Wilson, R. S., Rosenbaum, G., Brown, G., Rourke, D., Whitman, D., & Grisell, J. (1978). An index of premorbid intelligence. *Journal of Consulting and Clinical Psychology, 46*, 1554–1555.

Wilson, R. S., Rosenbaum, G., & Brown, G. (1979). The problem of premorbid intelligence in neuropsychological assessment. *Journal of Clinical Neuropsychology, 1*, 49–53.

Woodcock, R. W., McGrew, K. S., & Mather, N. (2001). *Woodcock-Johnson III Tests of Achievement*. Itasca, IL: Riverside Publishing.

Yesavage, J. A., Brink, T. L., Rose, T. L., Lum, O., Huang, V., Adey, M. B., & Leirer, V. O. (1983). Development and validation of a geriatric depression rating scale: A preliminary report. *Journal of Psychiatric Research, 17*, 37–49.

Zachary, R. A. (1987). *Shipley Institute of Living Scale: Revised Manual*. Los Angeles: Western Psychological Services.

Annotated Bibliography

BOOKS

Albert, M. S. (1988). *Geriatric neuropsychology.* New York: Guilford.

This book is a definitive text on the topic of geriatric neuropsychology. It contains chapters covering normal and abnormal aging, memory, language, and assessment issues. It was published before some of the more recent advances in neuroimaging but is still a broad and informative introduction to the area.

Ardilla, A., Rosselli, M., & Puente, A. E. (1994). *Neuropsychological evaluation of the Spanish speaker.* New York: Plenum Press.

This book summarizes the attempts of the authors to develop neuropsychological tests for Spanish-speaking individuals. It presents the normative data for multiple standard neuropsychological tests collected in Columbia over several years. A particular focus was on developing normative data for elderly Spanish-speaking individuals and Spanish-speaking individuals with limited educational backgrounds.

Clark, D. L., & Boutros, N. N. (1999). *The brain and behavior: An introduction to behavioral neuroanatomy.* Oxford, England: Blackwell Science.

This behavioral neuroanatomy book was written with the clinician in mind. It is helpful in understanding functional neuroanatomy, or the neuroanatomy that underlies certain behavior.

Grant, I. G., & Adams, K. M. (1996). *Neuropsychological assessment of neuropsychiatric disorders* (2nd ed.). New York: Oxford University Press.

This book contains chapters describing major test systems (e.g., Halstead-Reitan Battery, Boston Process Approach) and reviews of the application of neuropsychological techniques to a variety of clinical populations and problems.

Heaton, R. K., Grant, I., & Matthews, C. G. (1991). *Comprehensive norms for an Expanded Halstead-Reitan Battery: Demographic corrections, research findings, and clinical applications.* Odessa, FL: Psychological Assessment Resources.

This book is comprised of up-to-date normative data for the basic tests from the Halstead-Reitan Battery and many tests not part of the original battery (e.g., Thurstone Fluency). The norms are demographically corrected for gender, age, and education.

Heilman, K. M., & Valenstein E. (Eds.). (1993). *Clinical neuropsychology.* New York: Oxford University Press.

This is a definitive compilation of chapters reviewing the classic neurobehavioral syndromes (e.g., aphasia, apraxia, amnesia, and neglect).

Jarvis, P. E., & Barth J. T. (1994). *The Halstead-Reitan Neuropsychological Battery: A guide to interpretation and clinical applications.* Odessa, FL: Psychological Assessment Resources.

This text was developed to instruct its readers how to systematically interpret and apply in a clinical setting the test results from administration of the Halstead-Reitan Battery.

Lezak, M. D. (1995). *Neuropsychological assessment (3rd ed.).* New York: Oxford University Press.

This book is a comprehensive general text that includes such topics as neuroanatomy, neuropathology, the procedures involved in neuropsychological evaluation, and an encyclopedic description of neuropsychological tests.

Loring, D. W. (1999). *INS dictionary of neuropsychology.* New York: Oxford University Press.

The International Neuropsychological Society sponsored this topic dictionary in order to standardize terminology in the field of neuropsychology. This comprehensive work contains entries from adult and developmental neuropsychology and from neurology, clinical psychology, cognitive psychology, neurosurgery, neuroimaging, neuroanatomy, psychiatry, rehabilitation, and multiple other areas relevant to neuropsychology. This book is also useful because it contains the many abbreviations and acronyms that are found in medical records.

McCaffrey, R. J., Williams, A. D., Fisher, J. M., & Laing, L. C. (1997). *The practice of forensic neuropsychology: Meeting challenges in the courtroom.* New York: Plenum Press.

This book addresses the particular issues confronting the neuropsychologist who enters into the forensic arena and who uses neuropsychology in legal matters. The book includes chapters discussing the history of forensic neuropsychology and special problems associated with it. It also contains chapters that address forensic evaluations in traumatic brain injury, including the special issues pertaining to mild traumatic brain injury. Also discussed are general clinical issues such as fixed versus flexible batteries, determination of premorbid functioning, and special issues relating to testimony.

Mitrushina, M. N., Boone, K. B., & D'Elia, L. F. (1999). *Handbook of normative data for neuropsychological assessment.* New York: Oxford University Press.

This book discusses the issues of norms in neuropsychological assessment and then presents a comprehensive review of the normative data for 17 commonly used tests. For each test the authors include a brief history of the measure, its relationship with demographic factors, a method for evaluating the normative data, a summary of the status of the norms, and summaries of the normative studies.

Nussbaum, P. D. (1997). *Handbook of neuropsychology and aging.* New York: Plenum Press.

This book contains 35 chapters focused on the assessment and treatment of geriatric populations. The editors have tried to integrate topics in geropsychology and neuropsychology with excellent discussions of psychiatric disorders, dementia, and pharmacology.

Reynolds, C. R. (1998). *Detection of malingering during head injury litigation.* New York: Plenum Press.

The book contains chapters describing a variety of current approaches to the assessment of malingering. The chapters cover base rates and test sensitivity and specificity, forced-choice techniques for detecting malingering, detecting malingering through clinical techniques, different fixed test batteries and the MMPI-2, as well as the detection of malingered memory disorders and commonsense approaches to the evaluation of malingering.

Reynolds, C. R., & Fletcher-Janzen, E. (1997). *Handbook of clinical child neuropsychology (2nd ed.).* New York: Plenum Press.

This text covers a full range of topics in pediatric neuropsychology, including neurodevelopment, assessment and diagnosis, and intervention techniques from a developmental perspective. It is intended for those already working in the field and serves as a good reference for the practicing neuropsychologist.

Rogers, R. (Ed.). (1997). *Clinical assessment of malingering and deception* (2nd ed.). New York: Guilford Press.

Although not specific to neuropsychological assessment, this book is invaluable in exploring the issues of detection of malingering in various clinical disorders. It explores the issue of malingering in relation to posttraumatic disorders, psychosis, amnesia, and substance abuse. The book also includes chapters on children and deception as well as assessment techniques for the detection of malingering.

Spreen, O., Risser, A. H., & Edgell, D. (1995). *Developmental neuropsychology.* New York: Oxford University Press.

This text is a comprehensive overview of pediatric neuropsychology. It covers early neural and cognitive development, issues in developmental neuropsychology, developmental disorders, and functional disturbances in various areas such as attention, language, and learning.

Spreen, O., & Strauss, E. (1998). *A compendium of neuropsychological tests: Administration, norms, and commentary (2nd ed.).* New York: Oxford University Press.

This book is a compilation of the most commonly used measures in neuropsychological assessment. The authors discuss general assessment issues such as history taking and report writing and then present a description of each neuropsychological measure, its source, and its purpose, as well as administration, scoring, normative data, and comments on reliability and validity.

Yeates, K. O., Ris, M. D., & Taylor, H. G. (1999). *Pediatric neuropsychology: Research, theory and practice.* New York: Guilford.

This book contains review chapters focused on the major medical disorders of childhood with neuropsychological consequences. It includes discussions of assessment and neuroradiology.

JOURNALS

Applied Neuropsychology. Publisher: Erlbaum.

> *This journal is oriented toward clinical neuropsychology and clinically relevant topics. It publishes articles and case studies dealing with assessment, brain functioning, neuroimaging, neuropsychological treatment, and rehabilitation.*

Archives of Clinical Neuropsychology. Publisher: Pergamon.

> *This journal contains articles concerning the psychological aspects of the etiology, diagnosis, and treatment of disorders of the central nervous system. It also publishes articles dealing with delivery and evaluation of services, ethical and legal issues, and approaches to education and training. The* Archives of Clinical Neuropsychology *is sponsored by the National Academy of Neuropsychologists.*

The Clinical Neuropsychologist. Publisher: Swets & Zeitlinger.

> *This journal publishes in-depth discussions of matters related to educational, clinical, and professional issues important to the neuropsychologist engaged in clinical practice.*

Cortex. Publisher: Masson.

> *This international journal presents articles concerning the study of interrelations of the nervous system and behavior with a particular focus on the effects of brain lesions on cognitive functions.*

Journal of Clinical and Experimental Neuropsychology. Publisher: Swets & Zeitlinger.

> JCEN *publishes scholarly research concerned with behavioral impairment associated with neurological disorders and neurological dysfunction. It includes articles focused on the etiology, course, and prognosis of brain diseases, scientific issues related to psychological assessment in brain disease, and the biological bases of cognitive functions.*

Journal of Forensic Neuropsychology. Publisher: Haworth Medical Press.

> *This journal contains articles dealing with forensically related neuropsychological topics. The journal accepts empirical studies, articles about court rulings and legal findings, position papers, commentaries, and case studies.*

Journal of International Neuropsychological Society. Publisher: Cambridge University Press.

> JINS *publishes research papers in both the experimental and clinical or applied areas of neuropsychology. Topics covered include development of cognitive processes, brain-behavior relationships, adult and child neuropsychology, developmental neuropsychology, speech and language disorders, and issues related to behavioral neurology, neuropsychiatry, neuroimaging, and electrophysiology.* JINS *is the official publication of the International Neuropsychological Society.*

The Journal of Neuropsychiatry and Clinical Neurosciences. Publisher: American Psychiatric Press.

This is the official journal of the American Neuropsychiatric Association. It publishes articles concerning clinical, educational, and research links between neuroscience and behavior in the broad field of neuropsychiatry.

Neuropsychiatry, Neuropsychology, and Behavioral Neurology. Publisher: Lippincott Williams & Wilkins.

This multidisciplinary journal presents articles containing original data on theoretical concepts, basic brain processes, and major clinical issues in the areas of neuropsychiatry, neuropsychology, and behavioral neurology. It is the official journal of the Society for Behavioral and Cognitive Neurology.

Neuropsychologia. Publisher: Elsevier Science.

This journal is an international journal of the neurological, behavioral, and cognitive sciences. Neuropsychologia presents papers promoting the study and understanding of human and animal behavior and cognition and papers integrating experimental, clinical, and theoretical neuropsychological contributions. In addition, this journal publishes articles focusing on the analysis of cognitive disorders resulting from injury or disease of the central nervous system.

Neuropsychology. Publisher: American Psychological Association.

This journal publishes original, empirical research investigating the relationship between the brain and cognitive, emotional, and behavioral functioning across the life span. Applied, clinical research with relevance to experimental investigations is encouraged.

Neuropsychology Review. Publisher: Kluwer Academic/Plenum Publishers.

This publication presents original evaluative review articles concerning significant topics in neuropsychological assessment, neurobehavioral aspects of neurological disorders, and theoretical analyses of human brain function. Neuropsychology Review is an official publication of the National Academy of Neuropsychology.

Psychological Assessment. Publisher: American Psychological Association.

This journal publishes primarily empirical articles on the research, development, validation, application, and evaluation of clinical psychological assessment instruments, as well as articles on clinical judgement and decision making, methods of measurement of treatment process and outcome, and dimensions of individual differences as they relate to clinical assessment.

Index

ABCN. *See* American Board of Clinical Neuropsychology (ABCN)
ABPN. *See* American Board of Professional Neuropsychology (ABPN)
ABPP. *See* American Board of Professional Psychology (ABPP)
Acalculia, 211
Achievement, tests of, 115–118
Adaptive Behavior Assessment System (ABAS), 125, 126
ADHD. *See* Attention-Deficit/Hyperactivity Disorder (ADHD)
Agnosia, 133, 212
Agraphia, 212
Alexia, 212
American Board of Clinical Neuropsychology (ABCN), 2, 3, 35–37
American Board of Professional Neuropsychology (ABPN), 2, 3, 35, 36–37
American Board of Professional Psychology (ABPP), 2, 3, 30, 35–37
American Psychological Association (APA), 2, 3, 29, 30, 31, 32, 34, 36, 37

Division 40, 2, 3, 25, 33, 34, 37, 38
Symposium on Clinical Neuropsychology, 1, 3
American Sign Language, 87–88
Amnesia, 212–213
APA. *See* American Psychological Association (APA)
Aphasia, 7, 86, 88, 89, 133, 135, 151, 213–214
Apraxia, 133, 214
Attention, tests of, 104–106
Attention-Deficit/Hyperactivity Disorder (ADHD), 163
Attention-Deficit/Hyperactivity Disorder Test (ADHDT), 126, 163
Audiotaping, 58. *See also* Third-party observers
Auditory Continuous Performance Test (ACPT), 105

Base rates, 145–147
Batteries. *See* Test batteries
Beck Anxiety Inventory (BAI), 126, 172
Beck Depression Inventory–II (BDI-II), 126, 172
Beck Youth Inventories, 126, 127

Beery-Buktenica Test of Visual-Motor Development (VMI), 118, 119

Behavior, tests of, 125–129

Behavioral observations, 61–65, 74–78

Behavior Assessment System for Children (BASC), 126, 127, 163

Benton, Arthur, 23

Benton Visual Retention Test–Fifth Edition (BVRT), 109, 110

Bilingualism and cultural issues, 139–140, 164–166

Blind Learning Aptitude Test, 87

Board certification, 30, 32, 33, 35–37
    ABCN, 35–37
    ABPN, 36–37
    vanity boards, 37

Booklet Category Test, 107

Boston Diagnostic Aphasia Examination (BDAE-III), 13, 88, 90, 113, 156

Boston Naming Test (BNT), 87, 88, 90, 113, 156, 170

Boston Process Approach (BPA), 14, 15, 19–21, 22, 81, 155–157

Brain, W. R., 15

Brief Test of Attention (BTA), 105

Broca, Paul, 10

Buschke Selective Reminding Test (Buschke SRT), 109, 110

California Verbal Learning Test (CVLT), 13, 156, 169

California Verbal Learning Test–Children (CVLT-C), 109, 111

California Verbal Learning Test–Second Edition (CVLT-II), 109, 110–111, 157

Category Test, 15, 17, 94, 107–108, 135. See also Halstead-Reitan Neuropsychological Battery [HRB], tests of

CERAD, 170

Children, assessment of, 159–164
    complicating factors in, 160
    differences from adults, 161
    general considerations in, 164

Children's Category Test, 107, 108

Children's Depression Inventory (CDI), 126, 127

Children's Memory Scale (CMS), 85–86, 109, 110

Christensen, Anne-Lise, 18

Clinical neuropsychologists:
    definition of, 26, 32–33
    education and knowledge base, 25–31
    training, expertise, and credentials, 33–37

Clinical neuropsychology:
    definition of, 3–5
    history of, 1–3
    major organizations, 37–38
    training programs, 34

Clock Test, 118, 119

Cognitive neuroscience, 10

Cognitivism, vs. empiricism, 12–14
Cohort effects, 167
Comprehensive Test of Nonverbal Intelligence (CTONI), 88, 101
Computerized Test of Response Bias (CARB), 122–123
Conners' Continuous Performance Test–Second Edition (CPT-II), 105
Conners' Rating Scales–Revised (CRS-R), 126, 127, 163
Controlled Oral Word Association Test (COWAT), 107, 108

Data, qualitative vs. quantitative, 153–157
Delirium/confusional states, 46, 57, 74, 214
Dementia, 45, 152, 168, 214–215
Design Fluency Test, 21
Dichaptic Perception Test, 21
Dichotic Listening, 21
Digit Vigilance Test (DVT), 105, 106
Diplomate. See Board certification
Division 40. See American Psychological Association (APA), Division 40
Dot Counting Test (DCT), 122, 123
Dysexecutive Syndrome, 215

Emotions, behavior, and personality, tests of, 125–129

Empiricism, vs. cognitivism, 12–14
Ethical guidelines, 80
Executive functions, tests of, 107–109
Expressive One-Word Picture Vocabulary Test (EOWPVT-2000), 113, 114
Expressive Vocabulary Test (EVT), 113, 114

Factitious disorders, 175
False positive errors, 139, 165–166, 172
Finger Oscillation Test, 15, 95, 121. See also Halstead-Reitan Neuropsychological Battery [HRB], tests of
Finger Tapping Test. See Finger Oscillation Test
Fodor, Jerry, 10
Folstein Mini-Mental State Exam (MMSE), 170

Gall, Franz Joseph, 10
Geriatric patient, assessment of. See Geroneuropsychology, assessment in
Geroneuropsychology, assessment in, 166–171
general considerations in, 171
Geschwind, Norman, 19, 155
Golden, Charles, 18, 155
Goldstein, Kurt, 11, 15
Goodglass, Harold, 19

Gray Oral Reading Test–Fourth Edition (GORT-4), 115, 116

Grip Strength, 95, 121. *See also* Halstead-Reitan Neuropsychological Battery [HRB], tests of

Grooved Pegboard, 121. *See also* Halstead-Reitan Neuropsychological Battery [HRB], tests of

Halstead, Ward, 11, 13, 15, 16, 17, 133, 135, 139

Halstead-Reitan Neuropsychological Battery (HRB), 4, 11, 12, 14–17, 22, 92, 93–95, 135, 136, 139, 154

tests of, 93–95

Hays-Binet, 87

Head, Henry, 15

Hemianopsia, 215

Hemispatial neglect, 135, 215

History gathering, 44–45

content:

birth and development, 46, 53–55

current situation, 46, 55–56

demographic information, 46

educational history, 46, 51–52

family background, 46, 55

legal history, 46, 56

medical history, 46, 47, 48–49

military history, 46, 56

presenting problem, 46–47

psychiatric history, 46, 49–51

vocational history, 46, 52–53

sources, 44–45, 61

Holism, vs. localization, 9–12

Hooper Visual Organization Test (VOT), 118, 119

Houston Conference, 3, 4, 26–31

Intelligence:

screening, 101–102

testing of, 100–101

tests of, 102–104

International Neuropsychological Society (INS), 1–2, 3, 25, 37, 38, 226

Interview, clinical, 56–61

behavioral observations in, 59–60, 61–65

communication in, 60–61

establishing rapport, 59

setting, 58

Jackson, Hughlings, 11, 15

Judgment of Line Orientation, 118, 119

Kaplan, Edith, 19–21, 155–157

Kaufman Adolescent and Adult Intelligence Test (KAIT), 103

Kaufman Assessment Battery for Children (K-ABC), 115, 116, 162

Kaufman Brief Intelligence Test (K-BIT), 102

Kaufman Functional Academic Skills Test (K-FAST), 115, 116

Kaufman Survey of Early Academic and Language Skills (K-SEALS), 113, 114

Kaufman Test of Educational Achievement (K-TEA), 115, 116, 162

Language functions, tests of, 112–115
Lashley, Karl, 11, 15
Learning and memory, tests of, 109–112
Localization, 6, 135, 136, 137, 182, 188. *See also* Holism, vs. localization
Luria, Alexander, 10, 17, 21, 154–155
Luria Nebraska Neuropsychological Battery (LNNB), 14, 15, 17–19, 22, 81, 95–96, 97, 154, 155
Luria's Neuropsychological Investigation, 18

Malingering, 73–74, 121–122, 173–179
    definition of, 173
    signs and symptoms of, 179
    tests of, 122–125
Mattis Dementia Rating Scale (Mattis DRS), 170
Meehl, Paul, 145
Memory Assessment Scale (MAS), 109, 111
Mesulam Cancellation Tests. *See* Verbal and Visual Cancellation Tests
Milner, Brenda, 21
Minnesota Multiphasic Personality Inventory–Adolescent (MMPI-A), 126, 127–128

Minnesota Multiphasic Personality Inventory–2 (MMPI-2), 126, 128, 172
Modularity, 10
Motivational disorders, differential diagnoses in, 174, 175
Motor-Free Visual Perception Test–Revised (MVPT-R), 118, 119
Motor functions, tests of, 120–121

Naglieri Nonverbal Ability Test–Individual Achievement, 88
National Academy of Neuropsychology (NAN), 2, 3, 26, 32, 33, 37–38, 58
National Adult Reading Test (NART-2), 99, 152
Neglect. *See* Hemispatial neglect
Nelson-Denny Reading Test, 115, 117
NEPSY: A Developmental Neuropsychological Assessment, 86, 96–98, 157
Neurobehavioral Cognitive Status Examination, 170
Neuroimaging techniques, 10, 133, 134
Neuropsychological assessment, approaches:
    Benton, Arthur, 23
    British, 23
    Canadian, 21
    European, 21, 23
    fixed vs. flexible, 5, 20, 91–92, 153–157

Neuropsychological assessment (*continued*)
  qualitative vs. quantitative, 153–157
  general guide for, 207–210
  test batteries (*see* Test batteries)
  uses of, 5–8
Neuropsychological Impairment Scale (NIS), 126, 128
Neuropsychological resources:
  assessment, 92
  books, 38–39, 227–229
  journals, 38–39, 230–231
Neuropsychological tests:
  ABAS (Adaptive Behavior Assessment System), 125, 126
  ACPT (Auditory Continuous Performance Test), 105
  ADHDT (Attention-Deficit/Hyperactivity Disorder Test), 126, 163
  BAI (Beck Anxiety Inventory), 126, 172
  BASC (Behavior Assessment System for Children), 126, 127, 163
  BDAE-III (Boston Diagnostic Aphasia Examination), 13, 88, 90, 113, 156
  BDI-II (Beck Depression Inventory–II), 126, 172
  Beck Youth Inventories, 126, 127
  Beery-Buktenica Test of Visual-Motor Development (*see* Neuropsychological tests, VMI [Beery-Buktenica Test of Visual-Motor Development])
  Blind Learning Aptitude Test, 87
  BNT (Boston Naming Test), 87, 88, 90, 113, 156, 170
  Booklet Category Test, 107
  BTA (Brief Test of Attention), 105
  Buschke SRT (Buschke Selective Reminding Test), 109, 110
  BVRT (Benton Visual Retention Test–Fifth Edition), 109, 110
  CARB (Computerized Test of Response Bias), 122–123
  Category Test, 15, 17, 94, 107–108, 135 (*see also* Halstead-Reitan Neuropsychological Battery [HRB], tests of)
  CDI (Children's Depression Inventory), 126, 127
  CERAD, 170
  Children's Category Test, 107, 108
  Clock Test, 118, 119
  CMS (Children's Memory Scale), 85–86, 109, 110
  COWAT (Controlled Oral Word Association Test), 107, 108
  CPT-II (Conners' Continuous Performance Test–Second Edition), 105
  CRS-R (Conners' Rating Scales–Revised), 126, 127, 163
  CTONI (Comprehensive Test of Nonverbal Intelligence), 88, 101

CVLT (California Verbal Learning Test), 13, 156, 169

CVLT-II (California Verbal Learning Test–Second Edition), 109, 110–111, 157

CVLT-C (California Verbal Learning Test–Children), 109, 111

DCT (Dot Counting Test), 122, 123

Design Fluency Test, 21

Dichaptic Perception Test, 21

Dichotic Listening, 21

DVT (Digit Vigilance Test), 105, 106

EOWPVT-2000 (Expressive One-Word Picture Vocabulary Test), 113, 114

EVT (Expressive Vocabulary Test), 113, 114

Finger Oscillation Test, 15, 95, 121 (*see also* Halstead-Reitan Neuropsychological Battery [HRB], tests of)

Finger Tapping Test (*see* Neuropsychological tests, Finger Oscillation Test)

GORT-4 (Gray Oral Reading Test–Fourth Edition), 115, 116

Grip Strength, 95, 121 (*see also* Halstead-Reitan Neuropsychological Battery [HRB], tests of)

Grooved Pegboard, 121 (*see also* Halstead-Reitan Neuropsy-

chological Battery [HRB], tests of)

Hays-Binet, 87

Hooper Visual Organization Test (*see* Neuropsychological tests, VOT [Hooper Visual Organization Test])

Judgment of Line Orientation, 118, 119

K-ABC (Kaufman Assessment Battery for Children), 115, 116, 162

KAIT (Kaufman Adolescent and Adult Intelligence Test), 103

K-BIT (Kaufman Brief Intelligence Test), 102

K-FAST (Kaufman Functional Academic Skills Test), 115, 116

K-SEALS (Kaufman Survey of Early Academic and Language Skills), 113, 114

K-TEA (Kaufman Test of Educational Achievement), 115, 116, 162

MAS (Memory Assessment Scale), 109, 111

Mattis DRS (Mattis Dementia Rating Scale), 170

Mesulam Cancellation Tests (*see* Neuropsychological tests, Verbal and Visual Cancellation Tests)

MMPI-A (Minnesota Multiphasic Personality Inventory–Adolescent), 126, 127–128

Neuropsychological tests (*continued*)

MMPI-2 (Minnesota Multiphasic Personality Inventory–2), 126, 128, 172

MMSE (Folstein Mini-Mental State Exam), 170

MVPT-R (Motor-Free Visual Perception Test–Revised), 118, 119

Naglieri Nonverbal Ability Test–Individual Achievement, 88

NART-2 (National Adult Reading Test), 99, 152

Nelson-Denny Reading Test, 115, 117

NEPSY, 157 (*see also* Test batteries)

Neurobehavioral Cognitive Status Examination, 170

NIS (Neuropsychological Impairment Scale), 126, 128

PAI (Personality Assessment Inventory), 126, 129

PASAT (Paced Auditory Serial Addition Test), 105, 106

Perkins-Binet, 87

Portland Digit Recognition Test, 177

PPVT-III (Peabody Picture Vocabulary Test–III), 113, 114

Raven's Progressive Matrices, 102

RAVLT (Rey Auditory Verbal Learning Test), 109, 111, 164

RBMT (Rivermead Behavioral Memory Test–Revised Edition), 109, 111–112

RCFT (Rey Complex Figure Test and Recognition Trial), 109, 111, 118, 119–120

Recall-Recognition Test, 122, 123

Reitan Indiana Aphasia Screening Test, 17, 95, 113, 114–115

Rey 15-Item Test (*see* Neuropsychological tests, RMT [Rey Memory Test])

Rey-Osterrieth Complex Figure, 20, 153

RFFT (Ruff Figural Fluency Test), 107, 108

RMT (Rey Memory Test), 122, 123–124

ROWPVT-2000 (Receptive One-Word Picture Vocabulary Test), 113, 114

Ruff 2 & 7 Selective Attention Test, 105, 106

SB-IV (Stanford-Binet Intelligence Scale–Fourth Edition), 103

SCOLP (Speed of Capacity of Language Processing Test), 100

SDMT (Symbol Digit Modalities Test), 105, 106

Seashore Rhythm Test, 4, 15, 95, 133 (*see also* Halstead-Reitan Neuropsychological Battery [HRB], tests of)

Seguin-Goddard Form Board, 15, 133 (*see also* Halstead-Reitan Neuropsychological Battery [HRB], tests of)

Short Category Test, 107–108

SILS (Shipley Institute of Living Scale), 99–100

Stroop Color and Word Test, 107, 108

TMT (Trail Making Test) 95, 107, 108 (*see also* Halstead-Reitan Neuropsychological Battery [HRB], tests of)

Token Test, 23, 164

TOMM (Test of Memory Malingering), 122, 124, 177

TONI-3 (Test of Nonverbal Intelligence–3), 88, 102

TPT (Tactual Performance Test), 87, 95, 118, 120, 145 (*see also* Halstead-Reitan Neuropsychological Battery [HRB], tests of)

TSCC (Trauma Symptom Checklist for Children), 126, 129

TSI (Trauma Symptom Inventory), 126, 129, 172

TVPS-R (Test of Visual-Perceptual Skills–nonmotor–Revised), 118, 120

Verbal and Visual Cancellation Tests, 118, 120

Vigil (Vigil Continuous Performance Test), 105, 106

Vineland Adaptive Behavior Scales, 126, 129

VIP (Validity Indicator Profile), 122, 124

VMI (Beery-Buktenica Test of Visual-Motor Development), 118, 119

VOT (Hooper Visual Organization Test), 118, 119

VSAT (Visual Search and Attention Test), 105, 106

VSVT (Victoria Symptom Validity Test), 122, 124

WAB (Western Aphasia Battery), 113, 115

WAIS (Wechsler Adult Intelligence Scale), 4, 20

WAIS-R (Wechsler Adult Intelligence Scale–Revised), 20

WAIS-R NI (Wechsler Adult Intelligence Scale–Revised Neuropsychological Instrument), 20, 156

WAIS-III (Wechsler Adult Intelligence Scale–Third Edition), 72, 85, 88, 90, 103, 104, 136, 144, 157
Digit Span, 105–106
Letter-Number Sequencing, 72
Picture Arrangement, 137–138

WASI (Wechsler Abbreviated Scale of Intelligence), 101, 102

WCST (Wisconsin Card Sorting Test), 107, 108–109, 153

Neuropsychological tests (*continued*)
WIAT (Wechsler Individual Achievement Test), 115, 117, 162
WIAT-II (Wechsler Individual Achievement Test–Second Edition), 115, 117
WISC-R (Wechsler Intelligence Scale for Children–Revised), 88
WISC-III (Wechsler Intelligence Scale for Children–Third Edition), 88, 103, 104, 165
WJ-III (Woodcock-Johnson III Tests of Achievement), 115, 117–118, 162
WMS (Wechsler Memory Scale), 20
WMS-III (Wechsler Memory Scale–Third Edition), 27, 70, 72, 85, 109, 112, 144, 157, 179
Letter-Number Sequencing, 72
WMT (Word Memory Test), 122, 124–125
WPPSI-R (Wechsler Preschool and Primary Scale of Intelligence–Revised), 103, 104
WRAML (Wide Range Assessment of Memory and Learning), 109, 112
WRAT3 (Wide Range Achievement Test–Revision 3), 100, 115, 117, 162
WRAVMA (Wide Range Assessment of Visual Motor Ability), 118, 120

WRMT (Warrington Recognition Memory Test), 23
WRT (Word Recognition Test), 122, 125
WTAR (Wechsler Test of Adult Reading), 100
Nonneurological factors, 7, 28, 44, 50, 64, 67, 70
false-positive errors and, 139–140
Nonneuropsychological factors. *See* Nonneurological factors
Normality, 148–150
Note taking, 78–80
abbreviations for, 79

Paced Auditory Serial Addition Test (PASAT), 105, 106
Peabody Picture Vocabulary Test–III (PPVT-III), 113, 114
Perkins-Binet, 87
Personality, tests of, 125–129
Personality Assessment Inventory (PAI), 126, 129
Portland Digit Recognition Test, 177
Premorbid capacity:
assessment of, 98–100, 150–153
demographic formulas, 150–151
educational history, 51
hold vs. don't hold tests, 151–152
irregular word reading, 152
methods for estimating, 152
tests for, 99–100
vocational history, 53

Psychiatric disorders, assessment in, 171–173

Qualitative/quantitative data, 153–157

Rapport, establishing, 70
Raven's Progressive Matrices, 102
Recall-Recognition Test, 122, 123
Receptive One-Word Picture Vocabulary Test (ROWPVT-2000), 113, 114
Record keeping, 78–80
    raw data, release of, 80
    storage, 80
    See also Note taking
Reitan, Ralph, 1, 13, 16
Reitan Indiana Aphasia Screening Test, 17, 95, 113, 114–115
Reliability, test, 141–145
    definition and types of, 143
    inter-rater, 143, 144
    test-retest, 143
Report writing:
    general guidelines, 182
    maxims, 183–189
    organization of sections, 189–192
    outline, 189
    sample report, 192–205
Rey Auditory Verbal Learning Test (RAVLT), 109, 111, 164
Rey Complex Figure Test and Recognition Trial (RCFT), 109, 111, 118, 119–120
Rey 15-Item Test. *See* Rey Memory Test (RMT)

Rey Memory Test (RMT), 122, 123–124
Rey-Osterrieth Complex Figure, 20, 153
Rivermead Behavioral Memory Test–Revised Edition (RBMT), 109, 111–112
Ruff Figural Fluency Test (RFFT), 107, 108
Ruff 2 & 7 Selective Attention Test, 105, 106

Seashore Rhythm Test, 4, 15, 95, 133. *See also* Halstead-Reitan Neuropsychological Battery [HRB], tests of
Seguin-Goddard Form Board, 15, 133. *See also* Halstead-Reitan Neuropsychological Battery [HRB], tests of
Sensitivity/specificity, 4, 5, 13, 14, 42, 43–44, 138–141
Shipley Institute of Living Scale (SILS), 99–100
Short Category Test, 107–108
Somatoform disorder. *See* Motivational disorders, differential diagnoses in
Special needs:
    aphasia, 88, 89
    hearing impairments, 81, 86, 87–88, 89
    input and output channels, 86–87, 89
    motor impairments, 81, 86, 88–89
    visual impairments, 81, 86, 87, 89

Specificity. *See* Sensitivity/speci-
ficity
Speed of Capacity of Language
Processing Test (SCOLP), 100
Stanford-Binet Intelligence Scale–
Fourth Edition (SB-IV), 103
Stroop Color and Word Test, 107,
108
Symbol Digit Modalities Test
(SDMT), 105, 106

Tactual Performance Test (TPT),
87, 95, 118, 120, 145. *See also*
Halstead-Reitan Neuropsy-
chological Battery [HRB],
tests of
Test administration, 82–84
balancing test order, 72
behavioral observations in, 74–
78
encouragement, 84
establishing rapport, 59, 70
feedback, 84
modifications, 87
optimizing motivation and alertness, 72–74
optimizing performance, 67–68,
163, 169, 173
steps in, 83
structuring the test situation,
70–72, 74
test procedures and standards,
80–82, 83
testing conditions, 68–69
testing the limits, 82
timing, 83–84

Test batteries:
Boston Process Approach
(BPA), 14, 15, 19–21, 22, 81,
155–157
Halstead-Reitan Neuropsychological Battery (HRB), 4, 11,
12, 14–17, 22, 92, 93–95, 135,
136, 139, 154
tests of, 93–95
Luria Nebraska Neuropsychological Battery (LNNB), 14,
15, 17–19, 22, 81, 95–96, 97,
154, 155
NEPSY: A Developmental Neuropsychological Assessment,
86, 96–98
See also Neuropsychological assessment, approaches
Testing conditions, 68–69
Test interpretation, 42
using test norms, 147–150,
166
See also Validity, test
Test of Memory Malingering
(TOMM), 122, 124, 177
Test of Nonverbal Intelligence–3
(TONI-3), 88, 102
Test scoring, 84–86
computer scoring programs, 85–
86
errors, 79, 85
Test selection, 90–92
appropriateness, 90–91
comprehensiveness, 91
referral question, 90, 91
Test session, structure of, 70–72

Test of Visual-Perceptual Skills–
nonmotor–Revised
(TVPS-R), 118, 120
Third-party observers, 57–58
Token Test, 23, 164
Trail Making Test (TMT) 95, 107,
108. *See also* Halstead-Reitan
Neuropsychological Battery
[HRB], tests of
Trauma Symptom Checklist for
Children (TSCC), 126, 129
Trauma Symptom Inventory (TSI),
126, 129, 172

Validity, test:
construct, 14, 132, 135–138
content, 132, 135–138
criterion or predictive, 131, 132–
135
ecological, 14, 131, 135
See also Base rates
Validity Indicator Profile (VIP),
122, 124
Verbal and Visual Cancellation
Tests, 118, 120
Victoria Symptom Validity Test
(VSVT), 122, 124
Videotaping, 58. *See also* Third-
party observers
Vigil Continuous Performance Test
(Vigil), 105, 106
Vineland Adaptive Behavior Scales,
126, 129
Visual, visuospatial, and visuo-
tactile functions, tests of,
118–120

Visual Search and Attention Test
(VSAT), 105, 106

Warrington, Elizabeth, 23
Warrington Recognition Memory
Test (WRMT), 23
Wechsler Abbreviated Scale of In-
telligence (WASI), 102
Wechsler Adult Intelligence Scale
(WAIS), 4, 20
Wechsler Adult Intelligence Scale–
Revised (WAIS-R), 20
Wechsler Adult Intelligence Scale–
Revised Neuropsychological
Instrument (WAIS-R NI), 20,
156
Wechsler Adult Intelligence Scale–
Third Edition (WAIS-III), 72,
85, 88, 90, 103, 104, 136, 144,
157
Digit Span, 105–106
Letter-Number Sequencing, 72
Picture Arrangement, 137–138
Wechsler Individual Achievement
Test (WIAT), 115, 117, 162
Wechsler Individual Achievement
Test–Second Edition (WIAT-
II), 115, 117
Wechsler Intelligence Scale for
Children–Revised (WISC-R),
88
Wechsler Intelligence Scale for
Children–Third Edition
(WISC-III), 88, 103, 104, 165
Wechsler intelligence scales, 72, 87,
104, 136–137, 150

Wechsler Memory Scale (WMS), 20

Wechsler Memory Scale–Third Edition (WMS-III), 27, 70, 72, 85, 109, 112, 144, 157, 179
Letter-Number Sequencing, 72

Wechsler Preschool and Primary Scale of Intelligence–Revised (WPPSI-R), 103, 104

Wechsler Test of Adult Reading (WTAR), 100

Werner, Heinz, 19–20, 155

Western Aphasia Battery (WAB), 113, 115

Wide Range Achievement Test–Revision 3 (WRAT3), 100, 115, 117, 162

Wide Range Assessment of Memory and Learning (WRAML), 109, 112

Wide Range Assessment of Visual Motor Ability (WRAVMA), 118, 120

Wisconsin Card Sorting Test (WCST), 107, 108–109, 153

Woodcock-Johnson III Tests of Achievement (WJ-III), 115, 117–118, 162

Word Memory Test (WMT), 122, 124

Word Recognition Test (WRT), 122, 125

About the Authors

Nancy Hebben is an Assistant Clinical Professor of Psychology in the Department of Psychiatry at Harvard Medical School. She holds a doctorate in clinical psychology with a specialty in Neuropsychology from Wayne State University in Detroit, Michigan, a degree which she earned in 1979. She was an intern with Edith Kaplan at the Boston Veterans Administration Medical Center from 1978 to 1979. Then as part of a National Research Service Award, Dr. Hebben did a three-year postdoctoral fellowship in neuropsychology at the Massachusetts Institute of Technology, where with Suzanne Corkin she studied pain perception in patients undergoing cingulotomy for chronic pain and intractable psychiatric disorders. In 1982 she began at the McLean Hospital as the Chief Consultant in Neuropsychology, a position she held until 1998 when she modified her position to Attending Psychologist and began to focus primarily on her private practice. As a clinical neuropsychologist Dr. Hebben has provided neuropsychological assessments of over 3,500 children, adults, and geriatric patients, and she has supervised more than 3,000 neuropsychological assessments by numerous predoctoral and postdoctoral fellows specializing in neuropsychology. Dr. Hebben is board certified in Clinical Neuropsychology by the American Board of Professional Psychology. She has taught a course in Clinical Psychology each fall for over ten years at Harvard University Extension School, and she has published numerous papers on topics in clinical neuropsychology and pain perception. Dr. Hebben is a coauthor with Dr. Milberg and Dr. Kaplan of the chapter, "The Boston Process Approach to Neuropsychological Assessment" in the book *Neuropsychological Assessment of Neuropsychiatric Disorders,* edited by Kenneth Adams and Igor Grant. Dr. Hebben has consulted with attorneys in Massachusetts, Connecticut, Florida, Illinois, Michigan, New Hampshire, Rhode Island, New York, and South Carolina in both civil and criminal cases on issues of brain damage, head injury, competence, and lead intoxication.

William Milberg is an Associate Professor of Psychology in the Department of Psychiatry at Harvard Medical School. He is also the Associate Director for Research of the VA Boston Healthcare GRECC (Geriatric Research, Education, and Clinical Center). He holds a doctorate in clinical psychology with a specialty in Neuropsychology from Wayne State University in Detroit, Michigan, a degree which he earned in 1978. He was an intern with Edith Kaplan at the Boston Veterans Administration Medical Center from 1978 to 1979 and a postdoctoral fellow at Harvard University in the Department of Psychology from 1979 to 1980. In 1981 he joined the GRECC, where he conducts basic and clinical research on the neuropsychology of cognition. He has taught formal courses in neuroanatomy and neuropsychological assessment at Harvard University for more than fifteen years and directs a pre- and postdoctoral clinical training program in Geriatric Neuropsychology under the auspices of the GRECC. Dr. Milberg is a frequent lecturer on topics related to cognitive assessment in older adults. Dr. Milberg has published over 70 papers and chapters on various topics in the neuropsychology of higher mental functions. He is a coauthor with Dr. Hebben and Dr. Kaplan of the chapter, "The Boston Process Approach to Neuropsychological Assessment" in the book *Neuropsychological Assessment of Neuropsychiatric Disorders,* edited by Kenneth Adams and Igor Grant. He is also board certified in Clinical Neuropsychology by the American Board of Professional Psychology.